Women i
for Irish

Women in the Struggle for Irish Independence

JOSEPH MCKENNA

McFarland & Company, Inc., Publishers
Jefferson, North Carolina

ISBN (print) 978-1-4766-8041-5
ISBN (ebook) 978-1-4766-3856-0

LIBRARY OF CONGRESS AND BRITISH LIBRARY
CATALOGUING DATA ARE AVAILABLE

Front cover image: studio portrait of Countess
Constance Markievicz in uniform with a gun, circa 1915,
reproduced after the 1916 Easter Rising (author's collection)

Printed in the United States of America

McFarland & Company, Inc., Publishers
Box 611, Jefferson, North Carolina 28640
www.mcfarlandpub.com

Table of Contents

No better allies than women can be found. They are in certain emergencies more dangerous to despotism than men. They have more courage, through having less scruples, when their better instincts are appealed to by a militant and just cause in a fight against a mean foe.

—Michael Davitt

When trimmers and compromisers disavow you, I, a poor slum bred politician, raise my hat in thanksgiving that I have lived to see this resurgence of women.

—James Connolly

Introduction

Ireland at the opening of the twentieth century faced three great challenges: the fight for independence, the rise of organized labor, and the struggle for female suffrage. The interconnectivity between all three was to be the women of Ireland, who in an understated way helped shape Ireland's destiny.

But—and there is always a *but*—the suffragist struggle was opposed by the Irish Parliamentary Party at Westminster. The Party's leaders had been blackmailed into opposing it, by the British government, in exchange for support for Home Rule. The Church, both Catholic and Protestant, and the emerging provisional Unionist government of Ulster were also opposed to this extension of the franchise. The republican movement in the south was initially indifferent to the rights of women. In their minds, the independence of Ireland came first. The suffragettes' best hope was to align themselves with the socialist struggle of Larkin and Connolly. Both men advocated equality of the sexes. As most of the leading suffragettes were of the upper, or middle class, however, supporting labor was an anathema. Yet the Marxist socialism of James Connolly offered them their best hope. In Connolly they had a champion who believed in the equality of women in a socialist Worker's Republic. Padraig Pearse, leader of the nationalists, had initially a very narrow view of the part women should play in the forthcoming struggle for independence. "While the women would have ambulance and red cross work to do," he suggested, he "would not like the idea of women drilling and marching in the ordinary way, but there is no reason why they should not learn how to shoot." Not that he was advocating that they should shoot. That was men's work, after all.

Many of the educated middle-class suffragists of the South, and indeed some in the North, had upon its foundation, joined the nonpolitical Gaelic League. It was seen as a benign form of nationalism—art, literature, drama, and language. There were those within the new society, however, members of the secretive Irish Republican Brotherhood, who saw it as a recruiting vehicle for a more extreme view on Irish nationalism. They were dedicated

1

to the violent overthrow of British rule in Ireland. It was a natural progression, later, when the Irish Volunteers had been formed in the support of Home Rule, that the women of Ireland should do their bit. This culminated in the formation of Cumann na mBan. Branches were established throughout Ireland as well as in Scotland and England. This new women's society saw itself as a support group to the Irish Volunteers, raising money to arm them and training as nurses and cooks to assist them. The support these women offered gave them some future hope of electoral equality as a reward for loyalty. In 1916, in varying degrees, the three groups—suffragettes, socialists, and nationalists—all came together at the time of the Easter Rising. They must have drawn comfort from the wording of the declaration of Irish independence which began:

> IRISH MEN AND WOMEN: In the name of God and of the dead generations from which she receives her old tradition of nationhood, Ireland, through us summons her children to her flag and strikes for her freedom.

Here was a perceived promise of equality, a promise from both socialists and nationalists. The part that the women played in that glorious week of Easter is recorded in some depth in the Witness Statements compiled by the Bureau of Military History during the 1940s and '50s. There is sadness and there are tears in the accounts, but also fun and laughter amidst the horrors.

The failure of the Rising saw the execution of those men most sympathetic to the equality of women: James Connolly, Thomas McDonagh, and a latecomer to that equality, Padraig Pearse. Now the women had to fight their cause once more. In this they were helped by the "Widows," the wives and mothers of the executed leaders of the Rising. Through their husbands and sons, they exercised influence and brought the various groups of women together in Cumann na dTeachtaire. As a pressure group, it succeeded in securing four seats on the Sinn Fein executive. Though a minority, this representation did give them a chance to have their voices heard and thus to formulate policy.

When the War of Independence broke out, it was not Cumann na mBan as an organization, but rather individuals and nonmembers, that proved to be most effective. Indeed, the most effective women—Lily Mernin, Linda Kearns, Moya Llewelyn Davies, and Eileen McGrane—were explicitly told not to join nor associate themselves with Cumann. They were to remain aloof and thus avoid suspicion as they spied on the British administration and provided intelligence for Michael Collins. Then there are the unseen actors who played their part in the establishment of an independent Irish state, women like Lily Brennan, Mary McGeehan, and Nancy O'Brien, unknown today even by Ireland's feminist writers. They were never acknowledged as participants in the great struggle, though some recorded their experiences to the compilers at the Bureau of Military History. One of them, just as an example, was Lily Brennan. She went to work in London in 1918 as a trainee in an advertising firm. While there, seeking friendship among the community, she completely immersed herself in all things Irish:

> I was in the Gaelic League Central Branch which was in the neighborhood of Blackfriars Bridge. I was also in a Sinn Fein Club near St. Paul's and in the Self-Determination League which generally met at the Gaelic League headquarters.... In this way I got to know most of the prominent people in the Independence Movement in London.

She was quietly approached one day and asked to work for Art O'Briain, the unofficial, and clandestine, "Republican" ambassador in London. It was he who dealt with all aspects of the Republican cause in England. It was to him that the couriers from the various Republican departments in Ireland reported. One such was Sam Maguire; as Lily Brennan relates, he was "the key man in England for the purchase of arms for the Republican Army headquarters here." O'Briain, as Brennan continues, "knew Michael Collins very well. It was he who molded him [when he was living in London at the turn of the century] and initiated him into the whole idea of military republicanism."

Mary McGeehan, a member of the London branch of Cumann na mBan, played a more dangerous part, as she herself reveals in her witness statement to the Bureau of Military History:

> On one occasion when I was coming home on a holiday I was asked to bring over some revolvers to Dublin. I handed them to P.S. O'Hegarty in his bookshop at the corner of Duke Street and Dawson Street, and I still remember my disgust at his gruffness and complete lack of appreciation of the risk I had run.
>
> On another occasion I met a man at King's Cross railway station. He arrived by train dressed as a laborer and carried a little tin trunk such as a laborer might have for his clothes. He laid the trunk which I knew was filled with guns and ammunition, at my feet. We pretended to be lovers and we stuck close together until we got to Euston by tram, I think. Not knowing the way into the station he laid down the trunk on the side walk and went over to ask a policeman the way. At Euston I saw him into the train where he placed the trunk under the seat. We parted affectionately and he arrived safely in Ireland with his luggage.

The Witness Statements, as indicated, cast a light on the activities of the women involved, whose relevance is perhaps not fully appreciated as yet. Their accounts touch upon others, the great and the good. There are many others, whose stories are yet to be revealed. Some left their accounts with the Bureau. Others were briefly brought to mind, in their obituaries, which appeared in the 1960s and '70s, in the pages of the *United Irishman*. Just as male writers in the past have written women out of the national struggle, feminist writers of today have largely written men out of the struggle for female suffrage. Where are William Thompson, Thomas Haslam, John Stuart Mill, Francis Skeffington, James Cousins, and James Connolly in the female pantheon? Let us not repeat the mistakes of the past in rewriting history. Where men have made contributions to the struggle for equality, these contributions should be recognized and applauded. In the meantime, this is an account of the part played by the women during those momentous years, and of their ultimate betrayal by lesser men.

List of Abbreviations

AOH   Ancient Order of Hibernians
DMP   Dublin Metropolitan Police
DUTC   Dublin United Tramways Company
ICA   Irish Citizen Army
IPP   Irish Parliamentary Party
IRB   Irish Republican Brotherhood
ISF   Irish Women's Suffrage Federation
ISRP   Irish Socialist Republican Party
ITGWU   Irish Transport & General Workers' Union
ITUC   Irish Trades Union Congress
IWFL   Irish Women's Franchise League
IWRL   Irish Women' Reform League
IWSF   Irish Women's Suffrage Federation
IWSLGA   Irish Women's Suffrage & Local Government Association
IWSS   Irish Women's Suffrage Society
IWWU   Irish Women's Worker's Union
MP   Member of the British Parliament
NSWS   Irish Women's Workers' Union
NUDL   National Union of Dock Laborers
NUWSS   National Union of Women's Suffrage Societies
RIC   Royal Irish Constabulary
TUC   Trade Union Council
UVF   Ulster Volunteer Force
UWLU   Ulster Women's Liberal Unionists
WSPU   Women's Social & Political Union

1

Suffragists and Suffragettes

Agitation within the British Parliament for an extension to the franchise was the result of the economic power of an emerging industrial middle class during the early nineteenth century. By degrees, they wrested control from a rural-based aristocracy, concentrating power in the city. The result was the passing of the Great Reform Act of 1832. The legislation, *An Act to amend the representation of the people in England and Wales*, increased the electorate from about five hundred thousand to eight hundred thousand, extending the vote to approximately one in five men. Two separate Reform Acts followed that same year for Ireland and Scotland. In all cases the operative word in the Act was "males." There was to be no vote for women. At the time there was little vocal opposition from either men or women. Women simply did not count.

However, as early as 1817, English philosopher and social reformer Jeremy Bentham had taken up the case for female suffrage in his *Plan of Parliamentary Reform in the Form of a Catechism*. In this, and in his other works, he advocated equal rights for women. His was a very simple, but true philosophy, that laws and government policies should promote the greatest happiness of the greatest number of individuals. Students of Bentham's philosophy included the Irish duo of social reform, William Thompson and Anna Wheeler. They jointly wrote a book entitled *An Appeal of One Half the Human Race, Women, Against the Pretensions of the Other Half, Men....* It was published in 1825 by Longman, Hurst, Rees, of Paternoster Row, London, wherein they argued in favor of extending the vote to women. In this they might be credited as being Ireland's earliest suffragists. Their argument echoed that of Bentham, that the happiness of the greatest number of both men and women would be increased if both sexes had equal rights in civil and criminal law. Interestingly, their thesis argued that only a socialist system could deliver the fullest possible happiness for the greatest number.

William Thompson, born in Cork in 1775, was a political and philosophical writer, championing the cause of social equality in all its forms. His earlier paper, *An Inquiry into the Principles of the Distribution of Wealth*, published in 1824, became an influential work on the subject, influencing the emerging Karl Marx. Thompson is perhaps better known, though, as a champion of women's rights, with his coauthored work, *An Appeal....* It argued logically for women's rights to social and political equality. At the time, women had very few rights. They were subject to their fathers, and later to their husbands. It was a patriarchal society, and middle-class women were mere adornments—birds in a gilded cage. Thompson's cowriter, Anna Doyle Wheeler, was born in County Tipperary in 1785. She was the daughter of a Church of Ireland vicar. At the age of fifteen, she married the nineteen-year-old Francis Massey Wheeler, the son of a baronet. It was not a happy marriage, and in 1812, Anna fled Ireland with her two daughters for Guernsey, and the home of an uncle, Sir John Doyle, the island's governor. Here, and later in London, she met the important philosophers and political thinkers of her time, people who were to influence her future life and beliefs. Included in this number were Jeremy Bentham, mentioned above, James Mill, John Stuart Mill, Robert Owen, Frances Place, William Thompson, and Frances Wright. In 1823, Anna moved to France, where she met Charles Fourier, philosopher, socialist, and feminist. With his permission, and as a means of earning a living, she translated his and other writers' works into English. In 1825, now returned to England, she, and William Thompson put their shared beliefs on paper to be published as an *Appeal of one half of the Human Race....* Though published under William Thompson's name, in its introduction, he credits Anna as the source of many of the ideas in the work. He wrote, "The following pages are the exclusive produce of your mind and pen, and written with your own hand. The remainder are our joint property, I being your interpreter and the scribe of your sentiments."

By 1829, Anna was firmly established in London, and in that year she is known to have given a lecture on the rights of women to a mixed audience at a nonconformist chapel near Finsbury Square. In the following year, 1830, a paper written by her, *Rights of Women*, was published in the *British Co-operator.* Anna Doyle Wheeler also wrote a number of articles under the pseudonym of "Vlasta," a legendary sixteenth-century Swedish woman who led an army of women against the oppression of men. By 1832, renewing her contacts with France, Anna became associated with the journal *Tribune des femme,* a magazine aimed at working-class women. The periodical was unique in that it only published articles by women, for women, relating to women's affairs. Anna Wheeler's former collaborator, William Thompson, died in 1833, and soon after, Anna Wheeler returned to England. By 1840, due to ill health, she was obliged to withdraw physically from the struggle for feminine equality. She continued to correspond, and champion, fellow feminists. Anna Doyle Wheeler, a largely unknown early champion of women's rights, died in 1848, at the age of sixty-three.

Anna Doyle Wheeler

All over Britain and Ireland by the mid-nineteenth century, middle-class women were talking about female suffrage—votes for women. It was inevitable that at some stage these talks would be formalized into an organization. Prominent English suffragette Emmeline Pankhurst wrote of those early days:

I was fourteen years old when I went to my first suffrage meeting. Returning from school one day, I met my mother just setting out for the meeting, and I begged her to let me go along. She consented, and without stopping to lay my books down I scampered away in my mother's wake. The speeches interested and excited me, especially the address of the great Miss Lydia Becker, who was the Susan B. Anthony of the English movement, a splendid character and a truly eloquent speaker.[1]

In Ireland, Maeve McGarry was also introduced to the struggle for equality at a young age. In her witness statement to the Bureau of Military History, she wrote of her childhood:

My mother ... was also interested in the Suffragette movement and brought me into it. She spoke at meetings in Hyde Park. Pethwick Lawrence and his wife came to Dublin to speak at a meeting and they stayed with us. There were many public processions in which I marched.

Within the British Parliament, there was some support for female suffrage by more enlightened members. In 1866, John Stuart Mill presented the first women's suffrage petition to the House of Commons. It contained over fifteen hundred signatures; twenty-five Irish women appended their names. Eloquently, Mill proclaimed:

We ought not to deny to them, what we are conceding to everybody else—a right to be consulted; the ordinary chance of placing in the great Council of the nation a few organs of their sentiments—of having, what every petty trade or profession has, a few members who feel specially called on to attend to their interests, and to point out how those interests are affected by the law, or by any proposed changes in it.[2]

The petition proved to be no more than a momentary diversion in the doings of the House, however—nothing to be taken seriously. It was dismissed with little debate. Throughout the country, though, women were awakened to the cause of female suffrage. Societies were started in London, Edinburgh, and Manchester. In the following year, on 7th June, Mill presented a Second Reform Bill petition to Parliament advocating an extension of the suffrage. It also fell at the first hurdle. In response, the National Society for Women's Suffrage was founded. The Manchester branch of the society was formed in January 1867, the same year that the Parliamentary vote was extended to male heads of households. The organization held its first public meeting at the Manchester Free Trade Hall. As well as campaigning for the right to vote, it and the other branches of the campaign also supported changes to legislation regarding the position of married women, who had no civil existence in law. Married women at the time had no property or monetary rights; they could not divorce their husbands or claim any rights over their children. Access to higher-level education was also denied to them, as was entry into the higher professions, such as medicine or law.

A campaign by the NSWS was launched nationwide to repeal the Contagious Diseases Act. The legislation was a sensible attempt by the government to combat the spread of venereal diseases especially among the members of the armed services. In essence, though, it gave recognition, and thus, by implication, approval, to prostitution, and thus was seen by the Society as a threat to family life. In essence, under the law any woman could be taken into custody and subjected to a medical examination. The act, in the eyes of the female suffrage movement, introduced sexual double standards. Soldiers and sailors were not likewise examined. In the campaign to overturn this ill-thought-out legislation, we are introduced for the first time to two pioneers of Irish female suffrage: from Belfast, Isabella Tod, and from Dublin, Anna Haslam. Despite continual representation by them and others, the Act was not finally repealed until 1886.

Anna Haslam was born Anna Maria Fisher in 1829, to a liberal Quaker family living in Youghal, County Cork. Her family were noted for their philanthropic works, especially during the famine of the 1840s, when Anna helped in a soup kitchen. Anna married a fellow Quaker, Thomas Haslam, from County Laois, in 1854. The couple met while teaching at the Ackworth School in Yorkshire. The Haslams moved to Dublin in 1858. Here Anna taught knitting and lacemaking to young girls, later setting up a small lacemaking business of her own in Rathmines. In her first year in Dublin, she attended a talk at Blackrock, County Dublin, by Anne Robertson, a feminist speaker. Possibly through her influence, Anna was one of the signatories of John Stuart Mill's petition of 1866. Getting to know them, Mill opened correspondence with the Haslams during 1867 and 1868, in an attempt to boost enthusiasm for the feminist cause in Ireland. Thomas was a firm supporter of equality for men and women, and from 1868, he wrote a number of papers on women's suffrage and birth control. By 1869, the National Society for Women's Suffrage, established in London, had opened branches in Edinburgh and Dublin. Annie Robertson, of Blackrock, County Dublin, was appointed as honorary secretary of the Dublin Branch. In April 1870, she organized a public meeting in the Molesworth Hall in Dublin. The theme was the "electoral disabilities of women," and it was addressed by English suffragist leader Millicent Fawcett. Her speech was later reprinted in the *Freeman's Journal*. Listed in the audience of the meeting was Isabella Tod, more of whom later. Thomas Haslam, the much-ignored husband in feminist writings, was an active believer in human rights and the equality of women. His views on marriage and childrearing reflected his wide reading on social issues. In 1868, he wrote a treatise on birth control, a subject not generally associated with men at the time—nor, indeed, at the present. Thomas also produced a periodical called *The Women's Advocate* in 1874. Though it was a short-lived journal, the thrust of so much of the material published was the right of women to a more positive legal status.

On 26th January 1876, a suffrage meeting was held at the Exhibition Palace Hall, Earlsfoot Terrace, in Dublin. Among the speakers were two suffragettes from England: the Quaker Eliza Sturge, niece of Joseph Sturge, slave abolitionist, and prominent electoral reformer; and Lydia Becker, secretary of the Manchester Suffrage Society. Also on the platform was the increasingly influential Isabella Tod. Out of this meeting was formed the Dublin Women's Suffrage Society, which came into being one month later, on 21st February 1876. Anna Haslam was appointed joint secretary. Over the years, the Society evolved into the Irish Women's Suffrage and Local Government Association (IWSLGA). Most of its original members were drawn from the Society of Friends. Importantly, a number of prominent and influential men attended its meetings. These included Sir William Wilde, the Queen's surgeon in Ireland and the father of Oscar Wilde; Sir Robert Kane; the Reverend Lloyd, provost of Trinity College; the Reverend Mahaffy, also of Trinity College; and Sir John Gray, M.P. Though the membership was just one shilling a year, within the means of working women if paid in small sums over the course of the year, the DWSS remained an exclusive largely middle-class Quaker movement.

Isabella Tod, the other influential woman, referred to above, was born in Edinburgh in 1836. She came from a Presbyterian Scots-Irish family. Her mother was from County Monaghan. Isabella moved to Belfast with her family in the 1850s, when she was in her twenties. Again, through the influence of Anne Robertson, Isabella was drawn toward progressing female suffrage. She contributed to a number of newspapers and magazines, including the *Northern Whig* and the *Dublin University Magazine*. Isabella was prominent in the foundation of the North of Ireland Women's Suffrage Society, later to become the Irish Women's Suffrage Society. Articulate, she represented the Irish viewpoint as part of a larger English-led campaign, on the issue of married women's property rights—or lack of them. She was the only female witness to appear before a select committee of the House of Commons in 1868 to discuss the matter, thus indicating her importance to the movement. Isabella and the other women involved were successful in their endeavors when, in 1870, the first of a series of acts giving married women more control over their money and property was passed. That same year, promoting the rights of women, Isabella and Anne Robinson took to the road and began organizing feminist meetings across Ireland.

Meanwhile in England in that same year, Dr. Richard Pankhurst (later to marry Emmeline Goulden), a barrister and supporter of women's suffrage, drafted an enfranchisement bill known as the Women's Disabilities Removal Bill. It was introduced into the House of Commons by Jacob Bright, a Manchester M.P. and the brother of progressive Birmingham M.P. Joseph Bright. The bill advanced to its second reading by a majority of thirty-three votes, but it was killed off by direction of the Liberal Party prime minister, W.E. Gladstone. Now was not the time, he decided. There were more important issues. Also in 1870, Queen Victoria, whom one might think would have been sympathetic to the cause of female suffrage, expressed other views. Discovering that the Viscountess Amberley had become president of the Bristol and West of England Women's Suffrage Society, she wrote:

> I am most anxious to enlist everyone who can speak or write to join in checking this mad wicked folly of "Women's Rights," with all its attendant horrors, on which her poor feeble sex is bent, forgetting every sense of womanly feeling and propriety. Lady Amberley ought to get a good whipping. Were women to unsex themselves by claiming equality with men, they would become the most hateful, heathen and disgusting of beings and would surely perish without male protection.[3]

Ignoring such irrational thought by the monarch, back in Ireland in 1871, Isabella Tod cofounded the North of Ireland Women's Suffrage Society. As its secretary, she established links with the London Women's Suffrage Society. In agreement, the combined societies now lobbied for the vote in municipal elections and the right for women to become Poor Law Guardians. The thinking behind this was that if they could show female competence in these two areas, this would further promote the cause of Parliamentary female suffrage. Looking for other ways to progress improvements for women, in 1873, Isabella began campaigning to promote university education for women. In support of this, she published a paper in the following year entitled *On advanced education for girls in the upper and middle classes.* Her lobbying, and that of others, saw the successful passing of the Intermediate Education Act in 1878, and the University Act of 1879, which extended higher education to women. This advance was checked, much to the chagrin of the women graduates, by the fact that women were forbidden entry into many of the professions.

Isabella, and one or two other members of the NIWSS, then took the suffrage campaign out on the road. They gave lectures to mixed audiences, first in the towns of the northeast, before moving on and finishing in Dublin. It would seem most likely that she and Anna Haslam met up. However, it was not until three years later that the campaign in Dublin really took off with the establishment of a Dublin branch of the Women's Suffrage Association (DWSA).[4] This followed a public meeting held in the Exhibition Palace Hall, Earlsfort Terrace, Dublin. The

Isabella Tod

first meeting of the Dublin branch was held on 21st February 1876, in the Leinster Hall. It was chaired by a male suffragette supporter, Charles Eason, who, along with his wife, had a history of supporting the female cause. The inclusion of men in the movement was to become a positive feature of the DWSA, to the extent that it was noted in the records of the movement: "Co-operation with men has been a distinguishing feature of the policy of the Association from the first."[5] An annual membership subscription was set at one shilling per year. Yet despite this small amount, the DWSA remained a very middle-class organization. Though the DWSA remained a small organization, barely rising above fifty members, it participated wholeheartedly in the cause of women's suffrage in Ireland. Promoting the cause in 1874, Isabella Tod summarized the case for equality:

> [Women are] citizens of the state, inheritors with men of all history which ennobles a nation, guardians with men of all the best life of the nation; bound as much as men are bound to consider the good of the whole; and justified as men are justified in sharing the good of the whole.[6]

While it failed to influence the Parliamentary vote, the DWSA was more successful in local government issues. It witnessed reform in the Women's Poor Law Guardian bill of 1897, and the Local Government Act of 1898, which allowed women to run for office in district council and poor law boards. In 1899, some 115 women were appointed as district councilors or poor law guardians. The DWSA could claim some part in that success for democratic change.

There was good news from one part of the United Kingdom. In November 1880, the Isle of Man granted female suffrage in an amendment to the Manx Election Act of 1875. Meanwhile, between 1879 and 1884, and recognizing her talents, the English branch of the Women's Suffrage Society invited Isabella to give talks in London, Glasgow, Bristol, Manchester, Newcastle, Cambridge, Exeter, Dover, and Cheltenham. She had emerged from a regional spokesperson, to become a national one, on the question of female suffrage. However, about this time, 1884, Isabella turned her attentions toward other causes, dissipating her participation in the women' struggle. Her new crusade was the temperance movement, but with a female emphasis. As early as 1874, she became involved in the establishment of the Belfast Women's Temperance Association. What prompted her to redirect her efforts is uncertain. It would seem that her idea was that if drink-related issues were dealt with, then that would improve the lives of women. She established a home for alcoholic women and set up canteens for working-class Belfast factory girls. In 1893, Isabella became vice president of the Irish Women's Total Abstinence Union. It took up most of her time. One of the leading lights of her age, Isabella Tod was lost to the cause of female suffrage.

Middle-class women were also lost to the campaign for suffrage by the founding of the nationalist Ladies' Land League, an adjunct of the banned Land League founded by Michael Davitt and Charles Stewart Parnell. The aim of the two societies was the destruction of landlordism in Ireland and better rights for tenant farmers. In Parliament, the prime minister, W.E. Gladstone, sought to end the agitation by passing a well-intentioned, but ill-thought-out and incomplete Land Act in 1881. This legislation set up fair rents, and many tenant farmers benefited from it. Subtenants, however, who were the greater majority of farmers, and who were not covered by the act, were not helped. Parnell and the other Land League leaders spoke out against the Act in a series of speeches, pointing out its failures. Agitation followed. Davitt, and later Parnell, were arrested on a charge of incitement to violence, under the Coercion Act, on a charge of "reasonable suspicion" of promoting violence. Other Irish M.P.s and regional leaders of the Land League were also arrested. Parnell's response was to issue a manifesto to the tenant farmers of Ireland to pay no rent. Agrarian violence continued, and if anything, escalated. The British government proclaimed the Land League, under the terms of the Coercion Act, to be an illegal association. In response the Ladies' Land League was founded to continue the agitation. The female organization showed themselves capable of organizing and operating a countryside campaign. From his prison cell, Parnell agreed to negotiate an end to the violence if the government would settle the rent arrears problem. Parnell was released, and an Arrears of Rent (Ireland) Act was passed, solving the problem. The women involved in the Land campaign now had a nationalist agenda, for it was Parnell's belief that the destruction of landlordism in Ireland might also lead to the overthrow of British power in Ireland.

In England, in 1884, a Reform Bill was presented in Parliament. It was to be a further reform of Britain's system of voting. The Bill concentrated on rural areas bypassed by the 1867 Reform Act, which had dealt with urban areas, notably the emerging industrial towns and cities. The Conservative Party saw it as a cynical ploy. The Liberal Party, which introduced it, was aiming at the poorer people in the counties as opposed to the great landowners. These they believed would be natural Liberal supporters. While in its early stages, representation was made by the various female suffrage groups throughout Great Britain, for the inclusion of women. Anna Haslam, honorary secretary of the DWSA, wrote to the newspapers making the case for women. Her letter appeared in the English newspaper, the *Daily Express*, in April 1884:

> The only debatable argument is whether we [women] shall be included in the present Franchise Bill or be compelled to go on agitating, petitioning, addressing public meetings, interviewing members of Parliament memorializing Cabinet Ministers … for another ten or fifteen years, to the exceeding waste of time of these energies which we might be devoting to the improvement of our educational, sanitary, licensing, poor law and other systems which greatly need reform.

After making concessions to the lords, the bill was passed into law. The Reform Act extended the vote to all adult householders, and men who rented unfurnished lodgings, to the value of ten pounds a year. It increased the electorate to 5,500,000. It did nothing for women, none of whom were given the right to vote regardless of wealth. In Belfast, however, change was coming. A bylaw of 1887 was passed, granting rate-paying women the right to vote in municipal elections. Nine years later, in 1896, Belfast M.P. William Johnston introduced the Women's Poor Law Guardian (Ireland) Bill, to bring it in line with England and Wales. It was successfully carried through all its stages in the House of Commons without opposition. The DWSA threw its support into implementing its recommendations. Here was a chance to show that women could take up the responsibilities. In the process, Anna Haslam visited a number of workhouses in England and Wales to better understand how they were run. With strong DWSA support, eleven ladies were elected as poor law guardians. What they offered was a more compassionate approach to workhouse inmates and indicated the capabilities of women, given the opportunity. By 1898, thirty-five women had been elected as poor law guardians.

In Dublin, the fight for female suffrage continued, but it began to stall. By 1896, the DWSA had only forty-three members. They were drawn almost exclusively from the Quaker movement. In October of that year, Anna Haslam traveled to Birmingham to attend a national suffrage conference. The con-

ference proposed the joining together of the disparate organizations to build
a National Union of Women's Suffrage Societies. Both the DWSA and its
Belfast equivalent became founding members. Mrs. Haslam was appointed
to the London executive.

Lack of support for the suffrage campaign in Ireland was to some degree
also due to the cultural revival of Irish nationalism, offering other outlets to
women. Home Rule was in the air. The people were being encouraged to look
upon themselves no longer as "West Britons," but as Irish men and women.
The Gaelic Athletic Association was founded in 1885. It rejected English
sports in favor of national pastimes. Perhaps the real impetus was the establishment of the Gaelic League in 1893. Its original intention was the promotion
of the Irish language, culture, and customs. Its founders—Douglas Hyde, a
Protestant, and Eoin MacNeill, a Catholic—believed that in the restoration
of the language they could show to the world that Ireland was a separate
nation. The League was nonsectarian and right from the outset strove to
remain independent, and outside, of politics. For this reason, many Unionists
and Protestants joined, only to find that their political beliefs softened toward

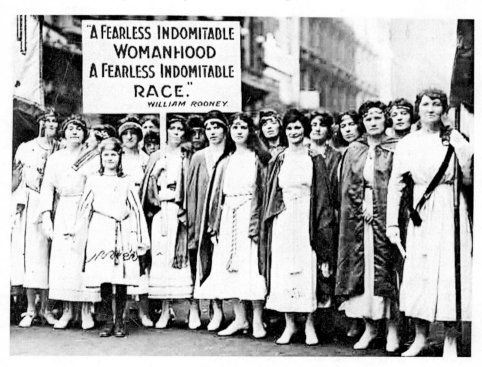

By 1905, Irish suffragettes also incorporated ideas of nationalism into their philosophy.

Irish nationalism. By 1903, there were six hundred branches of the Gaelic League throughout the country. For the moment, the fight for women's suffrage in Ireland had stalled.

In 1898, the government passed a further Local Government Act, strongly influenced by the participation of the Irish M.P.s at Westminster, which included Michael Davitt. It brought into line the 1884 Act, giving equal rights to women. Women who qualified could

> now enjoy all the franchises possessed by their English sisters together with the lodger franchise not yet conferred upon the latter. They now also enjoy all the franchises possessed by their fellow countrymen except the parliamentary; and if they have not yet obtained seats upon the County and Borough Councils, there is every probability that these will be thrown open to them at no very distant date.[7]

Previously in 1897, the proposed British-based National Union of Women's Suffrage Societies (NUWSS) was eventually founded. It brought together more than twenty disparate societies under one fold. Its leader was the very able Millicent Garrett Fawcett. The new organization began undertaking public meetings, organized petitions, wrote letters to politicians, published pamphlets, and handed out free literature. It was largely an educated middle-class organization, with contacts within the British Establishment. It is doubtful whether, in their minds, their struggle for female suffrage extended beyond their own class. It must have come as a surprise to them when, in March 1901, working-class women presented a petition to Parliament. Some thirty-seven thousand working women from the textile industry called for female suffrage. This petition was followed up by further petitions from working women in Yorkshire and Cheshire. The petitions were collected by maverick suffragists Esther Roper and Eva Gore-Booth. A few years earlier, Eva, the daughter of an Irish Ascendancy family, and her sister Constance (later the Countess Markievicz) helped found the Sligo Women's Suffrage Association. Now based in Manchester, Eva and her partner, Esther Roper, became involved in the Manchester, Salford, and District Women's Trade Union Council, as well as the Independent Labor Party. Unlike the NUWSS, the Roper-Gore-Booth movement was working class–based. The suffrage movement in Lancashire had become socialist. In 1902, in their next venture, the two women began collecting signatures and calling for votes for women from female graduates all over Great Britain and Ireland. One of the signatories was Irishwoman Hanna Sheehy Skeffington, later to become a highly influential figure in the Irish suffrage movement. The activities of Roper and Gore-Booth in the north of England brought the two into contact with the Pankhursts, and both Roper and Gore-Booth supported the establishment of the more radical Women's Social and Political Union (WSPU) in 1903.

The Pankhursts, like many other young, educated middle-class women supporters of the cause, thought that Fawcett's almost benign form of agitation was not enough. They became frustrated at the lack of activity and so broke away to form a new organization. "Deeds, not words," became their watchword. They took to the streets to promote their cause, even protesting, rather aggressively, it was suggested, outside the House of Commons. As a consequence, members were arrested on spurious charges, such as obstructing the police, and were imprisoned. The *Daily Mail* coined the term "suffragette" for those women who took part in this form of militant protest. Their more aggressive form of agitation did bring the women's struggle back to the fore. Actions had done more than all the letter writing of the NUWSS.

Perhaps fearful of losing support to the militants, in 1907, Fawcett organized a London march. More than three thousand women and men took part in the march through the capital. The weather was atrocious, with rain lashing down. There were few spectators. The demonstration became known as the "Mud March." Its success was limited; certainly it had little effect on some gentlemen in Parliament. On 8th March, the Women's Enfranchisement Bill, known popularly as the Dickinson Bill, passed its first reading in Parliament, but was talked out, quite deliberately, on its second reading. In response, seventy-five suffragettes were arrested when members of the WSPU angrily attempted to storm the Houses of Parliament.

English and Irish suffragettes. Left to right: Flora Drummond, Christabel Pankhurst, Jessie Kenney, Nellie Martel, Emmeline Pankhurst, and Charlotte Despard.

The British suffragists perhaps overreached themselves when they tried to introduce their own brand of women's suffrage into Ireland, particularly in the north. These new organizations were, by and large, Unionist based, including the Conservative and Unionist Suffrage Association, the Church League for Women's Suffrage, and the Men's League for Women's Suffrage. The situation in Ireland was far more complex than in Britain. Ireland was struggling with Home Rule, opposition to Home Rule, and the rise of organized labor. All three elements derived support from the different classes of women within the suffrage movement. The Irish struggle was far from being a case of one brand of suffrage serving all. That said, in 1906, the Irish Women's Suffrage and Local Government Association (IWSLGA) was founded and led by the old campaigner Anna Haslam. It was based very much on the British model of Fawcett's National Union of Women's Suffrage Societies. It attempted to bring together all the other suffrage groups in Ireland under one banner. Enthused by the prospect of a combined organization whose aim was to secure the vote for women, many joined, including young university graduates such as Hanna Sheehy Skeffington and Margaret Cousins. Like the Pankhursts in England, they, too, became disillusioned after a while at the pacifist nature of the new movement, which contented itself with writing polite letters to the newspapers and appeals to M.P.s. In November 1908, Hanna Sheehy Skeffington and Margaret Cousins went to see Anna Haslam. In her joint autobiography with her husband, Cousins wrote:

> So a group of us went on November 6 to the dear old leader of the constitutional suffragettes, Mrs. Anna Haslam, to inform her that we younger women were ready to start a new women's suffrage society on militant lines. She regretted what she felt to be a duplication of effort.[8]

The two younger women broke away and set up the Irish Women's Franchise League (IWFL). It was influenced by the militancy of the Pankhurst's WSPU. The watchword of the new organization was "Suffrage first, before all else." Initially it was non-party political, and as such, it attracted young, middle class women regardless of their political leanings. Meetings were held on a weekly basis, weather permitting, in Dublin's Phoenix Park, and at other venues across the country. It started off with just twelve members, but by 1912, it had approximately one thousand members, making it Ireland's largest suffrage society. The movement expanded to include the Conservative and Unionist Women's Franchise League, the Munster Women's Franchise League, the Irishwomen's Suffrage Federation, the North of Ireland Women's Suffrage Committee, the Irish Women's Suffrage Society, and the Irishwomen's Suffrage and Local Government Association. The new organization attracted both nationalists and unionists. Problems arose, though, when the majority of members sought to align the movement within the context of the existing struggle for Home Rule, thus tying it to the nationalist cause. In the process, there was a disconnect with its Unionist members.

Hanna Sheehy, the IWFL cofounder, was born in Kanturk, County Cork, in 1877. She was from a nationalist background; her father and uncle were connected to the Irish Republican Brotherhood, and both had been imprisoned for their revolutionary activities. Her uncle, Father Eugene Sheehy, "the Land League Priest," was one of Eamon deValera's teachers in Limerick. The family moved to 2 Belvedere Place, in Dublin, and Hanna was educated at the Dominican Convent on Eccles Street. During 1896–1897, the family held an open house on the second Sunday night of each month. Regular visitors included the singer and soon-to-be writer James Joyce. As a young woman, Hanna was educated at St. Mary's University College for Women, and she was the first woman to graduate, gaining a BA in modern languages in 1899. She added an MA in 1902. Hanna worked briefly in Paris as an au pair before returning to Ireland and marrying Francis Skeffington in June 1903. The two were introduced by their mutual friend James Joyce, who was at university

Hanna Sheehy Skeffington

with Skeffington. Francis was a pacifist and feminist, believing in women's suffrage and a woman's right to higher education. They famously took each other's surnames, both becoming Sheehy Skeffington. The couple moved to Airfield Road, Rathgar, Dublin.

Margaret Cousins, like so many leading advocates of women's suffrage in Ireland at the time, was Protestant by religion. She was born Margaret

Elizabeth Gillespie at Boyle, County Roscommon, in 1878. She moved to Dublin in 1898 to study music at the Royal Irish Academy, from where she graduated with a degree in music in 1902. She married James Cousins in Sandymount in 1903. They were both involved in Dublin literary circles and included W.B. Yeats, James Joyce, George Russell, and the Sheehy Skeffingtons among their friends.

In England in 1908, a mass rally of between three hundred thousand and five hundred thousand suffragettes was held in Hyde Park in London. The prime minister, Herbert Asquith, who was totally against giving women the vote, refused to receive a delegation sent by them. Frustrated, the suffragettes began a campaign of window smashing. Government offices in Downing Street were a particular target, with messages demanding the vote, attached to stones, thrown at the windows. Arrests and imprisonment followed.

In 1909, Margaret Cousins was sent as a delegate to England to confer with the Pankhursts and to coordinate action. That summer she worked with the WSPU, declaring, "it was a helpful apprenticeship for our campaign later in Ireland."[9] Cooperation between the two groups was reciprocal. On Friday, 11th March 1910, Christabel Pankhurst spoke at the Round Room in the Rotunda, Dublin. The admission fee was two shillings, which helped the cause, but rather excluded working-class women. In 1910, Cousins attended the Parliament of Women in Caxton Hall, London. She took part in the mass protest of 18th November 1910 that followed, wherein three hundred women marched on the House of Commons when they discovered that Prime Minister Herbert Asquith had no intention of giving women the vote. The protest was brutally broken up by the police, the women being beaten, punched, and kicked before being thrown to the ground. The day became known as "Black Friday." Emmeline Pankhurst recounts the incident in her autobiography:

> The country was on the eve of a general election. This fact made the wholesale arrest and imprisonment of great numbers of women, who were demanding the passage of the Conciliation Bill, extremely undesirable from the Government's point of view.... So the Government conceived a plan whereby the Suffragettes were to be punished, were to be turned back and defeated in their purpose of reaching the House, but would not be arrested. Orders were evidently given that the police were to be present in the streets, and that the women were to be thrown from one uniformed or uninformed policeman to another, that they were to be so rudely treated that sheer terror would cause them to turn back.[10]

In response a few days later, keeping up the pressure, the suffragettes began breaking more windows of government departments. Margaret Cousins was arrested for smashing the windows of cabinet ministers' offices in Downing Street. She was sentenced to one month's imprisonment in Holloway Prison. Other equally militant members, who had chained themselves to the railings of public buildings, were likewise imprisoned.

Previously, Scottish WSPU member Marion Wallace Dunlop was sent to prison in June 1909 for willful damage. She petitioned the governor of Holloway, claiming that she was not a common criminal. Her view was that she was a political prisoner and should be treated as such: "I claim the right recognized by all civilized nations that a person imprisoned for a political offence should have first division treatment; and as a matter of principle, not only for my own sake but for the sake of others who may come after me, I am now refusing all food until this matter is settled to my satisfaction." She had adopted the suffragette's new weapon of the hunger strike to secure recognition of status. Others were to follow her. Fellow suffragette prisoner Margaret Palmer wrote of her first few days on hunger strike, which echoes Marion Dunlop's:

> To the Hunger-Striker, one day is the same as another, and each hour as it comes is exactly the same as the last. The day is spent sitting upright on one's chair, looking at nothing, doing nothing, but thinking, thinking always. The blood stagnates at the knees, one creeps over to the bed to seek a change of position and get relief, but none comes. At last too weak to sit upright, one is forced to lie down—still no relief; every pulse in the body throbs, throbs incessantly, the heart thumps heavily through the body to the back, no sleep will come, and the hours creep slowly, slowly on.
>
> It is this sickening monotony, the awful silence, the ever present evidence of punishment, the barred windows, and above all, the relentless enemy, waiting, watching, to take any possible advantage as one's bodily strength gives out inch by inch—these are the things which play such mental havoc with the Hunger-Striker.[11]

Unsure of what to do, the governor at Holloway appealed to Herbert Gladstone, the home secretary. His decision was that she should not be allowed to die in prison. There were to be no martyrs, he decided. After ninety-one hours without food, Marion Dunlop was admonished once more for her behavior and released.

The situation regarding the status of convicted suffragettes remained vague. In Ireland, following the arrest and imprisonment of Meg Connery for smashing windows, Margaret Cousins, the secretary of IWFL, wrote to the lord lieutenant in Dublin Castle, drawing his attention to the fact that convicted suffragettes were being categorized as common criminals rather than political prisoners, which would entitle them to certain privileges. From the Lord Lieutenant's office came the reply, later published in the *Irish Times*: "imprisonment was not an integral part of the sentence, but would follow necessarily upon failure to pay the damages and fines imposed by the court. Payment would avoid imprisonment, and in these circumstances His Excellency is not empowered to interfere with the course of the Law." By the time the letter appeared in the newspaper, Meg Connery had been released. While political status was denied—Britain has always maintained that she does not have political prisoners—the status of her political prisoners has been hidden under the classification of "first-class misdemeanant," or prisoners with privileges. Prisoners so classified were allowed the privileges under Rule 231 of free association, the right to wear their own clothes, have food brought in, have daily visits, books and letters, and exercise. Invariably suffragettes who went on hunger strike ensured their release before they had served their full sentence. No official wanted a dead suffragette on their hands.

A new organization, the Women's Tax Resistance League, was formed in 1909. Its platform was simple: Women should refuse to pay taxes if they did not have political representation. Their battle cry was "No vote, no tax." Aimed at middle-class women, the new organization had little real support. Court appearances followed for nonpayment of tax. Another idea for resistance concerned noncompliance with the census, which is taken in Britain every ten years. On 1st April 1911, a letter was published in the pro-Unionist *Irish Times*. It was written by Mary Earl of the Irish Women's Franchise League. She suggested that women should boycott the census, due to be taken the following evening. Her justification was that the statistics gathered would be used by Parliament, which consisted only of men, elected by men, to make laws affecting women. Therefore, women would be justified in flouting the law while they had no share in its enactment. Her argument was logical, and many middle-class women both in Britain and Ireland engaged in civil disobedience by being absent from home when the census was taken.

Within the Irish Parliamentary Party, there was some support for female suffrage by individual members. Using them, the IWFL launched a determined campaign to have female suffrage included in the forthcoming third Home Rule Bill. Asquith's liberal government was clinging to power. It needed the support of the Irish Parliamentary Party. The price of that support was Home Rule. Inclusion of female suffrage, though, was a step too far. Asquith was very much opposed to giving women the vote. He more or less blackmailed Irish Parliamentary leader John Redmond into dropping the idea. Asquith warned him that he would resign if Redmond pressed for female suffrage, thus triggering a general election. If the Conservatives won, and it was quite probable that they would, then Home Rule was dead in the water. If Redmond would drop female suffrage from the Bill, then Asquith would ensure that Home Rule became a reality. Redmond readily agreed. Meanwhile, the British government was faced with another attempt at limited female suffrage in the shape of the Conciliation Bill. If passed, the law would grant limited suffrage to one million women who owned property over the value of £10. In order to stabilize the political partnership with the Liberals, Redmond and the IPP gave their support to Asquith's government and refused to support the Bill. It was defeated by 222 votes to 208. In April 1912, when the third Home Rule Bill was introduced, there was no reference to female franchise.

Following some disgruntled letters to the newspapers over the failure of the Conciliation Bill, Irish M.P. John Dillon scathingly dismissed female suffrage: "Women's suffrage will, I believe, be the ruin of our western civilization. It will destroy the home, challenging the headship of man, laid down by God. It may come in your time—I hope not in mine." The Catholic Church, which held so much sway over its religious adherents, also condemned women's suffrage. Father Barry of the Irish Ecclesiastical Record gave his opinion that "allowing women the right of suffrage is incompatible with the Catholic ideal of the unity of domestic life and would fare ill with the passive virtues of humility, patience, meekness, forbearance and self-repression looked upon by the church as the special prerogative of the female soul."

Openly dismissed by the Irish Parliamentary Party, as well as the churches, both Catholic and Protestant, and ignored or belittled by the press, it became increasingly difficult for the suffragettes to get their message across. Outside of Dublin, access to many public halls was denied them. Speakers at outside public meetings, on temporary stages, were heckled, and posters advertising the meetings were torn down. As frustration grew, the response from the more militant suffragettes was inevitable. On 13th June 1912 members of the IWFL embarked on an episode of window smashing in public buildings, including the GPO, the Customs House, and at the very heart of British rule in Ireland—Dublin Castle. The response by the police was equally immediate and decisive. Eight leading activists were arrested and put on trial. Some two hundred women packed the courtroom. Hanna Sheehy Skeffington, Marguerite Palmer, sisters Jane and Margaret Murphy, and later Kathleen Houston, Marjorie Hasler, Maud Lloyd, and Hilda Webb were sentenced to either a fine or two months' imprisonment. They all refused to pay the fine and were sent to prison.

There then followed a very dramatic, if foolish action, which the *Sunday Independent* described as a "dastardly suffragette outrage." In July 1912, four members of the English WSPU, without consulting the IWFL, traveled to Dublin. There, by their actions, they brought the Irish suffrage movement into disrepute. The prime minister, having made known his support for Home Rule, was being feted by the leaders of the Irish Parliamentary Party in Dublin. Members of the IWFL met Asquith when he arrived by boat at Kingstown, shouted at him through megaphones, and paraded with posters along his route into Dublin, demanding votes for women. It was attention-seeking, promoting the cause, but not violent; par for the course, it could be said. As Asquith was conducted that evening through the streets of the city in a torch-light procession, in gentle remonstration, the Irish suffragettes rained down on him "votes for women" confetti from upper windows. Down below on the streets, the women protesting with their banners did not get off so lightly. They were attacked by Redmond supporters, thugs from the Ancient Order of Hibernians, who were "determined to punish womanhood for the acts of militant women from England." Supporters and innocent bystanders caught up in the fray were forced to take refuge in shops and houses. As the carriage carrying Asquith and Redmond crossed over O'Connell Bridge amid the cheers of the supporters of Home Rule, an English suffragette, Mary Leigh, threw a small axe into the carriage. Attached to it was a written message: "This symbol of the extinction of the Liberal Party for evermore." The axe missed Asquith, but struck John Redmond, who was sitting next to the prime minister, on the arm. He was not seriously hurt. Leigh meanwhile escaped into the crowd.

Later that night, the four suffragettes entered the Royal Theatre as the audience was leaving. Asquith was due to speak there the following day. Leigh, along with Jennie Baines (using the alias of Lizzie Baker), set fire to a chair and flung it over the edge of a box, into the orchestra pit. Gladys Evans set fire to a carpet. Up in the cinema projection room, they collected bottles of petrol, then threw in tins filled with gunpowder, and dropped lighted matches. There was a mild explosion, and the room was set alight. Hearing the disturbance, members of the staff were soon on the scene and quickly extinguished the small fires. As the Englishwomen fled, they were caught by other members of staff and by Sergeant Durban Cooper of the Connaught Rangers, who was on leave. As they waited for the police to arrive, one of the women in defiance shouted out, "There will be more explosions in the second house. This is only the start of it."[12] The women were arrested and tried at the Green Street Special Criminal Court in Dublin before Judge Madden, on a charge of "Serious outrages at the time of the visit of the British Prime Minister Herbert Asquith." The attorney general, no less, C.A. O'Connor, conducted the prosecution. This was as much a political as a criminal trial. Gladys Evans, daughter of a London stockbroker, was found guilty of conspiring to do bodily harm and damage property. Mary Leigh, formerly a schoolteacher, was charged with throwing the axe at Asquith, and taking part in throwing the burning chair into the orchestra pit. Jennie Baines, the third suffragette, was not identified as being at the theater, so no blame could be attached to her for the fire. However, she was sharing a rented room at a house in Mount Street with Mabel Capper, wherein was found flammable liquid and rubber gloves similar to those used in the arson attack. The trial lasted several days, and the defendants were described as "highly dangerous provocateurs." All were found guilty. Before passing sentence, Judge Madden pronounced that it was his "imperative duty to pronounce a sentence that is calculated to have a deterrent effect." Gladys Evans and Mary Leigh were sentenced to five years of penal servitude. Baines and Capper were sentenced to seven months each, but they were quickly let go. Leigh and Evans went on a hunger strike. Leigh was force-fed for forty-six days until her release on 21st September 1912. Evans was force-fed for fifty days until her release on 23rd October 1912, due to ill health.[13]

For Mary Leigh, it was not the first time that she had been force-fed. In a statement published by the WSPU in October 1909, she described her first time:

> On Saturday afternoon the wardress forced me into the bed and two doctors came in. While I was held down a nasal tube was inserted. It is two yards long, with a funnel at the end; there is a glass junction in the middle to see if the liquid is passing. The end is put up the right and left nostril on alternative days. The sensation is most painful—the drums of the ears seem to be bursting and there is a horrible pain in the throat and the breast. The tube is pushed down 20 inches. I am on the bed pinned down by wardresses, one doctor holds the funnel end, and the other doctor forces the other end up the nostrils. The one holding the funnel end pours the liquid down—about a pint of milk ... egg and milk sometimes used.

Lady Constance Lytton, imprisoned as Jane Warton in Walton Prison, Liverpool, gives a more graphic description of force-feeding:

> I was visited by the Senior Medical Officer at about 6 o'clock in the evening with five wardresses and the feeding apparatus.... I offered no resistance to being placed in position but lay down voluntarily on the plank bed. Two of the wardresses took hold of my arms, one held my head and one my feet. One wardress helped pour the food. The doctor leant on my knees as he stooped over my chest to get at my mouth. I shut my mouth and clenched my teeth. The sense of being overpowered by more force than I could possibly resist was complete, but I resisted only with my mouth. The doctor offered me a choice of a wooden or steel gag; he explained elaborately, as he did on most subsequent occasions, that the steel gag would hurt and the wooden one not, and he urged me not to force him to use the steel gag. I did not speak nor open my mouth. He seemed annoyed at my reticence and he broke into a temper as he plied my teeth with the steel implement. The pain of it was intense and at last I must have given way for he got the gag between my teeth, when he proceeded to turn it until my jaws were fastened wide apart. Then he put down my throat a tube. The irritation of the tube was excessive. I choked the moment it touched my throat until it had got down. Then the food was poured in quickly; it made me sick a few seconds after it was down and the action of the sickness made my body and legs double up, but the wardresses instantly pressed back by head and the doctor leant on my knees. The horror of it was more than I can describe. It seemed a long time before they took the tube out. As the doctor left he gave me a slap on the cheek, not violently, but as it were, to express his contemptuous disapproval. When the doctor had gone out of the cell, I lay quite helpless.[14]

Mary Clarke, the sister of Emmeline Pankhurst, was forcibly fed while in detention in Holloway Prison. She was released on 22nd December 1910, but two days later she was dead as the result of a burst blood vessel on the brain. Her death was attributed to her being force-fed. Clearly force-feeding had its dangers.

To the Irish suffragettes, the actions of the Englishwomen had a suggestion of imperial undertones. They had come to Ireland to show the Irish how to conduct their affairs. As a consequence, there was resentment on the part of the Irishwomen. The IWFL was quick to distance themselves from the actions of the English suffragettes. A statement, signed by a number of members, was issued denouncing the British suffragettes who had attacked the British prime minister on Irish soil. Hanna Sheehy Skeffington was later to write that she "deplored the fact that they [the Englishwomen] had not left the 'heckling' to the Irishwomen ... the best meaning English have blind spots where the Sister Isle is concerned."[15] In a letter published in the *Irish Citizen* (27th July 1912), IWFL secretary Margaret Cousins wrote, ""the IWFL had no connection with or knowledge of the action of English suffragettes in Dublin." Though angry at the intervention into Irish affairs, four of the imprisoned Irish suffragists, due for release within days, went on a sympathetic hunger strike. While the English suffragettes were forcibly fed, this was not the case with the Irishwomen, whose actions were seen as more passive and perhaps understandable.

THE
IRISH CITIZEN

AUGUST 15, 1914. - ONE PENNY

VOTES FOR WOMEN
NOW!
DAMN
YOUR WAR!

The Irish Citizen, a suffragette newspaper

They were soon released. On a second level, the behavior of the English suffragettes was seen in the public conscience as an attack on the man who was promoting Home Rule. This might perhaps explain the length of sentence imposed on Leigh and Evans and the more aggressive approach to their hunger strike. Although twenty-four more suffragettes would be imprisoned in Ireland, and most went on hunger strike, the Irish prison authorities did not forcibly feed them. Indeed, the Irish suffragette prisoners were treated with greater leniency, being considered as political prisoners rather than criminals, with all the privileges that allowed. Margaret Cousins, arrested with Margaret Connery and Barbara Hoskins for smashing windows in Dublin Castle, confirms a more lenient manner in the treatment of female suffrage prisoners. Cousins, who had served time in an English prison for her political activities, revealed in an article for the *Freeman's Journal* (28th February 1913):

> The Irish prison system [is] more humane than the English. We were addressed by our names, not by numbers as in Holloway ... we felt very well pleased that Ireland had come through its test so humanely and had not stained its history, as England had stained hers, by forcibly feeding suffrage prisoners.

The question of force-feeding Irish suffragettes remained in a state of limbo within the Irish penal system until the request for clarification by John

Boland, the governor of Tullamore Prison, to the chief secretary. He pondered the question, "if they are to be fed forcibly through the nose, will he give a reference to the legal authority for this practice."[16] The reply was a deathly silence. The governor took it that there was no lawful authority, and so did not instigate force-feeding. Tullamore had become the prison to which suffragette prisoners were sent. It achieved fame, if *fame* is the right word, in the case of the "Tullamore Mice," highlighted in the *Irish Citizen*. A number of suffragettes, including Marguerite Palmer, had been arrested for smashing windows in Dublin, and sentenced to six weeks' imprisonment for nonpayment of fines. They

NOTHING FOR THEIR "PANES."

Militant suffragettes smashed windows in Dublin Castle and in other notable buildings.

demanded to be treated as political prisoners. It should perhaps be admitted that they were treated as such, in all but name. They enjoyed privileges not available to common criminals. The women went on a hunger strike. The governor responded with his request to the authorities in the castle. In the absence of a reply, he withdrew a number of privileges, including the receiving of books, a fire in the cell (not enjoyed by convicted criminals), and the withdrawal of pillows. Failing to break the strike, the women were released under the "Cat and Mouse Act," and ordered to return within a fixed number of weeks to complete their sentences. Following their release, a mass meeting was held in the Dublin Mansion House, attended by all shades of the suffragette movement and others, to highlight their case. In the end, the "Mice" failed to return to prison as ordered, but no attempt was made to re-arrest them. Indeed, it would seem that Boland was glad to see the back of them.

In the period between 1912 and the outbreak of World War I, a number of provincial suffrage groups sprang up. The Munster Women's Franchise League was established in Cork, with further branches opening in Limerick and Waterford. In Galway, the Connacht Women's Franchise League came into being. In the north, the Irish Women's Suffrage Society was established, with branches in Belfast, Derry, and Bangor. The Irish Women's Suffrage Federation (IWSF) was established to bring these many disparate organizations under one banner. While their numbers grew, and they distributed pamphlets and flyers, what was really needed was a newspaper that could coordinate their actions.

In 1912, in order to give a greater voice to the call of women's suffrage in Ireland, husband and wife Francis and Hanna Sheehy Skeffington founded the *Irish Citizen,* a suffragette newspaper. Its motto was "For Men and Women Equally the Rights of Citizenship; For Men and Women Equally the Duties of Citizen-

TORTURING WOMEN IN PRISON

VOTE AGAINST THE GOVERNMENT

While no Irish suffragettes were force-fed, English suffragettes, guilty of arson in Dublin, were.

ship." The money to set up the newspaper was reputedly donated by an English suffragist couple, the Pethick-Lawrences. Editorship of the new paper was shared by Francis Sheehy Skeffington, who had a journalist background, and James, husband of Margaret Cousins. An eight-page weekly, it sold for just one penny, making it accessible to working-class women. Within one month, the paper was able to claim weekly sales of three thousand and an estimated readership of ten thousand, the paper being passed around after having been read. Francis wrote the unsigned editorials and other articles. James Cousins also initially wrote articles until the readership responded with articles and correspondence of its own. The following year, the Cousins, experiencing financial difficulties, left Ireland to work in England, before later traveling on to India, where the couple reengaged with female suffrage in the subcontinent.

With the third Home Rule Bill before the House of Commons, Hanna, Jane, Margaret Murphy, and Margaret Palmer sought to bring to the attention of the appropriate authorities, the cause of female suffrage. They engaged in an orgy of window smashing at Dublin Castle, the very heart of the British administration in Ireland. For this, on 20th June 1912, they were convicted of willful damage and sentenced to a month in prison. They were imprisoned in Mountjoy, with all the privileges of political prisoners.

Francis likewise kept up the pressure in the *Irish Citizen*. His fear was that the Irish Parliamentary Party, after Home Rule was established, could not be trusted to give the vote to women. On 13th July 1912, he wrote:

> The Bill as it stands [before Parliament] ignores the change that has taken place since 1893; its electoral provisions are identical with those of the last Home Rule Bill. Irish women have contributed to build up local government and to make it a success. We claim for them a free entry into the edifice of which they have helped to lay the foundations. To refuse them that entry is inconsistent with the spirit of Nationalism…. "We want Home Rule for all Ireland or no Home Rule," said Mr. Dillon lately; and all nationalists who have a sense of their duty to their fellow countrywomen will echo this declaration. Home Rule for men only would clearly not be Home Rule for all Ireland. The chief excuse urged for the exclusion of women is that "this is a matter for the Irish Parliament to determine itself." Now if the Irish Parliament were left to determine its own franchise from the beginning, there might be some point in this; but it is not so permitted. The franchise for the Irish Parliament is being fixed at Westminster; we should see then that it is fixed justly, and not on the basis of sex-inequality…. Moreover, those who argue that the existing franchise ought not to be changed until it is done by the Home Rule Parliament are themselves, with astonishing inconsistency, assisting the Imperial Parliament to make a still more drastic change in the franchise. Manhood suffrage is not being left to the Irish Parliament to decide on; if the Government's Franchise and Registration Bill be carried into law before or simultaneously with the Home Rule Bill, then the Irish Parliament will be elected from the beginning, not on the existing register, but on the new Manhood Suffrage Register. The Irish Party, led by Mr. Redmond, are Supporting that Manhood Suffrage Bill; and that shows the hollowness of their pretence that "this must be left to the Irish Parliament." Their real motive, it is evident, in refusing to allow the Local Government Register to be incorporated in the Home Rule Bill is hostility to the cause of women.

Previously Hanna Sheehy Skeffington had been more hopeful with regard to Home Rule. On 8th June 1912, she had written, "Home Rule or no Home Rule, Westminster or College Green, there is a new spirit abroad among women; whether the vote is reluctantly granted by a Liberal Government or wrested from an Irish parliament, to women in the end it matters but little."

A fair number of suffragettes were prepared to give the IPP the benefit of the doubt. Susanne R. Day of the Cork branch of the MWFL warned (*Irish Citizen*, Feb. 1913) that if suffragettes were actively opposed to Home Rule, it would alienate the cause of female suffrage. She argued that only after the success of Home Rule should the suffragettes go to the Irish government and demand the vote. Her view was echoed by Helen Morony (22nd Feb.) that an anti–Home Rule stance would seriously damage the cause of female suffrage in Ireland.

As the Home Rule Bill passed through its many stages, in the edition of 17th May 1913, the *Irish Citizen* posed the question, "What do suffragists want?" The answer took the form of a catechism:

"What do suffragists want?"
"Votes for Women."
"What does this mean?"
"That women should be allowed to vote at the elections of members of Parliament, just the same as men are."
"Does that mean that you want every woman to have a vote?"
"No."
"Why not?"
"Because every man has not got a vote. Men have to qualify for the vote in certain ways—they have to be owners or occupiers of certain property, or lodgers in rooms of a certain value. What we ask is that women who qualify in the same way should have the same right to vote as the men who qualify."

One can see the logic of the thinking. The paper was pushing for limited suffrage for women. It was not fighting the greater battle for universal suffrage. In some ways, though, particularly from a socialist perspective, it was seen as selfish suffrage, extending the vote to the mainly upper middle-class, or votes for "ladies" only. The newspaper itself was middle-class, as is seen in the content and the advertisements that appeared, largely appealing to a middle-class reader. Even Hanna Sheehy Skeffington's editorials and pieces reflect this. In one article she addressed the "servant problem." A number of letters, some from women later known to be linked to socialism, did appear in the *Citizen,* castigating the middle-class suffragettes of Ireland for seeking aggrandizement.

In their defense, the middle-class suffragettes argued that they only sought what the men of their class possessed. By and large, this was the aspiration of the leaders of the English campaign, too. Led by wealthy and aristocratic women, they likewise distanced themselves from the labor movement and the working class. Marion Duggan, writing as "M.E.," took the argument to its logical conclusion, turning the female suffrage argument on its head. In her article of 8th August 1914, she wrote:

I think the real point of issue is between those who want a "high franchise," votes for all who pay a large amount of taxes, and those who desire one person one vote. The time is at hand when there must be war between those who want votes to protect the rich, and those who want votes to help the poor. Government rests upon the consent of the governed, and the advocates of votes for gentry are faced with the difficulty of making their "social inferiors" obey laws as to which they have not been consulted.... Let us be honest with ourselves. Will we be content with votes for women, or do we mean to go on and work for votes for all women and men? Do we honestly believe that wealthy women or educated women, can be trusted to make laws for poor working women?

As early as 2nd August 1913, E. A. Browning suggested that the middle classes had little or no knowledge of the lives of working women, nor did they care:

> It has been said that one half of the world does not know how the other half lives, and this is certainly true of the women of Dublin. What the eye does not see, the heart does not grieve for, and, so far the eye of the women of the leisure classes has not seen, for instance, how the factory girl, in our town, lives, or how she works, what in fact life means to her; and so the heart has not sympathized, and the head has not troubled to do more than accept without challenge, the first casual information that comes to hand.

Even as late as June 1915, Lucy Kingston of the IWSF was writing in the *Irish Citizen* of the snobbery she had encountered among the more educated and middle-class feminists toward those less-well-off women. The interest of the middle-class suffragettes, she believed, was in maintaining the status quo of the class system. Yet despite the criticisms of elitism, the *Citizen* did begin recording female trade union matters. This was largely due to the efforts of Louie Bennett, a committed suffragette and socialist.

The *Citizen*, and by extension the suffragettes of Dublin, did, when made aware, develop a sense of social responsibility, extending beyond philanthropic works. They participated in the repeal of the Contagious Diseases Act, the establishment of the National Society for the Prevention of Cruelty to Children, and joined such organizations as the Philanthropic Reform Association and the Irish Workhouse Association to better the lot of their fellow citizens. In Kingstown (Dun Laoghaire), Rosa Bennett opened a children's crèche, later to become the Cottage Home for Little Children. They looked at the situation that other women found themselves in, particularly the poor, the vulnerable, and the oppressed. The *Citizen* during this period inquired into social issues that affected women. Giving women the vote, the paper contended, would improve their quality of life, and bring new standards of morality, compassion, equality, and justice into decision-making. Such an establishment would tackle the evils prevalent throughout society. These included the sexual exploitation and violence against women and children. The newspaper's weekly issues detailed court cases, cases that the courts refused to take seriously, and the handing down of light sentences. The paper criticized the legal system, biased in favor of the male perpetrators rather than the victims. In an article by Marion Duggan, *In the Courts,* published on 11th July 1914, she wrote of three such cases:

> Two cases involving sexual offences against little girls were before Mr. Hunt in the Northern Police Court on Monday, June 29th, and have been returned for trial at the City Sessions on 9th July.

John Madden, a "free laborer," now an ice cream seller, is alleged to have attempted to assault a child aged six years and eleven months in Lower Gardiner Street. Dr. Boyd Barrett deposed that the victim is suffering from venereal disease (gonorrhea). Bail refused. A Protestant clergyman is said to have gone bail in £20 for a man named Jones, resident in Drumcondra, who is accused of indecent conduct towards an eight year old girl.

The notorious Edelstein, when guilty of assaulting a girl of ten, was allowed by the recorder to go free, "on account of his services to his co-religionists." (The said co-religionists have since got the individual in question sent out of the country.

These were cases that were shamefully not recorded in the established Irish newspapers of the day, perhaps because the cases seemed so trivial in their eyes. If the suffragettes achieved anything, it was in exposing such wickedness and the seeming indifference to such wickedness by the authorities. The *Irish Citizen* asked the question: "Is it not time we had women on the bench and on the jury when such crimes as murderous and indecent assault receive nominal or no punishment?" The aim of women like Marion Duggan was to transform society through the promotion of female values.

At the opening of the Great War, the paper took up a pacifist stance that reflected the views of the Sheehy Skeffingtons. Throughout the war, the paper kept up a strong criticism, linking the war to male dominance. They failed to see that the First World War was a necessary war to halt German militarism. The atrocities against the people of Belgium, and the shooting of nurse Edith Cavall, had to be addressed and the aggressor defeated. The editorials and correspondence perhaps show the naivety of the editorship, and some of its readership, living in a would-be ideal world where you could talk to, and persuade, frightful people to behave. In the opinion of Hanna Sheehy Skeffington, women who helped the war effort, even though they might be nurses who tended the wounded, were "traitors." Fellow suffragette and friend Violet Crichton protested that Sheehy Skeffington's position was inhuman. The wounded had to be tended to, and women were needed to fill the vacated places of men who had gone off to fight. Sheehy Skeffington's naïve call for the setting up of an international peace movement among the women of Europe fell on deaf ears. Certainly, there was no response from German or Austrian womanhood once the war had begun, nor, indeed, from Emmeline and Christabel Pankhurst, her erstwhile English allies. Francis Sheehy Skeffington was critical of the Pankhursts for their lack of support, and in particular for their flag-waving patriotic support of the war. Miss E.A. Browning of the IRWL came to the defense of the Pankhursts and of those women engaged in war work. She criticized the double standards shown, whereby the Sheehy Skeffingtons and other Irish suffragettes supported militancy for their ends, but condemned men for using militancy to preserve the nation and destroy the evil that was the Kaiser's Germany. The more astute English suffragettes realized that they had to take up their share of war-work in the knowledge that their work would most probably be unrewarded. It was the right thing to do. The Galway branch of the IWSF, led by Mary Fleetwood Berry, broke ranks and followed suit. They took up fund-raising to aid the troops in the trenches. Berry instigated an annual meeting of the Galway War Fund Association.

Husband, Francis Sheehy Skeffington, was most vocal in his opposition to British Army recruiting in Ireland. After some forty public speeches, he was arrested and charged with prejudicing recruitment for His Majesty's forces. Sentenced to six months' imprisonment, he followed the suffragette tactic of hunger striking, adding a thirst strike on the sixth day. Never a completely healthy man, and in a weakened state, he was released before completing his sentence under the Cat and Mouse Act, as described more fully below. Eluding the authorities, Francis briefly escaped to America, but he returned in December 1915. In his absence, Hanna took over the running of the *Irish Citizen*. Upon his return, Francis resumed his editorship, treading more carefully along the path of pacifism. During the Easter Rising, he was arrested by the military while trying to prevent looting and was shot.[17] There was some suggestion at the time that it was because of his unpatriotic pacifist stance. Following his death, coeditorship of the *Irish Citizen* was taken over by Louie Bennett of the IWRL, suffragette, trade unionist, and peace advocate, and Mary Bourke-Dowling of the IWFL, who had been sent to prison for her suffragette activities back in November 1911.

Previously in Britain, a ruling by the speaker of the House of Commons wrecked any chance of the acceptance of an amendment to include women in a forthcoming Reform Bill then being discussed in Parliament. In response, a bombing and arson campaign was begun by the more militant suffragettes. Following arrests and hunger strikes, on 25th April 1913, the British government passed "An Act to provide for the Temporary Discharge of Prisoners whose further detention in prison is undesirable on account of the condition of their health." The suffragettes described it as the "Cat and Mouse" Act, by which hunger strikers were temporarily released rather than force-fed. Once they had recovered at home, they were later re-arrested to continue their sentence. The government desperately wanted to avoid women dying in custody and becoming martyrs to the cause. Tragically, Emily Wilding Davison, arrested nine times and force-fed forty-nine times, before the introduction of the "Cat and Mouse" Act, was killed when she attempted to disrupt the Derby. She stepped beyond the rail and attempted to attach a suffragette bunting to the bridle of the king's speeding horse, Anmer. It was a dangerous thing to do, and in the process, she was knocked down, and she died four days later of a skull fracture and internal injuries. Being a nation of animal lovers, a great deal of sympathy was extended to the injured horse. Nevertheless, tens of thousands of women and men (and it should not be forgotten that a large number of men supported the women's struggle) lined the streets of London as her coffin passed by.

In Ireland, the struggle for Home Rule, was reaching its culmination. The struggle for female suffrage was put on hold, as many of the militant suffragettes of old now threw their support behind the nation's aspirations. Everything else was to be put to one side: "The Nation first" became the country's new watchword. The *Irish Citizen*'s response was to condemn, often in a derogatory manner, the support given by fellow suffragettes to the nationalist struggle over that of votes for women. Mary McSwiney responded in a letter published in the 9th May 1914 edition of the paper:

> I am not a follower of Mr. Redmond—nor of Mr. O'Brien either—I use the word Nationalist to include all those who believe that self-government for Ireland is the most important question in this country at present, and must be paramount until Home Rule is attained. I do not put Party first; I put Ireland first.
>
> Mr. Redmond is offering the Irish people a very poor mouse after such years of labor; but, inadequate as the Home Rule Bill is, any Irishwoman who rejoices in its possible wrecking—because women are not included in it—is sadly in need of that clearer conception of the realities of the political position in Ireland which you so kindly desire for my poor self.
>
> I quite agree with you that there can be no free nation without free women; but the world—women included—has taken some thousands of years to realize the fact. Three years more, in our very exceptional circumstances, will not hurt us.

Those suffragettes who supported Home Rule were not deceived. They knew that there was no mention of women's suffrage in the Home Rule manifesto of the IPP. So vexed when she discovered that her own father, the Irish Parliamentary Party M.P. David Sheehy, had voted against women's suffrage, Hanna Sheehy Skeffington denounced him in the *Irish Citizen*.

As early as 1908, realizing that there was very little chance of women's suffrage being in the Home Rule Bill, and with perhaps a touch of sarcasm, Rose Lavery wrote in an article in the *New Irish Review*:

> Irishmen do not need to have indicated to them the hardship of being governed by those alien to them in temperament, ideals and traditions. An Englishman they say can never understand the needs of a country like Ireland. How strange then that all men should be considered gifted with the wonderful power of sympathetic interest which enables them to so easily understand the needs of women.

As the struggle for Home Rule reached its climax, passing its many stages, the suffrage movement in Ireland began to tear itself in pieces. The province of Ulster, with its high concentration of Presbyterians, was opposed to the separation of Ireland from British rule. Social, economic, and political reasons were cited. Perhaps the most telling was the religious issue. There was fear that a Roman Catholic Ireland would dominate and dictate.

Unscrupulous politicians played on the Protestant fear that Home Rule was Rome Rule. Prominent suffragist Isabella Tod made plain her Unionist stand. It caused consternation within her own suffrage movement. In some ways, her stand cut across her former liberal criticism of imperialist expansion. Ireland, semi-independent from Britain, yet still remaining within the British Empire, did not dissuade her. Other early Protestant pioneers of female suffrage, such as Anna Haslam, were also strongly Unionist and were likewise opposed to Home Rule. The Unionist suffragists began to align themselves with the more moderate English groups. Millicent Garrett Fawcett of the NUWSS gave them her support. She, too, was opposed to Home Rule. In Ulster, most Protestant suffragists followed suit in their support of Unionist opposition to Home Rule. Religion aside, Tod was of the opinion that Ireland should remain under British rule on the basis that breaking away would destroy Ireland's economic base. In truth, the British government was already doing so. Irish industries such as Dunlop's, the tire manufacturers, had been induced to relocate to Birmingham by generous tax concessions. Other companies were to follow. Britain's justification was that if there was war, commerce between the two islands could be jeopardized. As a consequence of her Unionist beliefs, Tod fell out with the nationalists within the IWSLGA, and she further angered them by her appointment to the executive of the Ulster Women's Liberal Unionists, the party of Herbert Asquith, the chief denier of women's rights. The UWLU went on to present a petition, signed by thirty thousand people, demanding that Home Rule should be abandoned. Old friendships across the religious divide sadly came to an abrupt end.

At Christmastime 1913, the IWSF sponsored "Suffrage Week in Dublin." The gathering brought together the various women's groups in Ireland, including the National Union of Women's Suffrage Societies, the Women's Freedom League, the Church League for Women's Suffrage, the Tax Resistance League, the Actresses Franchise League, the New Constitutional Society, and the Men's League. It was a combined conference and exhibition event. Not always serious, it had its lighthearted moments, too—Mr. Leggett-Byrne gave demonstrations of the tango. The highlight of the week, the conference aside, was a production of Ibsen's play *Rosmersholm*. Written in 1886, the play concerns the traditional ruling class relinquishing their right to impose ideals on the rest of society. The hidden message of the play, to its audience, hinted at a change in attitude by the government toward the vote.

The conference was all-embracing, reflecting the many affiliations of its members. There was a talk and debate by the socialists on the subject of "Women's Trade Unions and the Vote." Few working-class women would have gotten to hear the debate, however; tickets for admission were two shillings and sixpence. Working women could be discussed, but not necessarily included.

In 1913, up in Belfast, the Unionist Council leadership planned the setting up of a provisional government for Ulster in the event that Home Rule became law. The Ulster Unionist Women's Council wrote to the secretary of the Unionist Council, seeking clarification as to the position of women in any new Ulster government. Dawson Bates, the secretary, wrote back, a copy of the letter appearing in the local press:

> I am authorized to inform you that the draft articles of the Provisional Government already approved of by this Council include the franchise for women on the basis of the register for local government purposes.

So there it was; Ulster was on the point of giving women the vote—or was it? Matters drifted, but in the spring of 1914, Unionist leader Sir Edward Carson revealed to a deputation from the WSPU that he had never intended to give women the vote. He argued that they were fighting for the same treatment for the men of Ulster as the men of England were getting, and the women of Ulster would get the same treatment as the women of England got; he would not ask for special treatment for Ulster women. It would be inconsistent on his part to do so since he had never agreed with the suffrage movement.[18]

So, while the women of the south had reason to be angry with John Redmond and his anti-suffrage stance, so also did the women of the north. Ulster's champion, Sir Edward Carson, had reneged on an undertaking to include women's suffrage in a Provisional Ulster Unionist government. The suffragists of Ulster became suffragettes, with an outbreak of window smashing and other militant undertakings, including setting fires and the destruction of private property, notably the homes of intended leaders of a rebel Ulster government. The police arrested the WSPU organizer, Miss Dorothy Evans, and the secretary, Miss Midge Muir (an alias of Florence McFarlane), at their flat on University Street, Belfast. Explosive substances were found on the premises, indicating intent, and the women were accordingly charged. In court, five days later, on 8th April 1914, there was uproar as, in their defense, the two women demanded to know why Ulster politician James Craig was not appearing on the same charge. But then there was one law for Unionist patriots threatening civil war against the country they professed to love, and another for women advocating equality. The two women were sent to Belfast Prison on remand, and as expected, went on hunger strike. After four days, they were released under the Cat and Mouse Act. Barely ten days after their release, they were re-arrested while attempting to burn down Annadale House, Ballynafeigh. After three days on hunger strike, they were again released. The situation had turned to farce.

In Dublin, it was the same. The leadership of Sinn Fein, in the Republican party upon which Mary McSwiney and others had pinned their hopes, also indicated their lack of commitment to gender equality. For them, it was the nation first, and all else must be subjugated to that struggle. There was one hope: that of a socialist Ireland—a Workers' Republic, as proposed by James Connolly, its Marxist leader. He believed in sexual equality. As a consequence, a section of the IWFL moved more to the left, taking up the cause of socialism. Some IWFL leaders, such as Hanna Sheehy Skeffington and Countess Markievicz, shared a platform with Delia and James Larkin at the launch of the Irish Women's Worker's Union (IWWU). Markievicz declared, "Union such as now being formed ... will also be a means of helping you get votes." The link between the IWWU and the IWFL became closer during the Dublin Lockout of 1913, when Hanna Sheehy Skeffington, Constance Markievicz, and other suffragettes joined Delia Larkin to organize a soup kitchen in Liberty Hall to feed the workers and their families. They also distributed clothing and blankets to the destitute. More than three thousand children received a daily breakfast through their efforts until the lockout ended in 1914. A strong bond between the suffrage movement and the labor movement was forged. Where applicable, some suffragettes joined the IWWU, and some joined the Irish Citizen Army, whose ranks were open to both men and women.

Kathleen Houston is generally credited with being the last suffragette to be imprisoned in the south of Ireland. She was secretary of the Dublin Branch of the IWFL, and a close friend of Hanna Sheehy Skeffington. Her early connections to the struggle for female suffrage date back to 1910, in London, where she was first radicalized. In November of that year, she was sentenced to two months' imprisonment in Holloway after the Black Friday riot. Following her release, she attended the big suffragette rally at Caxton Hall, after which the crowd of women marched on Downing Street, home of the British prime minister. In the melee that followed, policemen as well as suffragettes were injured. In the process, 150 suffragettes were arrested, including Houston and Irishwomen Mrs. J. Earle and Miss Helen McDermott. Further imprisonment followed in 1911, when Kathleen, once more in London, was sentenced to one month's imprisonment at Bow Street Police Court, along with a number of other suffragettes, for smashing windows and causing malicious damage. Having served her sentence, she returned to Dublin. In June 1912, along with other suffragette malcontents, including Hanna Sheehy Skeffington, the Murphy sisters, and Margaret Palmer, Kathleen embarked on a window-breaking escapade. They were all arrested, of course, and tried on 12th July for "malicious damage to glass." Determined to stamp out this sort of protest, the judge bestowed harsher sentences upon them than heretofore in Ireland. They were given six months' imprisonment. Recognizing that theirs was a political rather than a criminal assault, they were given first-class misdemeanant status with all the privileges that such a status permitted.

Kathleen was released a month earlier on 8th November 1912. Work was found for her in administration that kept her out of the limelight for two years, until 1914. In April of that year, she was arrested for smashing windows at the post office at College Green in protest at the Cat and Mouse Act. She was arrested, tried, and convicted, and on 1st May, she announced that she was going on a hunger-strike. She was not force-fed, as she would have been if she had been convicted in Britain. After five days, she was released on medical grounds.

Up in Ulster, the crusade continued for a few months longer. While Mary McSwiney was appealing to the suffragettes in the south to get behind the nationalist campaign, up in the north the pro-Unionist suffragettes began displaying their anger at Carson's betrayal of granting female suffrage should an Ulster government come into being. They interrupted the meetings of Carson's would-be army, the Ulster Volunteer Force. They burned Major-General Sir Hugh McCalmont's home and destroyed five Unionist-owned buildings, including Wallace Castle, and twelve places of male authority. Orlands House, one of the palaces of the Catholic bishop of Down, was set on fire. The women went on to smash windows and cut telephone wires, but their favored weapon was arson. The grandstand at Newtonards Race Course was attacked; the teahouse at Bellevue Zoo, the Cavehill Bowling and Tennis Club, and Ballylesson Church in Lisburn were also attacked. Acid was poured onto the greens at Fortwilliam Golf Club. At Belfast Cathedral, a number of suffragettes interrupted a Sunday service. Standing up and with left hands raised, they began a two-minute tirade before sitting down once more to allow the service to continue. Things came to a head when Dorothy Evans (sent over from England to organize the Ulster campaign) and local women Mrs. Carson, Joan Wickham, and Lilian Metge attempted to blow up Lisburn Cathedral on 31st July 1914. That was going just too far. Breaking windows was one thing, but desecrating God's house was another, especially in puritanical Ulster. The women were arrested and held on remand to await trial. As she awaited trial, some of the pious souls of Ulster attacked Suffragette Lilian Metge's home, badly damaging it. The trial of the women was held on 8th August. As expected, they were found guilty and given an appropriate sentence for attacking a house of God. They were sent to Crumlin Road Prison, and there, on "A" wing, the women's wing, they declared their intention of beginning a hunger strike. After four days, on 12th August, they were released. It was a conditional release, in that they agreed to refrain from militant action during the "national crisis"—a euphemism for World War I. In Britain, the largest of the suffrage organizations, the nonmilitant National Union of Women's Suffrage Societies (NUWSS), led by Millicent Fawcett, announced the suspension of suffrage activities in order to concentrate on wartime relief work. Even the more militant Sylvia Pankhurst, though opposed to the war, supported the need for women to support the war effort in that it would be a "great unlocking of their energies." In return for such support, all suffragette prisoners were released.

Home Rule in the shape of the Government of Ireland Act received royal assent on 18th September 1914. Events had overtaken Irish politics, and with the outbreak of the Great War, implementation was postponed by the Suspensory Act of that same year. In reality, the Act never took effect. A fourth Home Rule Bill was enacted as the Government of Ireland Act of 1920, which partitioned Ireland.

2

Socialists and Trade Unionists

To understand what was going on in Ireland at the opening of the twentieth century, it is necessary to understand what was going on elsewhere in the rest of the industrialized world. Organized labor was flexing its muscles all over that industrialized world. There were popular disturbances and strikes throughout Europe, some with political implications. Between 1902 and 1904, there were general strikes in Belgium, the Netherlands, Luxembourg, Italy, and Sweden. In desperation, these governments sought to curb the power of the unions. The Swedish government passed anti-Trade union laws, permitting the arrest and imprisonment of pickets. In Britain, the Taff Vale judgment rendered trade union funds liable to seizure following legal action for damages. In France, the Loichot case served as a brake on radical trade unionism. In 1903, there were strikes in the textile and heavy industries of Germany and Russia, leading to revolution in Russia in 1905. Also in 1905, there was rioting by the unemployed in Britain, a contributory factor to the heavy defeat of the Liberal government in the general election of 1906. In 1909, in Catalonia, the industrial heartland of Spain, riots in Barcelona were targeted against the symbols of feudal repression; big-land owners and the Catholic Church. convents and churches, seen as an arm of that repression, were sacked and burnt. In Portugal in 1910, the monarchy was overthrown. From 1910, Britain was caught up in a wave of industrial unrest that swept the country. There were major stoppages on the railway and in the docks in 1911, followed two years later by a miners' strike. A Commission on Industrial Relations revealed that there were 1,459 strikes throughout Britain and Ireland, many of them unofficial. The number of days lost through industrial action was 10 million in 1911, 40 million in 1912, and 11.6 million in 1913. These include two stoppages in Ireland, in Dublin and Belfast. The strike in Dublin of 1911 led to some arrests, but it was relatively peaceful, compared to the carters' strike in Belfast. It led to rioting and civilian deaths. Social restlessness was building up to a dangerous level in Britain and Ireland. There was alarm in the government following the establishment of the "Triple Alliance" between the railway workers, the miners, and the transport workers unions. Each union agreed to support the other in times of strife. The British foreign secretary, Edward Grey, expressed concern that unless the government took part in talks with the unions, there would be a revolution.

The part played by women in the great socialist struggle for a Workers' Republic in Ireland, is set against this greater struggle. It was played out in Ireland's two main cities, Belfast and Dublin. At the opening of the twentieth century, the industrial city of Belfast contained the biggest shipyard in the world. There were thriving engineering works, distilleries, tobacco factories, rope works, and linen manufacturers. Some 36.2 percent of the men, and 70 percent of the women in the workforce, had manufacturing jobs.[1] Linen (Belfast was known as Linenopolis) factories employed about eleven thousand men in Belfast, and the shipyards employed seven thousand men. Engineering works took some six thousand, and iron and steel a further five thousand. Half of the forty-eight-thousand-plus women workers were employed in the linen industry and clothing manufacturing. Dublin, by contrast, lacked a true industrial base. There was brewing, of course, but its main industries were based around its dockers and transport workers. Of the two cities, Belfast's housing stock was largely the better of the two, due to its more recent construction dating from the 1840s. Dublin's housing stock was largely Georgian, overcrowded and unsanitary, particularly in central Dublin, north of the river. Over five thousand one-room tenements housed five or more people.[2] There was a higher mortality rate in Dublin, too, among babies and infants than in any other city of Europe, due to overcrowding. The main diseases were pneumonia and tuberculosis. It was so bad that Lenin judged that if there was a people's revolution in Britain, then it would begin in Dublin.

At the opening of the twentieth century, neither city was labor-organized. Liverpool-born James Larkin arrived in Belfast in January 1907, to change all that. Paying a poetic tribute in 1947 to Larkin, his successor as president of Dublin Trade Council, John Swift, declared:

> Then came James Larkin and his co-workers. Soon thousands of the despised rabble became ennobled with the dignity of trade union organization. Larkin taught them the duty of struggle, the imperative of rebelliousness.[3]

Larkin had been sent as a full-time organizer by the British National Union of Dock Laborers to organize the Irish ports. Very soon, following mass recruitment to the union, there was a series of strikes in Belfast, Cork, and Dublin for better pay. The 3,100 dockers, mainly casual workers, rarely earned more than ten shillings a week. An independent survey carried out at the same time estimated that the minimum cost of keeping a family was twenty-two shillings and five pence. As a consequence, mothers and children were sent out to work in an attempt to make up the difference. On 26th April, coal importer Samuel Kelly dismissed union members from his employment. As a consequence, the remainder of his men walked out. On 6th May, the men of the Belfast Steamship Company went out on strike. The lord mayor relayed Larkin's willingness to go to arbitration. The Steamship Company's owner, Thomas Gallaher, also founder of a well-known tobacco company, refused to negotiate. He believed that his men would be starved back to work if he just waited. Coal importer Kelly meanwhile capitulated and negotiated a pay raise, agreeing to recognize the union. With Gallaher refusing to negotiate, Larkin upped the stakes and began unionizing his mainly female tobacco workers. On 16th May, he called them out on strike. One thousand tobacco girls walked out. In England, NUDL general secretary James Sexton refused to admit the women to the union. With no means of support or strike pay, the girls were forced back to work the next day. It was an impetuous move on Larkin's part, and the tobacco girls paid the price. Elsewhere, Larkin demanded union recognition from all the other coal importers, which he got. On 20th June, Larkin upped the stakes, and demanded union recognition from all the shipping companies, which included the great British railway companies with their cross-channel steamers. They were more obdurate. Meanwhile the Presbyterian *Ulster Echo* played the orange card. They claimed that all the union leaders were Roman Catholics, and that this was part of a Fenian plot. Larkin responded to the attack by resigning his position in favor of Alex Boyd, a Protestant. Further intercession by the lord mayor with the employers was now met with a firm rebuff. With the aggressive Larkin standing down, matters had turned in favor of the employers. The coal quay employers now fought back and locked their men out. Following a police mutiny over pay and conditions, and with the threat of public disorder, the army was called in to patrol the streets. Strike-breakers, or "Black legs" as they were called, were brought in to replace the strikers. In the disorder that followed on the streets, troops shot dead three bystanders. The authorities, the larger employers, and the popular press manipulated the situation into a political and religious dispute. As a consequence, the strikers lost the support of the trade unions in Britain. NUDL general secretary James Sexton now denounced the strike. It had lasted for five months and ended in a defeat for the union. It had cost the NUDL £7,000 in strike pay. This perhaps was the real reason for the withdrawal of support. Larkin was bitter over the lack of support from the TUC, but more especially from his own union. The NUDL, in the shape of its general secretary, now sought to remove Larkin from the equation. He was ordered to go to Scotland to resolve a dispute in Aberdeen. Larkin refused to leave. He was looking at the bigger picture—organizing all the unskilled labor in Ireland, not just the dock workers. On 7th December

1908, Sexton suspended him from the union. This was a rude awakening. The British unions, Larkin came to realize, would never truly represent the interests of the Irish workers. What was needed was an independent Irish trade union.

As a consequence, Larkin remained in Ireland, and on 4th January 1909, the Irish Transport and General Workers' Union was founded. Its first head office was at 10 Beresford Place in Dublin. James Larkin was elected general secretary. In the preface to its rules, Larkin posed the question, "Are we going to continue the policy of grafting ourselves on the English Trades Union movement, losing our own identity as a nation in the great world of organized labor?" Larkin was committing to Ireland; not only as a trade unionist, but also as a nationalist. Funds from the Irish branch of the NUDL were transferred to the ITGWU. This brought about a sharp response from Sexton. He brought a case of misappropriation against Larkin, Thomas Fearon, and two other ITGWU leaders. The four were arrested and taken before the court. Sexton appeared as a prosecution witness. All four were found guilty. Larkin was sentenced to a year's hard labor. Fearon got six months, but the other two were released. Following a successful appeal by the Dublin Trades Council, both imprisoned men got early release. By 1911, the union membership had grown to eighteen thousand male workers. Perhaps curiously, given James Connolly's later stand regarding female participation, the ITGWU upon its foundation was not open to female membership. It was not that Larkin was a misogynist, more that he was steeped in working class tradition; men went out to work, and women stayed at home and looked after their husbands and children.

Pressure from the women workers for representation was realized in September 1911, when Larkin formed a separate union for women, the Irish Women Workers' Union (IWWU). At the formation of the new union, Larkin shared the speakers' platform with Hanna Sheehy Skeffington and Constance Markievicz. Sister Delia Larkin was appointed secretary, and Larkin himself became its president, thus overseeing—or controlling—both unions. In February 1912, the ITGWU took over the old Northumberland Hotel at 18 Beresford Place, renaming it Liberty Hall. The IWWU and the

Trade union leader James Larkin

National Sailors' and Firemens' Union (NSFU) were allocated offices in the building.

In unionized Cork, there were a series of strikes among the tram workers, then later the builders' laborers. The Cork Employers' Federation took a firm stand. They put forward a joint policy:

That we, the employers of Cork, hereby bind ourselves and the firms we represent as follows:

1. to immediately dismiss any employee who shall wilfully disobey any lawful order out of sympathy with any other strike or trade dispute;
2. that the vacancy so caused shall be filled forthwith by local labour if procurable, failing this that the vacancy be filled from any available source;
3. that any employee discharged shall not be employed by any member of the Federation.[4]

James Connolly, who had returned from America in 1910, was sent by Larkin to resolve the dispute. The Cork employers were adamant. They would not treat with the ITGWU. Connolly resolved the situation by renaming the Cork union, implying that it was no longer part of the ITGWU.

Negotiator James Connolly was born in Cowgate, Edinburgh, Scotland, to Irish parents in June 1868. Both his father and grandfather were laborers from County Monaghan. James was educated up to the age of eleven in the local Catholic primary school, then was taken out of education and sent out to work. At the age of fourteen, falsifying his age, he enlisted in the British Army under the alias of James Reid and served in the Royal Scots Regiment. He served several terms of duty in Ireland. Here he met, and fell in love with, Lillie Reynolds. With the prospect of being posted to India, he deserted the army, and he and Lillie fled to Scotland, where they married in April 1890. Connolly became involved in the Scottish Socialist Federation. At the time, his elder brother was its secretary. When brother John was sacked from his job working for Edinburgh Corporation for advocating

James Connolly, a committed feminist and Marxist, sought to establish a socialist republic in Ireland.

an eight-hour day, and needing to find another job, James stepped in as secretary. He also became involved in the Independent Labour Party, founded
by Keir Hardy, in 1893. Connolly became editor of *The Socialist* newspaper
and was a founding member of the Socialist Labor Party. Most of this work
brought little remuneration, so when he heard that the Dublin Socialist Club
was looking for a full-time secretary, with a salary of one pound a week, he
applied and got the job. The family moved to Dublin. With the new impetus
that Connolly brought, the club quickly evolved into the Irish Socialist Republican Party (ISRP). Founded in 1896, the new party drew the attention of
socialists all over Europe. Eleanor Marx sent a message of support. In Dublin,
Connolly found himself allied with nationalists Maud Gonne and Arthur
Griffiths in opposition to the Boer War, seen by them all as an imperialist
war of aggression.

In September 1903, the Connolly family emigrated to the United States,
the cause being a mixture of frustration at the slow progress of the socialist
movement and a need for Connolly to provide a steady income for his growing family. He obtained a number of low-paying jobs during his time there.
He became a member of the Socialist Labor Party of America, founded in
1906. In addition, he joined the Socialist Party of America and the Industrial
Workers of the World, the nemesis of capitalism. In 1907, Connolly founded
the Irish Socialist Federation in New York, renewing his ties with Ireland. In
1910, Connolly and his family returned to Ireland at Larkin's invitation. He
was appointed to a senior position within the Irish Transport and General
Workers Union. In 1912, along with others, Connolly founded the Irish Labor
Party as the political wing of the Irish Trades Union Congress.

Already existing at the time of Larkin's time in Belfast was the women's
union, the Textile Operatives' Society of Ireland, founded in 1893. It had a
membership of around 750. The union was affiliated to the Belfast Trades
Council, with William Walker acting as its first secretary. He was succeeded
by Mary Galway from 1896. With her at the helm, recruiting was stepped up,
new branches established, and a less passive approach was taken regarding
grievances.

Mary Galway was born in Moira, County Down, in 1864. She and her
family later moved to Belfast, where Mary, her parents, and sisters all became
linen workers. Mary joined the Textile Operatives Society, which was affiliated
with the Women's Trade Union League. Elected onto the executive of Belfast
Trades Council in 1898, she and Elizabeth Bruce represented the textile operatives as delegates to the Irish Trade Union Congress of that year.

Members of the Textile Operatives were largely unskilled women,
employed by the mills on the basis of their acceptance of lower wages. This
was resented to a considerable degree by the trade unions because women
workers, who provided cheap labor for employers, undercut men's wages.

The women worked a fifty-five-and-a-half-hour week, in poor conditions, high temperatures, poor ventilation, and noisy machinery, earning 40 percent less than their male colleagues. In 1897, Mary Galway, who had also taken up the cause of female suffrage, became president of the Textile Operatives. The fight was on for change. In 1906, some fifteen thousand textile workers went out on strike for higher wages. The mill owners laid off workers and closed some thirty factories to all workers. The strike became part of the greater Belfast Strike of 1907, which ended in disappointment for the workers. During the strike, Mary Galway took an active part, addressing rallies and collecting funds for her members. That same year, she was appointed the first woman on the Irish Trade Union Congress National Executive. Also in 1907, some skilled women workers were admitted into the all-male Flax Rougthers' Trade Union, much to Galway's annoyance. Her response was to fill the loss by admitting male workers who were not covered by other union membership into the Textile Operatives. Within the Flax Roughers' Union, it was now possible for the new women workers to bring attention to the wage differential between men and women, something not available in their former trade union. In 1910, Galway became the vice president of the Irish Trade Union Congress. Reaching such prominence enabled Galway to participate in a number of Parliamentary inquiries into work practices, resulting in better working conditions and reducing the workweek to forty-eight hours. In the process of all this, she perhaps neglected her original function, of fighting for the rights of the unskilled. In 1911, a wave of demonstrations and strikes by women workers across Britain brought the issue of low rates of pay before the TUC. On 4th October 1911, the unskilled textile mill workers of Belfast went out on strike. It was the result of a demand by the employers to speed up production. Also in the mix was a system of draconian fines employed by the mill owners against singing, laughing, and talking. In particular, combined singing was feared, in that it would produce solidarity, and thereby defiance, on a large scale. Galway condemned the strike as futile. James Connolly, recently arrived from Scotland, took their part and opened a women's section of the ITGWU, known as the Irish Textile Workers' Union. In the Belfast Trades Council, Galway turned on Connolly, accusing him of poaching members. Giving as good as he got, Connolly accused her of abandoning her members. In support of the struggle, Connolly appealed to the shipyard workers to blacklist the import of flax and the export of linen. In his fight, Connolly was joined by the increasingly influential Winifred Carney.

Carney was born in Bangor, County Down, in 1887, and educated at the Christian Brothers' School in Donegal Street, Belfast. She was for a time a junior teacher there, before leaving to qualify as a secretary and a shorthand typist. She gained work as a clerk, and in her independence away from home she joined the Gaelic League, took an interest in the suffragist movement, and became involved in socialist activities. In 1912, she met James Connolly and came under his influence, becoming a friend and confidante. With Connolly's encouragement, Winifred became secretary of the Textile Workers' Union. She was not slow in putting forward the demands of the new union. A copy of the demands was sent to the *Irish Citizen* for publication (28th Dec. 1912):

> We demand that the entire Linen industry be put under the Sweated Industries Act, which gives power to a Trades Board, on which employees and employers are requested to fix minimum wages for the whole. Under that Act the wages of women in the Clothing Operatives Trade has been already fixed at a minimum wage of 3d [three pence, U.K. pre-decimal coinage] per hour. Until the extension to the Linen Industry or that Act, we demand and pledge ourselves as a Union to fight for a Minimum Wage of 3d per hour for all qualified spinners, proportionate increases for all lower grades in the Spinning-room, and increases in the piece rates for the reeling-room and all departments in piece work; abolition of fines for lost time; all stopping to be at the same rates as the daily pay per hour. We also demand from Government the appointment of a competent woman Inspector for the Belfast District exclusively, in order that the inspection of our mills, factories, and warerooms may be a constant reality instead of the occasional farce it is today.

Winifred was also a nationalist. She joined Cumann na mBan soon after its foundation. Close to Easter 1916, Connolly invited her down to Dublin. She was with him in the GPO, reputedly with a typewriter and a Webley revolver. Following the failure of the rising, after a brief arrest, Winifred eventually returned to Belfast. In the general election of 1918, she stood as a Sinn Fein candidate up in the north but failed to win. Winifred continued to work for the ITGWU, joined the Labor Party, and got married. Her husband was George McBride, a Protestant, which alienated her from some former friends who might perhaps be described as religious bigots. In the 1930s, Winifred joined the Belfast Socialist Party, which morphed into a branch of the Communist Party of Great Britain. She died in 1943.

Winifred Carney, trade union leader in Ulster, became Connolly's secretary in Dublin.

During the 1911 strike, the

suffragists sought to use the crisis for enrolling the mill workers into their cause, linking their impoverished working conditions with the lack of women's rights. Leading suffragists were brought up from Dublin to address the mill women. Unfortunately, being middle-class women and having little experience of hard work, they failed to comprehend the situation. Suffrage was not uppermost in the minds of the impoverished and overworked mill workers. With their fine clothing and higher education, these higher-class ladies from Dublin were perceived as condescending. Helena Molony, of the Irish Womens' Workers Union, was scathing of these "missionaries," roundly attacking them in the pages of the suffragist newspaper, the *Irish Citizen,* for being elitist and having little appeal to the majority of Irishwomen. This cannot be said of all the Dublin suffragettes. Francis, husband of Hanna Sheehy Skeffington, and Kathleen Shannon, founding member of the IWFL, were also secretaries of the Socialist Party of Ireland, with links to the ITGWU.

Influential in nationalist, socialist, and suffragette circles, Helena Molony later became an actress at the Abbey Theatre. She was born in Dublin in 1883, the daughter of an inner-city grocer. Helena was drawn toward nationalism after hearing Maud Gonne speak near the Custom House in Dublin in 1903. She joined Gonne's movement, Inghinidhe na h'Eireann (Daughters of Ireland), and because of ability, became honorary secretary from 1907 to 1914. In 1908, she was appointed editor of the organization's monthly newspaper, *Bean na h'Eireann* (Women of Ireland). Nationalism apart, Inghinidhe was involved in a number of social campaigns. One of its campaigns was for the provision of help to poor women and children, and in particular the extension of school meals for poor children. The organization successfully pressured Dublin Corporation and other bodies to provide proper nourishing meals. In her newspaper column, "Labour Notes," Helena attracted the attention of James Connolly, at a time when she herself was being drawn toward socialism. "I knew little of Labour ideas. But I was always on the side of the underdog," she was to write. "Labour and the Nation were really one."[5] Connolly saw her potential and gave encouragement to Molony. He took time to guide and instruct her. "Connolly— staunch feminist that he was," she wrote, "was more than anxious to welcome women into the ranks on equal terms with men." Connolly understood that the trade union opposition to women was divisive and that it damaged the entire working class. Women, he considered, were a necessary part of the trade union movement. Their militancy and revolutionary fervor invigorated it, and improvements in their working conditions and wages would benefit those of men, as well. Louie Bennett also spoke well of Connolly in his support for women's suffrage. When the weekly IWFL meetings were held in Phoenix Park, during the good weather, Connolly sent stewards from Liberty Hall to protect the speakers from physical attacks by members of the Ancient Order of Hibernians, the foot soldiers of the Irish Parliamentary Party.

Now a committed socialist and trade unionist, Molony is credited with bringing a number of influential women within the nationalist movement into the socialist struggle, including Constance Markievicz and Dr. Kathleen Lynn. Here was a crossover from suffragist to nationalist to socialist—all three linked. Kathleen Lynn was born in County Mayo in 1874, the daughter of a Church of Ireland clergyman, Robert Young Lynn, and his wife, Catherine Wynne. In 1891, Kathleen attended Alexandra College in Dublin (a hotbed of the suffragist movement), matriculating from the Royal University of Ireland in 1893. She attended the Catholic University of Ireland's School of Medicine before graduating as a doctor from the Royal University of Ireland in 1899. As an intern, she worked at the Rotunda Hospital, the Royal Eye and Ear Hospital, and the Richmond Lunatic Asylum. With substantial experience, she was appointed the first resident doctor at Dublin's Adelaide Hospital. Here she was confronted by male opposition to her appointment, and she reluctantly turned the job down. Lynn sought further experience for a number of years in America before returning to Ireland, where she found work as a

duty doctor before becoming a general practitioner. Kathleen was involved in the suffrage movement, possibly dating back to her time at the Alexandra College. She was appointed to the executive committee of the Irish Women' Suffragette and Local Government Association (IWSLGA) in 1903. Lynn then joined the more radical British movement, the Women's Social and Political Union (WSPU), counting the Pankhursts among her newfound friends. In 1912, she was part of the mass movement to include women's suffrage in the forthcoming Home Rule Bill. During the 1913 lockout, her sympathies were with the workers. She worked alongside that other convert to socialism, Constance Markievicz, in the soup kitchens in Liberty Hall. Following the end of the strike, Markievicz asked Lynn to treat Helena Molony, who had suffered a breakdown following her tireless work during the lockout. Molony went to live with Lynn during her illness. Here, alongside Markievicz and Molony, Lynn was converted to the national struggle.

Helena Molony, suffragist, trade unionist, and nationalist, was influenced by Connolly.

Markievicz was born Constance Georgine Gore-Booth, on 4th February 1868, at Buckingham Gate, London. She was the daughter of Sir Henry Gore-Booth, fifth baronet. Following their father's example in feeding his tenants on his Irish estate in County Sligo in hard times, sisters Constance and Eva Gore-Booth were made aware of the poverty about them. Eva, as mentioned in the foregoing chapter, later became involved in the labor movement in the north of England. Constance, meanwhile, studied art at the Slade in London and the Academie Julian in Paris. While studying in London, she was activated into joining the National Union of Women's Suffrage Societies (NUWSS). Later in Paris, she met her future husband, Casimir Markievicz, a Ukrainian Pole, who styled himself as Count Markievicz. They married in London in September 1900. The couple, with their daughter, Maeve, and Casimir's son, Stanislas, by his first wife, settled down in Dublin in 1903. As a middle-class couple with connections, the Markieviczes moved in establishment circles, including artists, leading figures in the Irish revival movement, and future political leaders. In 1908, Constance became involved in nationalist politics. She joined Sinn Fein and Inghinidhe na h'Eireann (Daughters of Ireland), cofounded by fellow Ascendancy Anglo-Irishwoman Maude Gonne. Constance performed with Maud Gonne in a number of nationalistic plays in the newly established Abbey Theatre. In 1909, Markievicz and Bulmer Hobson founded Fianna Eireann, an Irish nationalist version of the Boy Scout movement. The boys were instructed in military drills and the use of firearms. Constance was briefly imprisoned in 1911 for taking part in a protest against the visit of King George V to Dublin. She fell under the spell of James Connolly, and upon its foundation, she joined the Irish Citizen Army. Advice she offered to other would-be women soldiers was, "Dress suitably in short skirts and strong boots, leave your jewels in the bank and buy a revolver."

Charlotte Despard was another woman from the Ascendancy who was attracted to socialist politics. In many ways, she was an extraordinary woman, turning her back upon everything into which she had been born. She was born Charlotte French, at Ripple in Kent, in June 1844. Her brother, John French, became a senior military commander of the British Army during World War I. He was later to prove her nemesis when he was appointed lord lieutenant of Ireland. Lacking any real education, for such a thing was felt unnecessary for a young woman of her social position, Charlotte attended a finishing school as was expected, with a view to marrying a rich young man. She did, indeed, marry. Her husband was Maximilian Carden Despard, an Anglo-Irish businessman, who had made his money as a cofounder of the Hong Kong and Shanghai Bank. He encouraged Charlotte in her writing, both prose and poetry, some of which was published. Maximilian died in 1890, leaving Charlotte a rich widow. There were no children from the marriage. Following her husband's death, Charlotte was encouraged to take up charity work. She devoted her time in ministering to the poor and was shocked at the level of poverty that she found in Nine Elms, an Irish slum district of London. Using her wealth, she set up working men's clubs, clinics, a youth club, and a soup kitchen. She became good friends with Eleanor Marx, wife of Karl, and became politicized. In 1894, she was elected as a Poor Law Guardian for Lambeth Poor Law Union. It gave her the opportunity of improving the lot of those forced to go into the workhouse. At this time, influenced no doubt by those around her, she converted to Roman Catholicism, a conversion not altogether approved of by her Protestant family. She joined the National Union of Women's Suffrage Societies (NUWSS) in 1906, and later the more militant WSPU. In 1908, then staying in Ireland and at the age of sixty-four, Charlotte joined Hanna Sheehy Skeffington and Margaret Cousins in forming the Irish Women's Franchise League. In 1913, she gave aid to the victims of the Dublin Lockout and set up the Irish Worker's College. She joined the Labor Party, and through the people she met, she was also drawn toward Irish nationalism. Charlotte, as a member of the Labor Party, was appointed to a committee of inquiry into conditions in Ireland, during the War of Independence, much to the chagrin of her brother. He, in fact, disowned her, even refusing to be reconciled on his deathbed in 1925. The job of the committee upon which she sat was to report on and collect evidence of atrocities committed by the police and army, particularly in Cork and Kerry. Later, following the end of the war, Charlotte joined the Communist Party of Great Britain, and became secretary of the Friends of Soviet Russia, following a visit to the Soviet Union, with Hanna Sheehy Skeffington. Charlotte Despard died in 1939, at the age of ninety-five, and she was buried in Glasnevin Cemetery. She was a most extraordinary woman.

Louie Bennett, perhaps less well known than the above three, was both a suffragette and a trade unionist. She was born in Temple Hill, Dublin, in 1870, into a middle-class background. The family were Protestant and Unionist. Her father, James Bennett, was a fine arts auctioneer and valuer with premises on Ormond Quay, Dublin. Louisa Elizabeth Bennett—"Louie," as she was more commonly known—was educated at home and later was sent to be educated at a boarding school in England. She attended Alexandra College in Dublin (a hotbed of female suffrage) before briefly studying music in Bonn, in Germany. At what stage she became interested in female suffrage is unknown. She herself suggested that it was through reading the novels of George Eliot, the pen name of the Nuneaton-born writer Mary Anne Evans. Louie Bennett was involved in the establishment of the Irish Women's Suffrage Federation (along with Helen Chenevix), the Irish Women's Reform League, and the Irish Women's Workers Union, reflecting her shift toward socialism. The IWWU was founded in September 1911. In 1916, as an officer of the union, Louie officially attended the Irish Trade Union Congress in Sligo, firmly establishing her as committed trade unionist. During the Lockout of 1913, Louie was involved in a scheme with the Lady Mayoress of Dublin to aid strikers' families. Coming under the spell of James Connolly, "a thorough feminist in every respect," as she declared of him, she also worked alongside Delia Larkin in the soup kitchens at Liberty Hall. Following the murder of Francis Sheehy Skeffington in 1916, Louie assisted, then became joint editor, with Mary Bourke-Dowling, of the suffragette newspaper the *Irish Citizen*. In a leader for the paper, she linked the suffrage movement with socialism when she wrote:

> The most notable development of the women's movement in Ireland during the past year has been the sudden growth of trade unionism amongst women workers. A year ago the members of the Irish Women's Workers Union numbered only a few hundreds; now they are over 2,000.[6]

Post–Easter Rising, Louie was joined by Helena Molony, Helen Chenevix, and Rosie Hackett, in a reorganized and revitalized IWWU, now independent of the ITGWU. She served as president of the Irish Trade Union Congress in 1932 and 1948. Louie never married. She shared a home with Helen Chenevix, at Killiney, County Dublin. Louie Bennett died in 1956 at the age of eighty-six.

Cissie Cahalan was born in Tipperary in 1876. She never became famous, certainly not in the mold of Constance Markievicz or Charlotte Despard, but she did make a difference to those around her. She was christened Mary Josephine Cahalan, but she was always known as Cissie, a familiar term for a sister. She was the daughter of a schoolteacher, but with little future in Tipperary, Cissie traveled to Dublin to better herself. Here she found work as a shop assistant, in the department store of Arnotts in Henry Street, a company founded in 1843. New to the city, Cissie got caught up in the excitement and was open to every new idea around her. She joined the Irish Women's Franchise League in 1908, and by diligence and commitment, she rose through its ranks, the only woman from a working-class background to achieve any prominence within this middle-class establishment. She became a close friend of Hanna Sheehy Skeffington. Through her job, Cissie joined the Irish Drapers' Association (IDAA), not perhaps the most militant of trade unions when she joined. By degrees, she became head of the female branch of the Association in 1912. Committed to the union, Cissie submitted articles to the trade union's journal, putting forward the notion of female equality. She also wrote articles that appeared in the *Irish Citizen*. One particular theme she championed was equal pay for men and women. This was in opposition to Louie Bennett's call, within the newspaper, for women-only trade unions. Cissie saw this as divisive. She maintained that if men and women were in the same union and being paid the same wages for doing the same job, then the employers could not play one sex off against the other, using lower-paid women to the detriment of men. Wearing her other hat, as a delegate of the IWFL, she sought the support of the Dublin Trades' Council for women's suffrage. By 1917, she was appointed to the executive committee of the IWFL. That same year, Cissie went to the Irish Trade Union Congress as a delegate of the IDAA. Now full of confidence, she took on Arnott's department store and succeeded in winning a 30 percent pay increase. In her quiet, little way, the unsung heroine who was Cissie Cahalan made a difference. She died in August 1948.

Likewise, Meg McCoubrey is only now coming to public attention. She was born Margaret Mearns at Elderslie near Glasgow in 1880. She is known as both a suffragette and a socialist, being a member of the Belfast Co-operative Movement. She married fellow Presbyterian and Irish trade unionist John Taylor McCoubry in 1906. Soon after, they moved to Belfast and from there to Ormeau in County Down. Margaret joined the Women's Social and Political Union (WSPU), possibly influenced by her husband and the trade unionists with whom he associated. She was certainly influential within the association, and she was chosen to represent the women of Ulster at their meetings in England. Margaret was also a member of the Irish Women's Suffrage Society (IWSS), founding a branch in Belfast city center, and so she was quite influential within Irish suffrage. As a radical socialist, Meg criticized the middle-class prejudices of some fellow suffragists in the pages of the *Irish Citizen.* She accused them of attempting to work only for a middle-class suffrage and ignoring the needs of working-class women. At the outbreak of World War I, she identified herself as a pacifist and ran a peace and suffrage campaign during the war. She put her case for peace in the pages of the *Irish Citizen.* On 27th Feb. 1915, Meg McCoubrey posed the moral question:

> What … would be the thought of a woman who looked down on a battlefield of slain and wounded? It would not be "there lie so many Germans, so many British, or so many French." It would be "so many mothers' sons!"

In June 1911, Larkin launched the *Irish Worker and People's Advocate.* Within the paper, he set himself up as the keeper of the public conscience, writing most of the front-page articles. He had been shocked upon his arrival in Dublin by the squalor of the city's tenement poor. In the columns of the paper, its title now reduced to *The Irish Worker,* he attacked the slum landlords, the sweatshop employers, lying journalists, corrupt politicians, and bullying policemen. The paper's first circulation was twenty-six thousand, rising to 94,994 by September, though it fell to a steady twenty thousand after that. Though socialist in nature, the newspaper was also staunchly Republican, reflecting not only Larkin's, but also Connolly's view that "the cause of labor is the cause of Ireland, the cause of Ireland is the cause of labor."

The women's section in the trade union's *Irish Worker*.

In February 1912, the ITGWU took over the old Northumberland Hotel at 18 Beresford Place, and renamed it Liberty Hall. The IWWU was allocated offices in the building. Forward-thinking, the union set up a number of societies at Liberty Hall in order to improve the social life of its members. Concerts and social events were arranged on Sunday evenings. The hall hosted plays and musical evenings, including performances from the Fintan Lalor Pipers' Band, established by Bob de Cour, secretary of the ITGWU branch in Aungier Street. In August 1913, the ITGWU took out a lease on Croydon Park in Clontarf. It was a large old house set on rambling grounds. The idea was that it would become a social center for the members and their families, somewhere to escape to out of the crowded tenement slums that they occupied. Again, the emphasis was on the general well-being of its members, with entertainment and cultural improvement. During the summer months, camps were organized on the grounds. It all helped to build up camaraderie among the union members.

The Irish Women Workers' Union, as mentioned above, was founded at a public meeting held on 5th September 1911, in the old Antient Concert Hall in Great Brunswick Street (now Pearse Street). Its formation had been mooted in an advertisement in the *Irish Worker,* on 12th August 1911. James Larkin, who had overseen its establishment, became the union's first president. His sister Delia was appointed its first secretary. Larkin's speech to the audience was "wildly cheered," it was reported. Constance Markievicz and Hanna

Sheehy Skeffington also spoke at the inauguration, linking membership of the new union with winning the vote. The IWWU, which Delia Larkin described as being "affiliated" to the ITGWU, was open to all women workers, regardless of their industry or the type of work they did. The IWWU established offices in Great Brunswick Street, but it was later allocated a room within Liberty Hall. Enrollment into the union cost sixpence, with a two-pence-a-week subscription. Though Dublin supplied most members to the union, branches were also opened in industrial Belfast, Dundalk, Wexford, and Cork.

Within weeks of its formation, the IWWU was involved in a successful dispute with Jacob's. The biscuit manufacturers were by far the largest employers of women in Dublin. The union acted after complaints by its members. Delia protested against the company's unfair punishments, sexual harassment, and management corruption. "Jacobs & Co," she claimed, "have no qualms of conscience whatever as far as the workers are concerned; they are out to make a profit, and make it they will, even though it be at the cost of ill-health and disablement to the girls, women and men of Dublin."[7] Men and women at Jacob's worked a fifty-hour week, mostly on piecework. Two-thirds of the women earned an average of between seven and ten shillings a week. Young girls just starting earned four shillings a week. Male laborers earned between fifteen and twenty-five shillings, which included overtime; craftsmen's and general builders' laborers earned over forty shillings. Craftsmen themselves, such as painters, carpenters, and plumbers, earned seventy-five shillings, or three pounds and fifteen shillings a week.[8] On 21st August 1911, about 350 men and women from the bakehouse went out on strike for better conditions. The company began advertising for strike-breakers, which led to skirmishes with the pickets at the factory gates. The police were called, and arrests were made. All the time, Jacob's was losing money. The management went over the head of the women's union and appealed to James Larkin to intercede. After some negotiation, the firm agreed to recognize the ITGWU, and working con-

Delia Larkin, secretary of the Irish Women Workers' Trade Union.

ditions and pay began to improve. The men received two shillings a week extra, the women got one shilling.

With that victory behind them, the IWWU took on other companies to improve wages and conditions, including Keogh's Sacks, where thirty-nine women went out on strike; the Pembroke Laundry, where fourteen women struck; the Somerset Linen Merchants; and the Savoy Confectionary Company. At the Somerset factory, though the strikers were not initially members of the union, they all joined for the greater protection that it offered. The IWWU paid them out four shillings a week in strike pay before a successful conclusion to the dispute. At the Savoy, the strike lasted some three months, largely brought to an end when the company began losing money over revelations that their products were adulterated. Within its first six months, the union paid out £172 in strike pay, but in exchange it won significant pay raises and a betterment of conditions for its increasing membership in Dublin.

R.M. Fox, who was later to write the official history of the Irish Citizen

Members of the Irish Women Workers' Union on the steps of Liberty Hall, Dublin. Delia Larkin is in the front center.

Army, published in 1943, described the IWWU leader, Delia Larkin: "She was tall and commanding in appearance, like her brother, and had a similar temperament, implacable to opponents, but with a friendly warmth to the people she trusted." Delia was born in Liverpool, in 1878, to Irish parents, James and Mary Ann Larkin. Her birth certificate names her as Bridget Larkin, but from a baby, she was affectionately known as Delia. Following the death of her father, James, in 1887, when she was just nine years old, her education was cut short when she was forced to go out to work to help support the family. As a young adult, she turned to nursing as a career, but by 1907, she was apparently running a hotel in Rostrevor, County Down. This was at a time when her brother James was the NUDL strike leader in Belfast. Brother and sister were in Dublin by April 1911, and Delia was living with her brother and his family at 27 Aubern Street, near Broadstone, as the census shows. Her occupation is given as teacher. At the time of her appointment as secretary of the IWWU, Delia was writing a regular column in the ITGWU's newspaper, *The Irish Worker*. Writing at the time of the formation of the women's union, its purpose, she explained, was simple: "all we ask for is just shorter hours, better pay that the scandalous limit now existing and conditions of labor befitting a human being." In her weekly column, she highlighted the working conditions of Dublin's laundry workers, food producers, domestics, clerical workers, and nurses. The aim of the union was to provide women with a voice, but it was more than just a vehicle for improving conditions and pay. The union developed a social life, which brought together women of varying social strata. There were discussion groups, weekly socials, annual outings, concerts, and dances. In 1912, Delia formed a choir from the union members. Later a drama group was founded, known as the Irish Workers' Dramatic Class. Intertwined throughout the union was an assertion of women's rights in the form of female suffrage. Delia Larkin represented the union within the suffrage movement and leading on from that came the union's demand for women's suffrage to be included in the Home Rule Bill. A mass meeting of the union's members, supported by the various suffragist movements, was held in the Antient Concert Rooms on 1st June 1912, in support of the proposal.

By 1913, the ITGWU, with the affiliated IWWU, was the largest and most militant trade union in Ireland. It claimed a membership of twenty thousand, with twelve thousand in Dublin. The negotiating power of the union over pay and conditions was seen as a threat by the city's largest employers. Under the leadership of William Martin Murphy, the Employers' Federation, as it became, set out to challenge Larkin and the growth of unionized labor. Murphy's employment policy was never to use unionized labor. On 21st August, when Murphy discovered that some of his employees in his newspaper-owned *Irish Independent* had joined the union, he dismissed half the workers in the dispatch department and about two hundred in the parcels section. Two days later, he issued his demand through the Employers' Federation, obliging all its employees to sign a form renouncing the Transport Union or face the loss of their positions. It read:

> I hereby undertake to carry out all instructions given to me by or on behalf of my employers and, further I agree to immediately resign my membership of the Irish Transport and General Workers' Union (if a member), and I further undertake that I will not join or in any way support this Union.

The conflict began on Tuesday, 26th August 1913, right in the middle of Horse Show Week, when the city was crowded. Some seven hundred men who worked for the Dublin Tramway Company, owned by Murphy, walked off their trams in an attempt to force a pay increase. Murphy had refused to recognize the ITGWU, and he now began sacking employees wearing the union's red hand badge. He employed "scab" labor to drive the trams, each tram guarded by a policeman standing beside its driver.

On the evening of the 26th, following speeches at Beresford Place regarding the strike, Larkin, Thomas Lawlor, and Dublin councilor William Partridge were arrested on the highly questionable charges of sedition and conspiracy and were bailed. Two days later, Larkin, now joined by James Connolly, lately returned from Belfast, spoke again publicly and announced that he would speak at a public meeting the following Sunday. On Saturday, 30th August, Connolly and Partridge were arrested. A warrant for the arrest of Larkin was also issued, but he was nowhere to be found. He was being sheltered at the home of Constance Markievicz, a convert to the socialist struggle.

That night, the police entered the working-class Corporation Street area of the city in an attempt to intimidate the people. Windows were broken, and people were roughed up. There were further clashes and baton

William Martin Murphy, leader of the Employer's Association, was vehemently opposed to the Irish Transport and General Workers' Union.

𝕴 𝖍𝖊𝖗𝖊𝖇𝖞 𝖚𝖓𝖉𝖊𝖗𝖙𝖆𝖐𝖊 to carry out all instructions given to me by or on behalf of my employers, and further I agree to immediately resign my membership of the Irish Transport and General Workers' Union (if a member) and I further undertake that I will not join or in any way support this Union.

Signed..

Address..

....

....

Witness..

Date..

The employers attempted to break the ITGWU by forcing their workers to sign this document.

charges on Burgh Quay and Eden Quay along the River Liffey, which led to the deaths of two men. In his book *Casement's Last Adventure,* Captain Robert Monteith recorded:

> I witnessed the murder of one of these unfortunate men. He was walking along Eden Quay when he was met by a mixed patrol of Dublin Metropolitan Police and the Royal Irish Constabulary. The strength of the patrol was about thirty-five, all more or less drunk. One of the Constabulary walked from the center of the road on to the sidewalk and, without the slightest provocation, felled the poor man with a blow from his staff. The horrible crunching sound of the blow was clearly audible fifty yards away. The drunken scoundrel was ably seconded by two of the Metropolitan Police, who, as the unfortunate man attempted to rise, beat him about the head until his skull was smashed in several places. They then rejoined their patrol leaving him in his blood. For saying, "you damned cowards," I was instantly struck by two policemen and fell to the ground, where I had sense enough to lie until the patrol had passed on.

The situation escalated over nonrecognition of the union throughout the city. On 30th August, mill owner Richard Shackleton sent a consignment of flour to Jacob's. Shackleton's had previously dismissed union members from its mills and had been blacklisted by the union. The ITGWU members at Jacob's refused to unload the wagon and were promptly sacked. Notices appeared around the factory banning the wearing of the union badge. Over the weekend, there were clashes with the pickets and the police in the city. The police arrested 168 people, most of them trade unionists. On Monday morning, 670 of the 1,060 of Jacob's male workers stayed out in support of their sacked colleagues. Things escalated when three girls wearing ITGWU red hand badges were told to remove them. Refusing, they were sent home. Similar demands were made of the other female union members, who also refused. By the end of the day, 303 women had been dismissed. Then, in consultation with the Employers' Federation, Jacob's declared a lockout.

One of the young women who was dismissed was the diminutive bakehouse worker Rosie Hackett. Rosanna Hackett, "Rosie" to all, was born in inner-city Dublin in 1893. In her teens, she got a job at Jacob's Biscuit Factory as a packer in the paper stores. Years earlier, on 22nd August 1910, she was one of the women who went out on strike for better pay. After some negotiation, the women received an increase. The delightfully diminutive Rosie was no shrinking violet. She stood up for what she believed in. She was one of the first to join the Irish Women Workers' Union following its establishment in August 1911. Rosie was on O'Connell Street on 13th August 1913, and she witnessed James Larkin's address to the crowds below. Following the lockout by the Employers' Federation, Rosie was one of the unsung heroines, cooking for the striking families in Liberty Hall. With the strike over, Rosie was not taken back by Jacob's. Work was found for her by the IWWU in their workers' cooperative shop, at 31 Eden Quay, adjoining Liberty Hall. She worked alongside Jinnie Shanahan and fell under the supervision and influence of Helena Molony. The co-op shop, in addition to selling goods, also made and sold working-men's shirts bearing the Red Hand crest of the ITGWU. The shirts sold at 2s. 6d. Hidden away in a back room of the shop was a printing press that produced the trade union's pamphlets and papers. The shop, which sold copies of *The Irish Worker*, *The Spark*, and *The Nation*, was raided by the police just prior to the Easter Rising, with a view to searching it. Rosie, barely five feet tall, if that, stood her ground and refused them further entry, She gave as good as she got in the shouting match that followed, until the arrival of an armed James Connolly. He saw the police off the premises, threatening "to drop them" if they did not leave. The printer, Christopher Brady, witnessed the confrontation and reported that Molony herself was present and already covering the police with her automatic. In the police report of the incident, Rosie is described as "the little girl in charge." Rosie was then trained up as a printer and worked part-time on the production line of the *Irish Worker*. With the formation of the Irish Citizen Army, Rosie joined up. She was instructed in first aid by Dr. Kathleen Lynn, with a view to assisting in the surgery in Liberty Hall. Rosie's coworker, Jinnie Shanahan, also joined the ICA.

Jane "Jinnie" Shanahan was born in South Dublin in 1891, the daughter of a bricklayer's laborer, Michael Shanahan. The family was living in a tenement, part of 52 Dolphin's Barn Lane, but by the 1911 census, they had moved to 22 Dawson Court, near St. Stephen's Green. Jinnie found work at Jacob's Biscuit Factory on Bishop Street, but as a member of the IWWU, she lost her position during the 1913–1914 strike and lockout. For a time, she worked in the Liberty Hall soup kitchen, helping to feed starving locked-out workers. From there she went to work at the union's cooperative shop, where she met little Rosie Hackett. Jinnie joined the Irish Citizen Army upon its foundation in November 1913. Though not offered a military rank, she effectively took command of the women's section, taking part in "all the Army maneuvers," and helping "in the training of recruits."[9]

On Sunday, 31st August, a small crowd of about five hundred gathered on Sackville Street (now O'Connell Street), enlarged by the curious and others out for a stroll that day. Despite the warrant for his arrest, Larkin, disguised as a bent and bearded invalid, succeeded in getting into the Imperial Hotel (ironically owned by Murphy). Standing on the balcony overlooking the street, he spoke for a few minutes to the people below before the police rushed the building and arrested him. As he was arrested, a roar went up from the crowd. In response, down below in the street, the police launched an indiscriminate attack on everyone, whether men, women, or children—anyone, in fact, within reach of their batons. James Nolan was killed outright; John Byrne died the next day from his injuries. The day became known as Bloody Sunday. An eyewitness relayed the story of the day's happenings to Connolly's daughter Nora:

> O'Connell Street was thronged. Not only by fellows like me …but by people who never gave a thought to Jim or us and were going home from twelve o'clock mass in Marlborough Street.… Suddenly a window in Murphy's Hotel opened, and a long fellow in a frock coat and a beard began to talk. I could hear what he said and was wondering who the old josser was, when the crowd began to yell, "It's Larkin!" And then a roar of cheering went up, and we rushed towards the hotel. At the same time about twenty peelers tore into the hotel. They came out in a few minutes with Larkin. The crowd gathered in and began to cheer Larkin and boo and jeer the police. A lad behind me yelled, "Hey!" the peelers have drawn their batons." The next thing I knew the peelers were upon us. I tried to get out of the crowd, but it was too thick. All you could hear was the thud, thump, crack of the batons as they fell on the heads of the crowd. There were screams and groans and yelps. There was no way to escape from the batons—the peelers came steadily on like mowing

machines, and behind them the street was like a battlefield dotted with bodies. Some of them were lying still, some twisting in pain. And the groaning! My God! Some of us tried to dodge round the peelers and get out of O'Connell Street down Princess Street. We raced for it. We weren't halfway down it when we met another bunch of peelers, and they came at us with their batons. We were in a trap. There was nothing but thuds, and cracks, and groans. I turned, thinking that I'd better chance O'Connell Street, and I don't remember anything after that. It was a massacre.[10]

That night, the police went on the rampage in the poorer parts of the city. This time, though, the poor in the Corporation Street buildings fought back with bricks, bottles, and other missiles, forcing the police to retire with injuries. At 2 a.m., when all was quiet, the police returned. In vengeance, they broke into houses, beating up the occupants without distinction of sex or age. Property was wantonly destroyed. One of the inhabitants of the Corporation Street Buildings, Mrs. Fanny O'Leary, later testified to an inquiry that between one and two o'clock in the morning, the police burst the door off its hinges and rushed in. They beat her brother Patrick, who was staying with her, until he was covered in blood. She heard them bursting into the flats below; another man had his arm broken. A widow who had lately buried her husband had her place smashed up by the intruders, and a baby just a few months old sustained a black eye. The later report of the commission looking into the police raids concluded that "willful damage was done without justification." Shamefully, no disciplinary action was recommended or taken.

On 3rd September, the Federation of Dublin Employers, representing some four hundred companies, demanded that all workers sign the document promising to leave the union or not to join any other union. Most workers refused. The lockout that followed paralyzed the city. Thousands were thrown out of work. By and large, the Irish Party at Westminster, William Martin Murphy, and the Employers' Federation, Sinn Fein and Arthur Griffith, the nationalists, the middle classes, and the newspapers all condemned the strikers rather than the employers. What had begun as a strike had evolved into class conflict, the middle classes fearing the strength of the working-class strikers. The Home Rule movement was conservative on social issues and was hostile to manifestations of social radicalism. Through his newspaper, the *United Irishman,* Arthur Griffith of Sinn Fein roundly condemned the strike, repeatedly attacking the ITGWU and urging the workers to join other trade unions. Strident trade unionism was not part of his brave new world of an independent Ireland. The poor should know their place within the scheme of things, he believed. In his vision of a new Ireland, free of British encumbrance, the social ladder would contain "a progressive and enlightened aristocracy, a prosperous middle class, and a contented working class." What James Connolly, a friend of his, thought of that is not recorded.

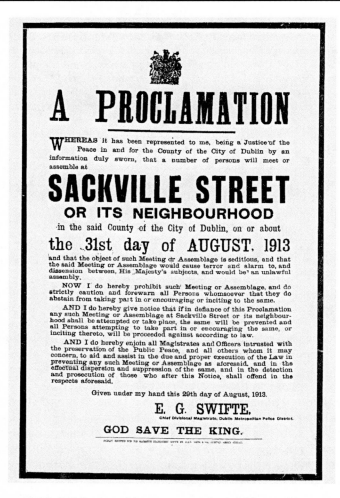

A proclamation forbidding a public meeting to be held by Larkin. Two men were killed when Larkin defied the authorities and the police overreacted, in what became known as Bloody Sunday.

The ongoing hostility of the police toward any form of public protest, and, indeed, toward the poor, saw the formation of a defense force drawn from the membership of the ITGWU. It was a disciplined force, trained up by Charles Armstrong, a reservist in the Royal Irish Rifles, with the assistance of a soldier from the Dublin Fusiliers. Armed with hurly sticks and trained to act on whistle signals, its role was to protect members' meetings from attacks by the police. With the arrival of the later food ships to feed the poor, the *Irish Times* (4th Oct. 1913) reported the defense force in action:

Quickly the food ship was made fast. And just at this moment a couple of hundred Transport workers, wearing picket badges and carrying sticks, marched down the quay under the command of Councilor [William] Partridge. They set about their function of maintaining order, and it must be admitted that they discharge it well.

At Liberty Hall, a visitor observed what happened next:

Orders for food coming by the foodships are distributed there in the upper rooms, while in the basement meals are always being cooked and distributed to the mothers and children who come in with tin cans and jugs for stew or cocoa and carry away under ragged shawls big loaves baked at the Co-op bakery. Every passage and landing is crowded with patient people, none of whom go empty away, for the organization as far as one can see is perfect.[11]

Liberty Hall became the center for the distribution of food and clothing for the workers who had been locked out. A reporter for the British Labor Party sponsored newspaper, the *Daily Herald,* wrote in the 24th December 1913 issue:

The work has grown to such proportions that five rooms in Liberty Hall are set aside for the various activities in connection with the administration of the Fund....

In one room women are working sewing machines making up serge and flannellette into warm clothing; another room is arranged as a warehouse, with wires stretched across the ceiling, from which hang the boots and clothes ready to be distributed every morning after the children had their breakfast.

I saw the piles of excellent whole meal bread, which with butter and cocoa, forms the children's breakfast.

At Jacob's, George Jacob resolved to fight back. He brought in a number of men from the company's Liverpool factory to maintain machinery and began recruiting new girls. By 15th September, the bakehouse was back to full production. The strikers were given until 15th October to return or be sacked. A loyalty bonus of two shillings a week was offered for those willing to cross the picket. There were scuffles when strikers and "scabs" clashed at the entrance to the factory, leading to arrests. On 3rd November, matters came to a head with a clash between mass pickets and strike breakers. One of the girl pickets, Mary Ellen Murphy, age sixteen, was sentenced to a month's imprisonment for boxing the ears of another girl and calling her a "scab." As conditions worsened, support for the strike crumbled. Some forty-three women returned before the deadline, driven by poverty and hunger.

In its 6th September 1913, issue, the suffragette newspaper the *Irish Citizen* announced its support for Larkin:

Mr. Larkin was the initiator of the vigorous resolution passed by the Irish Trades Congress, last Whitsuntide, in condemnation of the Government's attack upon freedom of speech and freedom of the press, and calling for the resignation of "that incapable irresponsible McKenna" [the Home Secretary, Reginald McKenna]. He also assisted to carry suffragist resolutions at the Dublin Trades Council, and his paper, the Irish Worker, has repeatedly attacked the Government's coercive policy towards the suffragists.

The men of Mr. Larkin's Union also frequently interfered, at the rowdy meetings in Dublin last year, to protect Suffragettes from the hooliganism of the Ancient Order of Hibernians—the body that is now organizing the strike breakers.

Larkin had established his suffragist credentials as early as 1909, not long after his arrival in Dublin. In the ITGWU program of that year, it advocated adult suffrage and equal voting rights in parliamentary and local elections for all women as well as men, at the age of twenty-one. In 1912, following the election of Dublin's first councilor, Sarah Harrison, Larkin was among the guests who attended the suffragists' celebrations.

On 2nd September, the Dublin Coal Merchants' Association began a lockout. Patterson's match factory followed suit. Realizing that he could not sustain the fight without help, James Larkin traveled to England to gain TUC support. In his absence, his sister Delia took effective charge of Liberty Hall. She, with a women's committee of volunteers from among her union members, strikers' relatives, and others, organized a soup kitchen for the feeding of the union members and their dependents. They provided daily breakfasts for three thousand children, lunches for nursing mothers, and the distribution of clothing. She is perhaps not fully recognized for this. Much of the credit is erroneously attributed to the more socially visible Constance Markievicz, especially by her hagiographer, Sean O'Faolain. He commented, much to Helena Molony's annoyance, that "Constance Markievicz abandoned her Boy Scouts for the time being and organized a food kitchen in the basement of Liberty Hall."[12] Much to their credit, the British Co-operative Movement sent food and clothing by the shipload. On 23rd September, the British Trades Union Congress dispatched the SS *Hare,* the first of eleven food ships, carrying a cargo of sixty thousand food parcels for the strikers and their families.

By 27th September, there were estimated to be twenty-four thousand people out of work. Estimates of their dependents could probably be magnified by a factor of five, or even six. With no money coming in, with all the strike pay gone, and despite the English intervention, genuine starvation and privation followed. At this crucial stage, with Larkin in prison, James Connolly was appointed general secretary of the ITGWU pro-tem.

Public opinion now turned against the strike leaders when they were attacked by the Catholic Church. Well-meaning ladies in London, Dora Montefiore and Lucille Rand, having heard of the suffering in Ireland, offered a scheme to provide the children of the strikers with a holiday in England. They, and Frances Greville, Lady Warwick, all members of the left-wing Social Democratic Federation, had launched a similar scheme for children in England during the London Dock Strike. The first group of Dublin children traveled to the home of influential suffragette leader, Emmeline Pethick Lawrence. At the dock, the children were treated with every kindness prior to sailing. When the Catholic Archbishop of Dublin, William Walsh, got to hear of the scheme, without consulting, he wrote a letter to all the Dublin newspapers condemning the scheme out of hand. His belief was that they would be placed with Protestant families. He wrote:

> The Dublin women now subjected to this cruel temptation to part with their help-less offspring are, in the majority of cases, Catholics. Have they abandoned their Faith? Well, if they have not, they should need no words of mine to remind them of the plain duty of every Catholic mother in such a case. I can only put it to them that they can be no longer held worthy of the name Catholic mothers if they so far forgot that duty as to send away their little children to be cared for in a strange land with-out security of any kind that those to whom the poor children are to be handed over are Catholics, or indeed persons of any faith at all.

Nothing could be further from the truth. The initial batch had been carefully housed with Catholic families in Liverpool. The genie was out of the bottle, though, and reason went by the board, whipped up by parish priests, who followed the archbishop's line. The practice of sending children to England was condemned. On 22nd October, there were "unseemly scuffles" at the dock where pickets of the Ancient Order of Hibernians stirred up the crowds to oppose the departure of more children. Amid the growing violence, the policy was forced to be abandoned. In the Albert Hall in London, George Russell, poet and writer, spoke out against "those super human beings" who "have so little concern for the human body at all, and that they assert it is better for children to be starved than to be moved from a Christian atmos-phere of the Dublin slums…. You have no idea what the slums of Dublin are like. There are more than twenty thousand families each living in one room." W.B. Yeats angrily wrote, "I want to know why the mob at the North Wall and elsewhere were permitted to drag children from their parents' arms and by what right one woman was compelled to open her box and show her mar-riage certificate; I want to know by what right the police refused to accept charges against the rioters." The Catholic church failed to offer an alternative scheme, nor did it set up kitchens to feed the poor. The children remained in Dublin to starve—but at least their souls were saved.

Connolly, who had been organizing the ITGWU up in Belfast, was sum-moned to Dublin in late October to be appointed general secretary pro-tem of the ITGWU. Larkin had been tried on 27th October and sentenced to seven months' imprisonment for "incitement and sedition." His imprison-ment was brief, and he was released. On 9th December 1913, Larkin attended a special meeting of the British Trades Union Congress in London. Accom-panied by James Connolly, William O'Brien, and Thomas McPartlin, Larkin railed against their lack of support, even though they agreed to continue financial aid to the strikers. Larkin, by his aggression, alienated the English trade unionists. Back in Dublin, another approach was made to the employers. On 18th December, representatives of the workers met with the employers, who agreed to withdraw the document forbidding membership of the ITGWU. In return, the workers were asked to renounce the sympathetic strike. By January, the workers began to drift back to work on whatever terms they could get. The epic struggle, which had lasted some six months, resulted in a crushing defeat for the workers. The strike officially ended on 14th February 1914. The women workers in Jacob's, some of the first to be locked out, were the last to return, in March 1914. Some of the more militant women, picked out as strike leaders, like little Rosie Hackett, were denied reinstatement.[13] The women's union paid a high price. Between four and five hundred women never got their jobs back. They had been beaten up, arrested, and imprisoned for their stand. One girl, fifteen-year-old Alice Brady, was shot and killed by a "scab." Membership in the ITGWU was banned at Jacob's. In its place, two, more compliant "house unions" were formed: the Dublin Biscuit Operatives' Labor Union & Benefit Society (Feb. 1914), and the Dublin Guild of Female Biscuit Operatives (Feb. 1916).

During the strike, tensions had developed within the labor movement and the Transport Union over the conduct of the strike. Relations between Larkin on the one hand, and Connolly and William O'Brien on the other, had become strained. Helena Molony in her witness statement, in an almost throwaway comment, revealed that between Larkin "and James Connolly there was a bitter feud. It was only a battle of temperaments, and I was on the side of James Connolly, with whom I had been in correspondence from 1908 in America."[14] Her loyalty was to have its rewards as will be shown.

By the autumn of 1914, after Larkin had set off for America, relations within Liberty Hall were fractious. There was a clash of personalities between James Connolly, the newly appointed acting secretary of the ITGWU, and Delia Larkin, a residue of the spat between Connolly and her brother. She was seen perhaps as a threat to his leadership, as the sister of the former secretary. Recollections by those present at the time suggested that he and Delia Larkin did not get on. A situation, perhaps manufactured, arose over the use of facilities at Liberty Hall by the women's union. The occupation of the largest room in Liberty Hall by the IWWU, without rent, was resented. There were other little niggling questions over housekeeping, and these mounted up. In the end, the IWWU was asked to vacate Liberty Hall. Added to this were financial difficulties relating to Delia Larkin's wages. Who should pay them? During the summer of 1915, the ITGWU gave up the lease on Croydon Park, where Delia had lived with her brother and his family. She was obliged to find a new home. Undermined at every turn, Delia left Dublin.

James Connolly, now completely in charge and without any opposition, appointed Helena Molony to take over the women's union. Some years later, when Delia returned to Dublin, she obtained work in the insurance section at Liberty Hall. She applied for reinstatement to the union that she had helped to found, but she was denied membership. She was told that she should join the Irish Clerical Workers' Union instead. They also turned her down. Perhaps driven by petty jealousies, it would seem that both unions feared the impact that she would make upon her return. Likewise, when Jim Larkin returned from America, the power that he had once yielded was also gone. With neither of the Larkins there to defend it, the IWWU, now led by Louie Bennett, came into conflict with the ITGWU when it began to recruit women workers. Though never a large union, the IWWU then went into terminal decline.

Between Larkin and Connolly, there was an ideological crossover. Larkin's fight was for the defense and recognition of trade unionism. Connolly, a Marxist, saw organized trade unionism as a vehicle for the establishment of a workers' revolution leading to a Workers' Republic. For that, though, it needed an army to protect its workers. On 13th November, at Liberty Hall, Connolly announced the formation of an Irish Citizen Army. In his witness statement to the Bureau of Military History (1766), William O'Brien recorded that Connolly announced:

> I am going to talk sedition. The next time we are out for a march I want to be accompanied by four battalions of trained men with their Corporals and sergeants. Why should we not train our men in Dublin as they are doing in Ulster?

The reference to Ulster relates to the formation of the Ulster Volunteer Force, an army established to fight Home Rule, particularly in the northeast of Ireland, a largely Protestant part of the country. Only days before Connolly's announcement, Eoin MacNeill, a prominent nationalist, published an article entitled "The North Began," calling for the formation of a southern volunteer force to ensure the fulfillment of Home Rule. Four days later, the intended formation of a Citizen Army was announced publicly, by Connolly, as recorded in the *Evening Telegraph* of 18th November:

> If we had a disciplined body of men there would be less danger of any of them falling against a policeman's baton. He hoped to see them soon on their route marches with their pikes on their shoulders … they had been promised the services of a competent military officer, the son of the distinguished Irish general who defended Ladysmith in South Africa during the second Boer War.

Captain Jack White was the son of the distinguished Irish general. Sandhurst-educated, Jack White was a veteran of the South African War, winning a DSO in the campaign. He had witnessed the police brutality in Dublin during the strike, and so wrote to Connolly to discuss a plan for the setting up of a defense force.

James Robert "Jack" White was born at Cleveland, Montague Place, Richmond, Surrey, England, in May 1879. The family's permanent residence was at Whitehall, Broughshane, County Antrim, in Ireland. Jack was the only son of Field Marshal Sir George Stuart White V.C. He was educated at Winchester College and later at the Royal Military College, Sandhurst. Here he was commissioned a second lieutenant in the 1st Gordon Highlanders in January 1899. In October, just prior to the embarkation of his regiment to South Africa, to fight the Boers, White was promoted to lieutenant. He took part in the Battle of Magersfontein (December 1899), the relief of Kimberley, and the Battle of Paadeberg (in February 1900). In further operations in the Orange Free State, White took part in the battles of Poplar Grove, Driefontein, Vet River, and Zand River. In May 1900, he and his regiment were part of the occupying force in Johannesburg and Pretoria. Mentioned in dispatches, White received the Distinguished Service Order (DSO) and the Queen's South Africa Medal with five clasps.

With the fighting over, White began to question Britain's right to subjugate the Boers. He grew disillusioned over the certainty of what he had been fighting for. Coupled to this was his perception of an arrogant British ruling class, lauding it over subject nations. He considered laying down his commission, but, following his father's appointment as governor of Gibraltar, in 1901, Jack became his aide-de-camp. While there, he married Mercedes "Dollie" Mosley, the daughter of a Gibraltar businessman. It proved to be an unhappy and somewhat acrimonious marriage. White returned to England, and in 1907, he resigned his commission. He spent a number of years traveling around the world, looking for some purpose to his life. The death of his father in 1912 saw his return to Ireland at a time of momentous change. Though of Ulster Protestant stock, he became a supporter of Home Rule. He wrote letters opposing Carson's anti–Home Rule stance and spoke on the same platform as George Bernard Shaw, and Roger Casement, in support of Irish nationalism. White was invited to speak in Dublin. Here he met James Connolly, and quickly identified with the workers' cause. It was a curious relationship. While identifying with the workers' cause, he himself admitted, "I clung to the comfortable suavities of my own class. I was not innocent of patronizing the cause I had adopted."[15] He was a man looking for a cause, rather akin to Constance Markievicz. Unlike Markievicz, who remained committed, though, White was constantly looking for new challenges. Leo Keohane in his biography of White has indicated that he was not always the easiest of people to get on with. For the moment, though, he was the right man at the right time, in the right place. In 1913, he put forward the idea of a workers' militia with the intention of putting "manners on the police."

White met Larkin at Liberty Hall, following Larkin's release from prison, to discuss the matter. At a meeting of the ITGWU, Larkin announced the outcome, "We are going to give the members of our union a military training. Captain White will speak to you now and tell you the plans he has, to create a great Citizen army." Members of the union were asked to attend the next day at Croydon Park at Clontarf, where those who wished would be enrolled. The Irish Citizen Army, Larkin announced, would fight for labor and for Ireland. The future playwright and soon to become its secretary Sean O'Casey records, "A last, long deafening cheer proclaimed the birth of the Citizen Army."

In response to the call, hundreds of men joined up. Of the women who joined, twenty-eight are known by name.[16] Right from the start, that they were more than subsidiaries of the men is indicated in the army notice, which appeared in the *Irish Worker* for 6th December 1913:

> After the Parade and Drilling of the Citizen Army at Croydon Park, a Great Procession will march through the streets to assure the delegates who will attend the British Trade Union Conference in London that Dublin is still determined to fight on. Men and girls must form up at Croydon Park.

As a result of police brutality, the Irish Citizen Army was formed.

The new recruits were formed into companies and drilled by Captain White. Clutching their broomsticks and hurlies, for want of rifles, they were sent out to protect the workers' demonstrations from police attacks. Connolly's daughter Nora, in her *Portrait of a Rebel Father,* describes a visit to Croydon Park, where she saw the Citizen Army training:

> Here were its members, marching now to the right, now to the left at the command of Captain White. He was tireless in drilling them and the men responded as tirelessly. Right and left they marched, round the field at the double, into columns and out of them. Once he stopped besides Connolly and he was in a rage. Some command he had given was misinterpreted. His hands were clenched and he was fairly gnashing his teeth.
>
> "Easy now, Captain," warned Connolly. "Easy now. Remember they're volunteers."
>
> "And aren't they great?" said Captain White, forgetting his rage in his admiration of the men.[17]

Gradually, the hurlies and the sticks were replaced by rifles smuggled in piecemeal from Glasgow, Liverpool, Holyhead, and London. Later, guns were appropriated from the volunteer landing at Howth. By early 1915, the Citizen Army was fully armed, and drilling at Croydon Park was carried out with an eclectic mix of British, Italian, and German rifles.

In January 1914, after six months, the strike was broken. Hungry, defeated workers were forced back to work; but the Citizen Army remained. With Larkin's departure to the United States soon after, the Citizen Army was taken over by his successor, the Marxist James Connolly. The Citizen Army that Connolly now forged was very much an egalitarian army, with the inclusion of women. Connolly believed in the emancipation of women to the extent that, following the assistance that she had rendered the strikers by working in Liberty Hall's soup kitchens during the great lockout, Constance Markievicz was appointed an officer in the Citizen Army.[18]

Breaking the strike, the employers now sought to break the union. They held the penalty of dismissal over the heads of the workers if they continued to remain members of the

Egalitarian, the ICA was open to both men and women. Connolly's daughter Nora became a soldier.

ITGWU. As such, many left the union, and drifted away from the Citizen Army, much to White's frustration. By 1916, its strength in Dublin had fallen to just 339, divided into twelve sections citywide. This decline had been accentuated by the creation of the Irish Volunteers two years earlier. Thousands who had originally been members of the ICA now joined the Volunteers. As the Citizen Army dwindled, a crisis meeting was held in Liberty Hall. A new constitution was put up for discussion. It agreed to the four articles listed below:

1. That the first and last principle of the Irish Citizen Army is the avowal that the ownership of Ireland, moral and material, is vested of right I the people of Ireland.
2. That the Irish Citizen Army shall stand for the absolute unity of Irish nationhood, and shall support the rights and liberties of the democracies of all nations.
3. That one of its objects shall be to sink all differences of birth, property and creed under the common name of the Irish people.
4. That the Citizen Army shall be open to all who accept the principle of equal rights and opportunities for the Irish people.

It was recommended that a standard uniform for the men be provided, to give them a feeling of dignity and belonging, that was lacking if they were dressed in their ordinary working men's clothes. The new uniforms were dark green in color, with broad, slouched hats of the same color, turned up on one side, fastened by the badge of the ITGWU's red hand. The uniform was to be common to both men and women. Training was increased, and nighttime route marches were begun.

The G. Department of the Dublin Metropolitan Police (DMP) continued to keep a regular watch on the increased activity of the remodeled ICA. Reports were submitted to Colonel Edgeworth Johnstone, chief commissioner of the DMP. There were reports of route marches and mock attacks on prominent buildings in Dublin. These were led by Connolly or his deputy, Michael Mallin, a former British Army soldier, now appointed chief of staff of the ICA. Countess Markievicz frequently took part in these escapades, it was reported, and it was further reported that women and boys went out with the men and engaged in these mock attacks. The boys were a Scout Corps of the ICA, formed in July 1914, under the command of Captain Walter Carpenter. Markievicz designed their uniforms, including hats turned up at one side and bright red ties. The boys were armed with .22-bore Winchester rifles, and they went through a weekly course of shooting practice, just like their elders and the women of the ICA.

Efforts were made, without authorization, by Captain White and Constance Markievicz to closer ally the Citizen Army with the Volunteers. These approaches were rejected by the more middle-class right-wing Volunteer leadership. When these overtures were discovered, both White and Markievicz were seen by some, notably the ICA'a secretary, Sean O'Casey,[19] as having conflicting loyalties. Frustrated, for he could do no more, Captain White eventually severed his connection with the ICA and joined the Volunteers. At a special meeting of the ICA Council, the honorary secretary, Sean O'Casey, moved:

> Seeing that Madame Markievicz was, through Cumann na mBan, attached to the Volunteers, and on intimate terms with many of the Volunteer leaders, and as the Volunteers' Association was, in its methods and aims, inimical to the first interests of Labor, it could not be expected that Madame could retain the confidence of the Council; and that she be now asked to sever her connection with either the Volunteers or the Irish Citizen Army.

The resolution was vigorously opposed. A vote of confidence in the Countess was proposed and was carried by seven votes to six. It was then moved that the secretary be called upon to tender an apology to Markievicz. O'Casey refused, and a few days later he offered his resignation. In his 1919 history of the ICA, O'Casey had his revenge, where in a moment of spite, he suggested that Connolly had deviated from his socialist principles:

> All proclaimed that Jim Connolly had stepped from the narrow byway of Irish Socialism on to the broad and crowded highway of Irish Nationalism ... its high creed became his daily rosary, while the higher creed of International humanity that had so long bubbled from his eloquent lips was silent forever and Irish Labor lost a leader.[20]

Connolly was being pragmatic. That old saying, England's difficulty is Ireland's opportunity, was much in Connolly's mind. An insurrection was coming, and it was vital that the ICA be part of it, otherwise the working class would have no say in a future Irish government. From the sidelines, Captain Jack White, who had drilled the union men into an army, observed:

> The two opposing interests cannot blend. They may combine to kick out foreign interference preparatory to having a straight fight between themselves.[21]

That was something that Connolly, likewise, was aware of. For the moment, though, Connolly knew that he would have to make common cause with the bourgeois that was the leadership of the nationalists. In June 1914, the ICA and the Irish Volunteers were brought together when the Wolfe Tone Committee invited both to take part in their annual ceremony at Bodenstown. O'Casey wrote of the occasion:

> It was the first time they had stood side by side ... and took orders from a common commander, and this drawing together was possibly a symbol of a union that would be finally cemented together with the blood of both organizations.[22]

From the start, Connolly had always been a believer in the equality of the sexes. In the revitalized Citizen Army, women now began to play a more active part. Markievicz was given a place on the Army Council. First aid and ambulance work were held in Liberty Hall under the guidance of another woman, Dr. Kathleen Lynn. The young women and girls were taught drill and rifle practice. A miniature rifle range was set up in Liberty Hall. The ever-loyal Helena Molony acted as secretary of this group.

In August 1914, France and Britain went to war with Germany. Irish Parliamentary leader John Redmond, fresh from his success in gaining Home Rule, called upon the Irish Volunteers to join with Britain in its war against Germany. It would be to Ireland's eternal shame if its young men did not go and fight, he contended. Connolly responded to the spurious argument in an article in the *Irish Worker*, on the 5th of September:

> If you are itching for a rifle, itching to fight, have a country of your own; better to fight for our country than for a robber Empire. If you ever shoulder a rifle, let it be for Ireland. Conscription or no conscription, they shall never get me or mine. You have been told you are not strong, that you have no rifles; start first and get your rifles after. Our curse is our belief in our weakness. We are not weak, we are strong.

At the end of the month, the Citizen Army turned out in all its strength in Dublin. Armed with rifles and bayonets, they marched from Liberty Hall to the Wolfe Tone Memorial near the arch in Stephen's Green. From a two horse–drawn open carriage, Connolly, Larkin, and Madame Markievicz voiced the opposition of Dublin citizens to Redmond's attempt to involve them in the war. Redmond's call led to a split in the Volunteer movement. Some 180,000 Volunteers went off to fight for Britain. They became known as the National Volunteers. Those remaining, just nine thousand, became the Irish Volunteers. Force of circumstance brought the Irish Volunteers and the Citizen Army closer together, to the extent that the ICA was looked upon as the apparent militant Left Wing of the Irish Volunteers. This was helped to a great degree by Connolly, who accepted the principles of nationalism as expounded by both Sinn Fein and the Irish Volunteers. In some ways, their view of nationalism was contradictory to the teachings of socialism, but expediency now outweighed doctrine. In truth, Connolly was well aware that the Volunteer leadership had no interest in improving the standard of life of the working class. Theirs was a very narrow view of nationalism. Everything else would be worked out after the establishment of an Irish Republic. For the moment, the nationalists needed an alliance with the ICA, if nothing more than to prevent them from starting a rising before the Volunteers were ready.

On the 17th of October, it was announced that Larkin would leave Ireland for a tour of the United States, in order to raise money for the union. In his place, as his deputy, Connolly was appointed to take command of the

Union, the Citizen Army, and the *Irish Worker*—all the reins of control. Over a short period of time following Larkin's departure, all of his appointees in the Union and the ICA were purged, to be replaced by Connolly's appointees. The socialist revolution was back on track.

A banner was placed above Liberty Hall that proclaimed, "We serve neither King nor Kaiser—but Ireland." This gesture of nationalism secured the bond between the ICA and the Irish Volunteers, bringing the two Republican armies together to the extent that Liberty Hall now became the center of Irish nationalism. Both sides were talking to each other, but both had separate agendas. On the night of 25 October 1914, the ICA joined with the Irish Volunteers in a torchlight procession around Dublin, culminating at St. Stephen's Green. Just then, a large body of Redmond's National Volunteers, headed by a marching band and returning from their Glasnevin parade, tried to force their way through the meeting. A thin line of Citizen Army men and a few Irish Volunteers formed an armed barrier across the road to prevent them. It was brave, but perhaps foolish; they were outnumbered by at least four to one. Just then Captain Monteith of the Irish Volunteers arrived with reinforcements. As ostentatiously as possible, he distributed ammunition to the Citizen Army men, which suggested to the National Volunteer leader that the men facing them were prepared to physically resist them. Colonel Nugent of the National Volunteers was persuaded to detour his men by way of Dorset Street. By their joint defiance, a strong bond had been formed by the Irish Volunteers and the Citizen Army.

In December 1914, the British government banned a number of Irish nationalist newspapers, including the *Irish Worker,* for having taken an anti-recruiting stance. The print works in Yarnhall Street were raided, and the machinery was dismantled. Connolly responded by acquiring another printing machine, which was installed in the ITGWU's new shop in Eden Quay, five buildings up from Liberty Hall. From there on 29th May 1915, Connolly launched *The Workers' Republic,* which continued in the same vein as its predecessor. Helena Molony was registered as the owner, but with Connolly retaining editorial control. In a further attempt to secure complete control of the socialist movement in Ireland, Connolly convened a meeting of the ITGWU at the end of July 1915. He proposed that the IWWU be reorganized. So, indeed, should the cooperative shop. He received agreement on both proposals. This was too much for Delia Larkin, who realized that there was a conspiracy to remove her. It was Connolly that announced her resignation. In her absence, the IWWU was disbanded, but it was brought back on Connolly's terms. The ever-influential Helena Molony, completely trusted by Connolly, was appointed union secretary *pro-tem.* Connolly appointed the new IWWU committee. It was comprised of "Mrs. Reilly, Mrs. Norgrove, Mrs Nolan, Miss M. Geraghty, Miss M. Ryan, Miss J. Shannon, and Miss Kinch."

The cooperative shop was closed down, a new committee was appointed, and the shop was reopened with Helena Molony as its new secretary. The manager was Jinny Shanahan, with Rosie Hackett as her assistant. These were all trustworthy women as far as Connolly was convinced, who shared with him a vision of an Irish Workers' Republic.

Connolly now looked at further reorganizing the ICA. He sought to purge the army of the waverers, those who saw the ICA as no more than a protective force for the union. He personally interviewed everyone, ascertaining their complete commitment to fight for Ireland's freedom, be it alongside the Irish Volunteers, or on their own. Having observed Cumann na mBan marching in formation, drilled, and smart of uniform, Connolly decided to reorganize the women at Liberty Hall into an auxiliary of the ICA. With this commitment from them all, and their acknowledged loyalty, Connolly had complete control. Now he planned an insurrection. The Volunteer leadership became concerned that Connolly would begin before they were completely ready. One evening in late January 1916, as Connolly left Liberty Hall alone, he was approached by four Volunteers and was persuaded to join them. Some alleged that he was kidnapped. He was held for three days in a house in Lucan, where members of the Volunteer Executive did their best to dissuade him from acting unilaterally. They divulged their plans to him, and he was delighted to discover a state of affairs that he had not suspected. Connolly agreed to work with them. He was sworn in as a member of the IRB and co-opted onto the secret committee. The rising was to be a joint venture.

In the week before Easter, instead of the starry plough flag, the old Irish national flag of green with a golden harp was raised above Liberty Hall as a show of unity. This followed a formal ceremony in front of the hall. Soldiers of the Citizen Army formed up on three sides around the front of the building. From a pile of drums, in the center of the square, the flag had been placed. The buglers sounded a salute, and the guard presented arms. Into the square stepped a young woman, Mollie O'Reilly, a member of the Women Workers' Union. She was also a member of the Citizen Army. Holding the flag to her breast, she walked into Liberty Hall. There, on the parapet of the roof, she fastened the flag to the staff, and with a pull of the lanyard, the flag was unfurled and billowed out to much cheering from those below. Observers from the G. Department of the Metropolitan Police took notes.

3

There Would Be Work for the Women

The Nationalists

There is a long tradition of the involvement of women in the national struggle. In particular, in early modern times, there was the Ladies' Land League, many of whose members were still around to influence the younger generation of 1916. The League was an offshoot of the Irish National Land League. It was founded in November 1879 by socialist Michael Davitt. Though born in Ireland, he was brought up in Lancashire in England. After attending infant school up to the age of just nine, he began working as a laborer in a cotton mill. When he was eleven years old, his right arm became entangled in the cogwheel of a machine, and it was so badly damaged that it had to be amputated. Support from a local benefactor, John Dean, permitted Davitt, upon his recovery, to return to education. In 1861, at the age of fifteen, he left school and went to work in the local post office. Davitt continued with his education at night school. Here he came under the influence of former Chartist Ernest Charles Jones. Apart from Jones's interpretation of socialism, the young Davitt also took an interest in social issues in his native Ireland. His interests brought him into contact with the Irish Republican Brotherhood, which he joined in 1865. Two years later, he became a full-time organizing secretary for the IRB in northern England and Scotland. In February 1867, Davitt was involved in an abortive Fenian raid on Chester Castle, to acquire arms for an Irish uprising. Three years later, Davitt was arrested at Paddington Station in London, awaiting the arrival of arms from a Birmingham gunsmith. He was sentenced to fifteen years in Dartmoor Prison. In 1877, following prolonged pressure in Parliament, Davitt and the other Fenian prisoners were released. Davitt returned to Ireland to a hero's welcome. He rejoined the IRB and was very soon appointed as a member of the Supreme Council. In 1878, Davitt went to America, where his family was now living, to engage in a lecture tour organized by John Devoy, leader of the Irish American Republican movement, Clan na Gael. Along with Devoy, he developed the strategy of landownership by the Irish people as a means to acquiring independence from England. Returning to Ireland in 1879, Davitt became involved in land agitation, under the slogan of "The Land for the People." A mass rally was held in Irishtown, County Mayo, on 20th April 1879, to campaign for the reduction of rents. Later that year. the Land League of Mayo was founded. Home Rule M.P. Charles Stewart Parnell grasped the fact that the destruction of landlordism in Ireland might also lead to the overthrow of British domination. Following talks between the two men, the Irish National Land League was formed at Castlebar, on 21st October 1879. Parnell was made president, and Davitt became one of its three regional secretaries. While Parnell and his nationalists obstructed and frustrated the doings of the British Parliament, in order to bring about support for Home Rule, Davitt and the Land League took on the landlords. Their intention was to abolish landlordism in Ireland and to enable tenant farmers to own the land that they farmed.

In 1880, Parnell, Davitt, and John Dillon went to the United States to seek Irish American funding. Residing in New York was Parnell's American mother, Delia, and his two sisters, Anna and Fanny. Guided by Davitt, all three women threw themselves into assisting the new movement. Again, with Davitt's help, Fanny established a women's league in New York in October 1880. Mother Delia became president of the New York Ladies' Land League. The two daughters became fellow committee members and embarked on a speaking campaign to fund the organization, resulting in thousands of dollars being sent to Ireland. Anna returned to Dublin, ready to assist her brother. With strong rumors that the leadership of the Land League in Ireland were to be arrested, Michael Davitt proposed that a women's organization should be set up to continue the work. Parnell was at first reluctant, but Davitt insisted. "No better allies than women could be found for such a task," he advocated. "They are, in certain emergencies, more dangerous to despotism than men." Eventually, but with reservations, Parnell and the other leaders agreed to Davitt's proposal. On 31st January 1881, the Ladies' Irish National Land League was founded, with Anna as its effectual leader.

In the British Parliament, the new prime minister, W.E. Gladstone, sought to end the agitation in Ireland and redress the wrongs of the past by passing a well-intentioned, but incomplete Land Act, in 1881.The legislation brought into being a land commission to review fair rents. Many tenant farmers benefited from it, but subtenants. however, the greater majority of the farmers, were not covered by the Act. It also failed to redress the problem of rent arrears and rent adjustment in the case of poor harvests. Parnell attacked the ill-thought-out Act, to the extent of making a personal attack upon William Forster, the chief secretary for Ireland. Unable to touch Parnell because of Parliamentary privilege, and fearing further agitation, Forster had Davitt arrested as a warning, on 3rd February 1881, on a charge of incitement to violence. On 13th October, outside of Parliament's jurisdiction, Parnell and others linked to the Land League were arrested under the new Irish Coercion Act, on a charge of "reasonable suspicion" of encouraging violence. In prison, Parnell issued a manifesto calling upon tenant farmers to pay no rent. With the arrests, the Ladies' Land League took over. They continued, and it is perhaps only fair to say, they efficiently reorganized the campaign. Detailed records were more accurately kept of money subscribed and dispersed. They compiled a complete record of every Irish estate and of the number of its tenants. To assist in this work, more than five hundred branches of the Ladies' Land League were established throughout Ireland. It was an extraordinary challenge, which they met. Following the "No Rent"

Michael Davitt, cofounder of the Land League, supported the foundation of a Ladies' Land League in 1879.

manifesto, many small farmers were evicted from the land for nonpayment of rent. The ladies were faced with the almost-impossible financial task of assisting these men and their families throughout the country. Added to their work was the growth of agrarian violence in retaliation for the evictions. Men were arrested and imprisoned. The Ladies' League then had to provide for their families, too. Credit for their activities was a little short in coming, particularly from some of the senior male members of the Land League. The exception was Andrew Kettle, a supporter and friend of Charles Stewart Parnell. He saw the true worth of Anna and the women who had to contend with the problems arising out of the No Rent manifesto:

> A better knowledge of the lights and shades of Irish peasant life, of the real economic conditions of the country and of the social and political forces which had to work out the freedom of Ireland than any person, man or women, I have ever met.... Anna Parnell would have worked the Land League revolution to a much better conclusion than her great brother.[1]

As the violence escalated, the meetings of the Ladies' League were continually raided by the police, in the mistake that the women were promoting the violence. In December 1881, the Ladies League was banned. Thirteen of its leaders were arrested and imprisoned, not as political prisoners like the men, but as common criminals. Those remaining free continued the struggle. Such behavior, women acting like men, received the odium of some members of the Catholic Church. Archbishop McCabe of Dublin ordered his priests "not to tolerate in your societies the women who so far disavow her birthright of modesty as to parade herself before the public gaze in a character so unworthy of a Child of Mary." Others, though, were more understanding. Archbishop Croke of Cashel, and several influential people, as well as ordinary priests, offered their support and their houses for meetings, perhaps seeing for themselves the misery of the poor and the attempts of the Ladies' Land League to help alleviate their sufferings.

Desperate to end the violence, in April 1882, Parnell and the other leaders were released under the Kilmainham Treaty. It was an agreement that they would end the violence. Depending upon which version you choose to accept, part of the agreement was that the Ladies League would be disbanded. Alternatively, disillusioned by the approach the men had taken in not continuing its pursuit of the No Rent manifesto to its logical conclusion, the ladies disbanded themselves in disgust. The breakup was clearly acrimonious, for the siblings never spoke to each other again. Anna, in particular, was resent-

The police breaking up a meeting of the Ladies' Land League.

ful at the poor treatment the Ladies' League received from the men. She wrote:

> I think now that, added to their natural resentment at our having done what they asked us to do, they soon acquired a much stronger ground for their annoyance in the discovery that we were taking the Land League seriously and thought that not paying rent was intended to mean not paying it.[2]

Years later, when she was an old lady, Anna was invited by the nationalist Inghinidhe na h'Eireann to give a talk on the Ladies' Land League. At the end of the talk, Frank Sheehy Skeffington, who had been in the audience, asked her, "What is your opinion of the Kilmainham Treaty, Miss Parnell?" Helena Molony recorded:

> She looked at him coldly, "Oh, I just think my brother found himself in an uncomfortable position, and he did what men usually do—got out of it in the easiest possible way for himself, regardless of the consequence to others."[3]

She was obviously not one to let bygones be bygones, even when it was her own brother. Fanny Parnell died in July 1882. Anna went to live in England but returned to Ireland from time to time, staying at Bray. She kept in touch with some of the ladies of Inghihidhe na h'Eireann, in particular Jennie Wyse Power, whom she had known from the Ladies' Land League days. She also contributed to the national cause, letting her name be associated as a supporter in 1908 of the Sinn Fein candidate in the North Leitrim election. Annie Parnell tragically drowned while swimming off the coast of Ilfracombe in Devon, on 20th September 1911. Before her death, she was able to witness the culmination of the Ladies' Land League struggle in the passing of the Land (Purchase) Act of 1903. This permitted Irish tenant farmers to buy out their freeholds, through the Land Commission, using British government loans repayable over a sixty-eight-year period. The Wyndham Land Purchase Act of the same year saw the breakup of large estates, many owned by absentee landlords, and the redistribution of the land to rural landholders. This Act was followed by the Laborers (Ireland) Act of 1906, and that of 1911, which paid county councils to build over forty thousand new rural cottages, each with an acre of land. By 1914, over 75 percent of the occupiers had full rights to their property and the land it stood on.

When the British war against the Boer Republics of South Africa began in 1899, many in Ireland were sympathetic toward the Boer cause, seeing it as a war of imperial aggression. In December 1899, Arthur Griffith, newly appointed editor of the *United Irishman,* and other members of a pro-Boer committee, arranged a series of public meetings to criticize the unjust attacks on the Boer Republics' independence. Among those who gave their support was James Connolly. Both he and Griffith spoke on the same platform. An open-air public meeting was called to be held at Foster Place, College Green, in Dublin later that month. The authorities in Dublin Castle "proclaimed" it—that is, banned it. Nevertheless, it went ahead. Crowds gathered, and at eight o'clock that night, a two-horsed wagonette drove up to Foster Place. Among the passengers were Griffith, Connolly, and Maud Gonne. Henry Dixon opened the proceedings, but all at once, an inspector of police, backed up by one hundred policemen in uniform and a large number of detectives from G. Division, shouted out that the meeting had been proclaimed, and therefore must not be held. Dixon ignored him and called upon Maud Gonne to speak. The inspector blew his whistle. At this a large force of mounted police galloped into the middle of the crowd in an effort to disperse them. Two mounted policemen took hold of the reins of the wagonette's horses, whipped them, and started them galloping toward Westmoreland Street, the vehicle's passengers hanging on for dear life. On the ground, the foot police scattered the crowd by use of their batons. Meanwhile, by Abbey Street, the driver of the vehicle was able to regain control. Arthur Griffith now attempted to address the crowd, but the police were soon upon them, and the horses were driven on again. Another stop was made at the Custom House, where James Connolly attempted to address the crowd. Again, the police scattered the crowd with brutality, and the would-be meeting was abandoned.

Maud Gonne now found herself the subject of abuse. A weekly magazine, *The Irish Figaro*, owned and edited by Ramsay Colles, made a derogatory reference to Maud Gonne. Griffith sprang to her defense, went to the magazine's offices, and there whipped the editor with a Boer whip. Colles later took him to court, where the magistrate imposed a fine, with the alternative of two weeks' imprisonment. Griffith refused to pay the fine and was imprisoned for ten days. On Easter Sunday 1900, fifteen friends met in the Celtic Society Rooms in Dublin. They had come together to publicly thank Arthur Griffith, who had defended Maud Gonne from the slur.

This memoriam to Griffith occurred shortly after a visit to the city by Queen Victoria. As part of the celebrations, the children of Dublin had been invited by the city council to a grand party in Phoenix Park. The queen's visit was an attempt by the British government to promote a patriotic appeal to Irishmen to enlist in the British Army in its war against the Boers. The fifteen friends came upon the idea of holding an alternative "patriotic" children's party. Moneys were collected, and the party went ahead in July of that year. Some thirty thousand children, it is alleged, paraded from Beresford Place to Clonturk Park. Arthur Griffith attended the party and was seen entertaining groups of children, handing out cakes, sweets, and bottles of mineral waters. All the food and drink had been supplied free of charge to the committee by the merchants and shopkeepers of Dublin. Here, among picnic celebrations and treats for the children, there were a series of anti-recruitment speeches. At the end of the day, some funds remained. It was decided that they should be put toward founding a permanent committee to promote further similar events. The new organization called itself Inghinidhe na h'Eireann, or the Daughters of Ireland.

Maud Gonne was elected president. Vice presidents were Alice Furlong, Jennie Wyse Power, Anne Egan, and Anna Johnston (known also by her pen name, Ethna Carbery). Other founding members included Helena Molony; Sinead O'Flanagan, who was later to marry Eamon de Valera; actresses Maire Quinn and Molly and Sara Allgood; physician Kathleen Lynn; Mary Macken, a leading member of the Catholic Women's Suffrage; Miss M. T. Quinn; Miss M. O'Kennedy; and Miss S. White. Later members included Mary McSwiney; actress Maire Nic Shiubhlaigh; Constance Markievicz; Margaret Buckley; Ella Young; Maire Gill; the writer Rosamond Jacob; Hanna Sheehy [Skeffington]; Alice Milligan; and Marcella Cosgrave, formerly of the Ladies' Land League. The objects that they set themselves were:

1. The re-establishment of the complete independence of Ireland.
2. To encourage the study of Gaelic, of Irish literature, history, music and art, especially among the young, by the organizing and teaching of classes for the above subjects.
3. To support and popularize Irish manufacturers.
4. To discourage the reading and circulation of low English literature, the singing of English songs, the attending of vulgar English entertainments at theatres and music halls, and to combat in every way English influence, which is doing so much injury to the artistic taste and refinement of the Irish people.
5. To form a fund called the National Purposes Fund for the furtherance of the above objects.

The new organization set to work by advertising its objectives. It provided weekend classes and entertainment for children. It hired halls to stage short patriotic plays and *tableaux vivants* on themes from Irish mythology. The movement brought together influential members from the various national organizations, such as the Gaelic League and the National Literary Society, which evolved into the Abbey Theatre. Maude Gonne herself took an interest in the theater, and later in 1902, she had a brief career as an actress, where she played the part of Cathleen Ni Houlihan in Yeat's play of the same name.

In 1908, the Inghinidhe launched a monthly magazine, *Bean na h'Eireann,* edited by the ubiquitous Helena Molony. She herself wrote the Labor Notes, bringing her to the attention of James Connolly. Prominent nationalists like Padraig Pearse, Thomas MacDonagh, and Constance Markievicz all wrote articles for the magazine. Regular features included Labor Notes, votes for women, politics, Irish language, gardening, fashion, and a children's section.

Mary McSwiney, suffragette and nationalist

Maude Gonne, Inghinidhe's first president, was born Edith Maud Gonne at Tongham, near Farnham, Surrey, England, in December 1866. She was the daughter of Captain Thomas Gonne of the 17th Lancers. Following the death of her mother, Edith, Maud was sent to a boarding school in France to be educated. At the age of sixteen, she accompanied her father to his new posting in Dublin. Here she developed an interest in Irish affairs. Following the death of her father, Maude, as she preferred to be called, returned to France. She met and became the partner of a nationalist politician, Lucien Millevoye. They were together for some time in Paris before Maude returned to Ireland. Here she became involved in a campaign to secure the release of Irish political prisoners in British jails. Involved in the campaign was Anne Egan, the wife of James Egan, arrested alongside John Daly in 1884, when an agent provocateur planted a bomb in the possession of Daly.[4]

While in Dublin, Maud moved in artistic circles, drawing the admiration of the poet William Butler Yeats and the friendship of Lady Gregory. Perhaps finding Dublin a little too parochial, Maud returned to Paris in 1890. She took up her relationship with Millevoye once more, and between 1893 and 1895, she bore him two children, Georges and Iseult. Georges died while still a child; Iseult was passed off as Maud's niece when she returned to Ireland to avoid scandal. Here Maud again involved herself in Irish politics. She traveled throughout the United Kingdom and the United States, promoting Ireland's cause for independence. In 1897, Maud, along with Arthur Griffith and Yeats, organized protests against the Queen Victoria Diamond Jubilee celebrations in Ireland. At Easter 1900, Maud was instrumental in the founding of Inghinidhe na h'Eireann.

Once more back in France in 1903, Maud married Major John McBride, who had led the Irish Transvaal Brigade against the British during the Second Boer War. She was infatuated with this nationalist hero. Maud had turned down a proposal of marriage by Yeats, because she considered that he was insufficiently nationalist. The McBrides had a son, Sean, born in 1904. Having had an adventurous life, McBride's now-mundane life led to heavy drinking and the physical abuse of his wife. The marriage ended. McBride returned to Ireland, where he played a minor role in the Easter Rising. At its end, McBride was executed, not so much for what he had done over that Easter week, but rather for his earlier "treason" in South Africa. Maud herself returned to Ireland in 1917. She survived the War of Independence and the civil war that followed. Maud Gonne published her memoirs, *A Servant of the Queen,* in 1938. The queen in question was the old Irish queen, Caitlin Ni Houlihan. Maud died in Ireland in 1953 at the age of eighty-six.

Maud Gonne cofounded Inghinidhe na h'Eireann (Daughters of Ireland), a nationalist organization.

Fellow founding member Jennie Wyse Power was born Jane O'Toole in Baltinglass, Wicklow, in 1858. As previously mentioned, she became a member of the Ladies' Land League in 1881 and was a friend to both Anna and Charles Stewart Parnell, a man whom she held in great esteem. Her youngest son, out of a family of four children, was named Charles Stewart Wyse Power in his honor. In 1883, Jennie had married John Wyse Power, then editor of the *Leinster Leader* newspaper and a member of the IRB. The couple moved to Dublin in 1885. Jennie, or Jinnie, as she was more popularly known, was a founding member of the Gaelic Athletic Association and an active member of the Dublin Women's Suffrage Association. In 1899, Jennie started a business at 21 Henry Street, right in the heart of Dublin city center. It specialized in the selling of fresh farm produce: eggs, butter, cream, honey, cakes, and other exclusively produced Irish goods. The business traded as the Irish Farm Produce Company. The shop also had a restaurant that attracted a nationalist clientele, including members of the Gaelic League and Sinn Fein. Jennie was a founding member of Sinn Fein. As such, she was very much aware of what was going on within the nationalist community. She joined Inghinidhe na h'Eireann at its inception, being appointed one of its vice presidents. As business expanded, Jennie opened a second shop at 21 Lower Camden Street, taking on additional staff, some of whom would figure in the Easter Rising and later War of Independence. Jennie became a Poor

Law Guardian in the North Dublin Union in 1903; a position she held until 1911. The following year, 1912, Jennie became the vice president of Sinn Fein, becoming very close to the center of the National movement. On 5th April 1914, at Wynne's Hotel in Dublin, she became a founding member of Cumann na mBan, and on 31st October, she became its first elected president. It was in her shop that the Proclamation of the Irish Republic was signed in 1916.

More perhaps should be said about Helena Malony, who recorded the early days of Inghinidhe in her witness statement (391) to the Bureau of Military History:

> I joined Inghinidhe na h'Eireann in 1903, three years after its foundation. It was my first active interest in Irish politics.... The Inghinidhe formed itself into a permanent society of Irish women pledged to fight for the complete separation of Ireland from England.... The means decided upon for the achievement of this object was the formation of evening classes for children, for Irish language, Irish history— social as well as political—the restoration of Irish customs to everyday life, Irish games, dancing and music.... Our first headquarters was at 196 Great Brunswick Street (now Pearse Street), afterwards we rented a whole house in North Great George's Street. Our President paid rent for the first year, and we subsequently paid it by sub-letting rooms to various societies, such as Gaelic League branches, etc. The extra house-room gave us more scope for our work with the children....
>
> Another important work of the Inghinidhe was the continuous anti-recruiting campaign, which was carried on year by year up to the first world war.
>
> In August 1903, on the evening when I went to join the Inghinidhe at their offices in 196 great Brunswick Street, I found a notice on the door [redirecting her to an alternative address]. The gate was opened for me, and I timidly entered. I had some trouble explaining to one of the Misses Meagher that I wanted to join the society. I was not known to any of them, and they were somewhat suspicious of a girl who wanted to join.... However, my enthusiasm was not to be damped, and I was told of days and hours of meetings, its works, rules, etc., so I felt I was received.

Jennie Wyse Power, a suffragette, was a member of the Ladies' Land League, Inghinidhe, Cumann na mBan, and Sinn Fein.

After eleven o'clock that night I walked home on air, really believing that I was a member of the mystical Army of Ireland.

Helena took part in the leafleting campaign out on the streets of Dublin, urging Irish girls not to go out with British soldiers. Sometimes they were chased away by the police and often risked being hit by the soldiers with their swagger sticks, but they persisted. Molony, in her witness statement, after describing her flirtation with the theater, then went on to describe the foundation of the magazine *Bean na h'Eireann,* whose subheading was "Freedom for Our Nation and the complete removal of all disabilities to our sex."

In the year 1907 we decided to start a woman's journal. I think that we Irishwomen, in common with the women of the rest of the civilized world, felt that the time had come when the point of view of women on the many aspects of social and national life, had to be expressed definitely.... There was at that date no paper expressing the view of complete separation from England, or the achievement of national freedom by force of arms.... We circularized a number of people whom we knew to be favorable to an Irish Ireland, asking them to help in the publication of a woman's national paper, by subscribing one shilling per month for six months, by which time we hoped to cover our printing bill by our advertisements. The plan succeeded, and Bean na hEireann as we called our little paper lasted just three years, and paid all its debts. By that time there were other national journals published [including a] woman's paper "The Irish Citizen" published by the Irish Women's Franchise League" and the need for our paper was not so urgent.

During its lifetime, *Bean na h'Eireann* attracted and brought into the movement more militant-minded people. Included was Constance Markievicz, who designed the title page and contributed drawings. People who wrote for *Bean* included Padraig Pearse and Thomas MacDonagh, alluded to above; Joseph Plunkett, the poet; Arthur Griffith; Roger Casement; A.E.; James Stephens; Maedhbh Cavanagh; Eva Gore Booth; "John Brennan"; and many others. Molony reflected:

I was pitch forked into the editorship, much against my will as I had no experience and no desire for such a responsible post. However, I carried on and the foregoing list of contributors make me feel that I cannot have been quite a failure as editor. Looking over some old copies in after years. One cannot help thinking that it was an odd kind of woman's paper. It was a mixture of guns and chiffon ... a funny hotchpotch of blood and thunder, high thinking, and home made bread.... It was through this little paper that Countess Markievicz came into the National movement.... She was already a staunch feminist, and she eagerly accepted our invitation to attend a committee meeting dealing with the forthcoming publication of Bean na h'Eireann.

In her writing of trade union matters, Helena came to the attention of James Connolly as she herself explains:

... James Connolly, with whom I had been in correspondence from 1908 in America. He edited a little Irish paper called "The Harp" in America and we exchanged views, as a result of a letter to William O'Brien about the "Bean" asking "Who is this lady? Find out about her and let me know."

O'Brien did, and the two corresponded, to the extent that upon his return to Ireland, Connolly ensured that Helena was given positions of authority within the socialist cause. She was a woman he could trust in the struggle to found a "Workers' Republic."

As well as educating the youth of Ireland, Inghinidhe also fed them. In 1910, concerned with infant mortality in Dublin, then the worst in any European city, the organization, along with the Women's Franchise League and other political and labor activists, set up school canteens to feed the malnourished schoolchildren in the worst areas of the city. They led the way by initially providing the meals at a cost of one penny a day. For those who could not afford it, the penny was waived, and most discreetly, to avoid embarrassing the child. The meals, it was decided, "should be a proper dinner, consisting of meat and vegetables every day, except Fridays or fast days when rice (cooked in milk) and jam was served." The Ladies Committee who ran the "Penny Dinners" supplied the food in large containers. Volunteers from Inghinidhe served it up and did the washing up. It took Parliamentary action before local authorities followed suit in providing hot meals for the children. Dublin Corporation was shamed into providing for its own children. Another of their projects was the promotion of home industries. By obstructive means, they forced stores to provide Irish-produced goods and actively promoted Irish men and women to wear and use Irish-manufactured goods in preference to British-made goods.

In 1911, King George and Queen Mary visited Dublin. The authorities in Dublin Castle, and the influential Unionists, ensured that the city was bedecked in Union Jacks and Royal Standards for their visit. Not everyone

Bean na h'Eireann, Inghinidhe's newspaper

welcomed them, however, especially the women of Inghinidhe na h'Eireann. Home Rule had been shelved, and even the more moderate nationalists felt angered. Counter demonstrations were mooted. Young men known to be sympathetic to the nationalist cause were recruited to help. They were given stones to throw at the decorations in order to cause general mayhem as the royal couple proceeded through the city's streets. Helena Molony took part in the demonstration. Following a meeting, she and Jennie Wyse Power were in a wagonette driven by Constance Markievicz, leading a march through the city in protest. Molony expressed her deep regret:

> To my amazement and deep disappointment not a stone was thrown, although hundreds of our followers from the meeting were walking behind. Some three or four stones remained in my handbag (which I never had any intention of using) but passing the corner of Grafton Street an illuminated screen displayed the portraits of King George and Queen Mary smug and benign, looked down on us. It, coupled with the absence of stone-throwing, was too much for me. I produced my stones and let fly, without warning. The police tried to close in but Madame Markievicz seized the reins, whipped up the horses, and we reached the top of Grafton Street—where we intended to disperse—in safety. As we descended from the brake a policeman emerged from the darkness and said, "Will I take her now sir?" to a nearby Inspector.

Molony was arrested and taken to Store Street Police Station. She was, after some difficulty, eventually bailed. She was subsequently charged with "Throwing stones and disorderly conduct," and she was sentenced to a fine of forty shillings or a month in prison. Her fine was paid for her. At the young men who had done nothing, she was angry, but she later came to realize that they had been obeying orders from the IRB. On the day of the demonstration, the young men had been ordered to make a pilgrimage to the grave of Wolfe Tone, twenty miles away, as a protest at the royal visit. As a protest, it was a little tame. In her witness statement Helena angrily recorded:

> … even now as I write (an old woman of sixty-six years) I think it contemptible. I would like if I were able to record the name of the man or men who were responsible for curbing the patriotic ardor of the young men of my time.

At the time, the IRB was just marking time, as it had done for a number of years. It was a silent spent force. But about this time, all of that was to change. The catalyst was Thomas J. Clarke, the fifty-year-old Fenian and former dynamitard who had arrived from America.[5] He rejuvenated the IRB by inviting young firebrand nationalists such as Sean McDermott, Bulmer Hobson, Cathal Brugha, and later Padraig Pearse to join the secret society. Their introduction caused a split in the organization. Its long-serving directorship, including Red Jack O'Hanlon and Fred Allen, were desperately hanging on to their positions. They used the threat of expulsion against the young men in a bid to maintain their leadership. The younger elements of the IRB in

Dublin had promised the women that they would join in the anti-royal visit. But then, as Sidney Gifford relates:

> Now the news came from the men's committee that they had decided to go to Bodenstown. It was only recently I heard from Pat McCartan what forced them to this decision. It was at the time of the split in the IRB and Fred Allen had given orders that there was to be no demonstration in the streets and these men, such as Sean McDermott, who had been speaking vigorously against the Royal visit, were now forced to climb down from the position they had advocated, probably on threat of expulsion. I remember how we pitched into poor Sean about the way they had let us down. All he said was "We had trouble."[6]

It was all very embarrassing for the young men of the IRB. Soon after, led by Tom Clarke, the old guard was ousted. Then with the deadwood out of the way, Clarke appointed his young men to senior positions within the IRB. There was talk among them of a rising.

A number of the young women attracted to Inghinidhe na hEireann came from Fenian backgrounds. Nationalism was in their blood. Maeve McGarry's nationalism came through her mother:

> My mother was always interested in the national movement as a young girl from Parnell's time. My father on the other hand did not agree with her outlook, although he never interfered with her national or political activities. He was very quiet and so my mother was able to bring up us children in the way she wanted.
> The first thing she wanted was to get schools for us to go to where the Irish language would be taught. My elder brother went to Newbridge. Milo went, of course, to Pearse's school. My sisters went to St. Louis's Convent, Monaghan. But a boarding school did not suit my health, so I went to Loreto, St. Stephen's Green.... My mother, who was always an Irish-Irelander, brought me to the Gaelic League—first to the Ard Craobh and then to the Cuig Cuigi branch.[7]

Others underwent a Damascene conversion. Sidney Gifford, described above, was one such young woman. Born in 1889, the youngest of twelve children, she was from a mixed family—a Catholic father and a Protestant mother. All of the children were brought up in the Church of Ireland. The family were Conservatives and Unionists. Sidney's father was a successful solicitor in Dublin. While the six sons remained true to the Establishment, the daughters rejected everything that was British. Elder sisters married rebels: Muriel married Thomas MacDonagh, and Grace married Joseph Mary Plunkett. Both husbands were among the executed leaders of the failed Easter Rising. Sidney was educated at the Church of Ireland's Alexandra College in Earlsfort Terrace, Dublin, and at the Leinster School of Music in Harcourt Street. One day, while leaving Alexandra College, everything changed, as she herself relates:

> The Royal University was opposite our school and one day I noticed there were scenes among the students. I asked my violin teacher, Mr. Griffiths, what it was all

about and he told me that the organist played "God Save the King" [the British National anthem], and a section of the students stormed the organ loft to stop it. I asked, "Why should they play God save the King in Ireland?" and he presented me with a copy of the *Leader,* the first paper of a national kind I had ever seen. I continued to read that paper every week, smuggling it home secretly.... I began then to read *Sinn Fein* and then wrote some articles for which I signed with the name "John Brennan." I had to take a nom-de-plume because I did not want my family or friends to know about these activities of mine.[8]

Through her writing, she came into contact with a number of literary figures in Dublin, including George Russell (A.E.), and she became a regular visitor to the Russells' Sunday evening soirees. Among those she met was Nora Dryhurst, a journalist who was formerly based in London, and a member of Inghinidhe na Eireann. At the time, in early 1908, Inghinidhe was planning the startup of its monthly newspaper, to be called *Bean na hEireann.* Dryhurst became its first editor. Sidney explains:

It was thus I became a great friend of Mme. Markievicz, Helena Molony, Miss ffrench-Mullen, Mme. McBride and Marie Perolz. I wrote regular articles for the paper on all sorts of subjects, sometimes using the penname of Sorcha Ni Annlain as well as John Brennan.

Minnie Ryan's interest in Irish nationalism was through her brother, then a student at Maynooth College. Mixing among other young men at the time, he developed an interest in Sinn Fein and the writings of Arthur Griffith. At home at holiday time, he could talk of nothing else, and soon Minnie became a convert. As she says in her witness statement to the Bureau of Military History, "We started to read papers about every single thing that was said by Arthur Griffith in connection with the Sinn Fein movement. Of course, Griffith was <u>the</u> man at that time." This was at a time "when the bulk of the people were satisfied with the Irish Parliamentary Party and with their efforts to get Home Rule." Later, when she was a teacher, about the middle of 1914, a branch of Cumann na mBan was established in London. Writing about the establishment of the Volunteers, she recalled:

Dr. Sophie Bryant was very enthusiastic about it. She was of Irish descent. She was headmistress of the North London Collegiate School where I taught. We had a very fine crowd there. We formed a branch of Cumann na mBan of which I was Hon. Secretary. We collected a good bit of money. When the war started in August 1914, Home Rule was put on the Statute Book, but there was no more about it. Shortly after Redmond began to advocate that our people should join the Allies to fight for the rights of small nations. The other side of the Volunteers would not have anything to do with that sort of thing and there was a lot of bad feeling which brought about a split. The Sinn Fein Volunteers were left where they were before, only rather worse, if anything, because a large number of the people, who had joined before then, were in favor of Redmond. Consequently we had to re-organize again. At the time I was still in London. I could see the danger of the money we had collected

being held up if I did not act quickly and bring it over to John MacNeill. Mrs. Stopford Green, who was President of the Branch, arranged for me to come over to Ireland in November.... I know nothing further about that Branch after November
1914. I don't think they met any more, because Cumann na mBan broke up over
there. That was the end of my career in London.... I came to Dublin in January 1915,
and took over some German classes from my sister in Rathmines Technical School.
This post, which left me a good deal of liberty, suited me very well at the time....
When we moved to 19, Ranelagh Road, Mrs Wyse-Power was delighted I had come
back. She said: "Here's one of the girls who has plenty of time. She can become one
of the secretaries of Cumann na mBan." I became one of the secretaries. We had
rooms in Dawson Street—No. 2, I think. The headquarters of the Volunteers was in
the same building. We had not the same rooms. Very often we would not see them,
because they only came in to us when they wanted to inquire about something.[9]

Previously in England, the Liberal Party was returned to power in the
general election of 1910, but with a shrunken majority. It became dependent
on the support of the Irish Parliamentary Party to govern. The price of
that support was a Home Rule bill. This was the third such bill, the previous
two having been defeated in the House of Lords. Things had changed in
Parliament, though, since the rejection of the second bill in 1892. Having
rejected the Liberal budget of 1909, Herbert Asquith's government introduced
a Parliament bill that limited the power of the lords. The resulting Parliament
Act curtailed the power of the lords and became the doorway to Home Rule.
The third Home Rule bill was introduced in April 1912 and passed through
all its stages in the Commons by January 1913. Twice it was rejected by the
lords as expected, but it could not be rejected a third time, in accordance
with the Parliament Act. The bill would become law in the early summer of
1914.

The majority of Protestants in the northeast of Ireland were bitterly
opposed even to this modest form of Home Rule, which still would have kept
Ireland within the Empire. Back in 1886 and in 1893, Home Rule bills had
produced anti-Catholic riots in Belfast. Fearful that "Home Rule would
become Rome Rule," it played on the fears of the Protestant population. Into
their midst came a new Protestant leader, Sir Edward Carson, a successful
Dublin lawyer. It was he who had prosecuted Oscar Wilde over his homo-
sexuality. Carson organized resistance to Home Rule, with the backing of the
Conservative Party. On 28th September 1912, religious services were held
throughout Protestant Ulster, and a Solemn League and Covenant was signed
by more than 218,000 men, some using their own blood. They pledged themselves to use "all means which may be found necessary to defeat the present
conspiracy to set up a home rule parliament in Ireland." Carson demanded
that Ulster be excluded from Home Rule. In 1912, illegal drilling began in
Ulster. Men were being trained as an army. They became known as the Ulster
Volunteer Force. Arms were smuggled in from Germany; 35,000 Mausers

and 2,500,000 rounds of ammunition. In September 1913, a provisional government was set up in Ulster to come into being on the day Home Rule became law. This was treason, and a capital offense for its leaders. At Newry, in County Down, Carson declared, "I am told that it will be illegal. Of course it will. Drilling is illegal … the Volunteers are illegal and the government knows they are illegal, and the government dare not interfere with them…. Don't be afraid of illegalities." Carson could speak so because he knew that he had the backing of the Conservative Party. Equally important was that Carson knew that he had the support of the British Army in Ireland. They would not go against him and the Loyalist Protestant population. When ordered to move against the UVF, General Sir Hugh Gough, commanding the 3rd Cavalry Brigade at the Curragh Camp, mutinously refused to obey a lawful order. Other officers, all of them Protestants and Loyalists, followed suit, preferring to resign their commissions than fight the Ulstermen. Sir Henry Wilson, chief of the Imperial General Staff and himself an Ulster Protestant, gave his support to the Curragh mutineers. At a time when the German army was rapidly expanding, and with conflict at some time in the near future seemed inevitable, now was not the time to start sacking senior officers. Following consultations in London, the mutineers were assured that they would not be used against the provisional Ulster government nor the UVF. All the officers were reinstated, and the orders were withdrawn.

In the south of Ireland, the nationalists viewed the UVF with disquiet. It was necessary, Eoin MacNeill believed, to raise an army in defense of the cherished dream of Home Rule. He wrote an article in the Gaelic League's newspaper, *An Claidheamh* (The Sword of Light), under the headline, "If the North, why not the South?" Members of the reinvigorated IRB read the article with interest. They sent an emissary to MacNeill, a cofounder of the Gaelic League and a cultural nationalist. They wished to ascertain whether he was prepared to implement his ideas of forming a new Volunteer organization in the south. MacNeill was only too willing. Twelve prominent nationalists were invited to Wynn's Hotel at 35–37 Lower Abbey Street to form a provisional committee. Among those present were Thomas MacDonagh, tutor of English literature in University College, Dublin; Padraig Pearse, founder of St. Enda's Irish School; and Eamonn Ceannt, a fellow founding member of the Gaelic League. All three were IRB men, from an organization pledged to the violent overthrow of the British and the establishment of an Irish republic. They praised MacNeill for his courage and gave him their full support. It was their intention to use MacNeill's volunteers to bring about Irish independence. In order to do this, it would be necessary for the IRB to control, or at least be in a position to influence, the more physical-force elements of Irish nationalism. In November 1913, *An Claidheamh Soluis* published an article calling for the setup of MacNeill's armed force of volunteers in defense of Home

Rule. A date was set on 25th November for the founding of the Irish National Volunteers at the Rotunda Rink in Parnell Square, Dublin.

The hall was packed to overflowing as MacNeill put the objectives of the proposed Volunteers. Very much in view of his pacifist nature, the would-be Volunteer movement, he declared, was not designed to oppose the Ulster Volunteers, but rather to cooperate if the occasion demanded in defense of their common country. It was to be nonsectarian and open to all who wished to join. Its aims were purely defensive, and it was not contemplating aggression or domination. There were speeches from the platform in support. Pearse spoke, declaring that citizenship involved the enjoyment of certain rights and the acceptance of certain duties, the most essential of which was the bearing of arms. During the course of the meeting, young men handed out enrollment forms. They included the aims and objectives of the Irish Volunteers:

1. To secure and maintain the rights and liberties common to the people of Ireland.
2. To train, discipline, and equip for this purpose an Irish Volunteer Force.
3. To unite, in the service of Ireland, Irishmen of every creed, and every party and class.

Laurence J. Kettle spoke from the platform. He announced, "There will also be work for women to do, and there are signs that the women of Ireland, true to their record, are especially enthusiastic for the success of the Volunteers." Unlike Connolly's ICA, this work was not to be in the ranks of the Volunteers.

Up in the gallery of the rink, in privileged position, sat a number of women, observing and listening to the speeches.[10] Some saw Kettle's statement as inclusivity for women. Some, though, must have felt disappointment, in that they would be relegated to support status. *What would be their part?* was the question. They decided to readjourn to a meeting room over the Queen's Theatre in Brunswick Street (now Pearse Street) to discuss the matter.[11] It was to be the inaugural meeting of Cumann na mBan (The Company of Women). A committee was formed pro-tem. Mrs. Eoin MacNeill acted as chairwoman, and Professor Agnes O'Farelly and Miss O'Rahilly served as committee members. Among the other women in attendance were members of Inghinidhe na hEireann, who then had a meeting place at 6 Harcourt Street, which they agreed to share with the new movement. In the fullness of time, Inghinidhe became a branch of Cumann na mBan.

On 2nd April 1914, a public meeting was convened at Wynn's Hotel in Dublin. Close to one hundred women attended. Agnes O'Farrely presided. A provisional committee was set up, consisting of O'Farelly, Agnes MacNeill, Nancy O'Rahilly, Mary Colum, Jennie Wyse Power, Louise Gavan-Duffy,

Maire Tuohy, and Maureen MacDonaghny. In the majority of cases, the committee members were wives, sweethearts, or sisters of the leaders of the Irish Volunteers. As such, this would bind the two movements closely together, but the women would always play only a supportive role. Later, the *Irish Citizen* condemned its "crawling servility to the men," while Sheehy Skeffington described Cumann na mBan as little more than "animated collecting boxes." This was in response to Alice Stopford Green's suggestion that the new women's organization's primary purpose "should be to collect money for the arming of their male counterparts." Sheehy Skeffington did mellow in her opinion when she herself became drawn more toward the nationalist movement.

At the meeting, the objects of the women's movement were then read out loud and agreed upon:

1. To advance the cause of Irish liberty.
2. Too organize Irishwomen in furtherance of this object.
3. To assist in arming and equipping a body of Irishmen for the defense of Ireland.
4. To form a fund for these purposes to be called the "Defence of Ireland Fund."

The subtext was that local branches, once formed, would keep in touch with their local Volunteer battalions, appear at the parades, and identify themselves with Volunteer work.

The suffragists who were present, who had initially perceived the new movement as promoting sexual equality, were annoyed that the principal aim was in supporting the Volunteers without any guarantee of suffrage. Experience had shown that the leaders of the Volunteers, as they now were, had previously been inclined to exclude women. The argument of the suffragists was blunted by Helena Molony, now also a soldier in the Irish Citizen Army. She proclaimed that there could be no free woman in an enslaved nation. She had nobly put women's suffrage second to the greater good of independence.

The direction of policy in the branches, it was agreed, would be carried out by a central Provisional Committee based in Dublin. Headquarters for the new movement were established at 6 Harcourt Street, Dublin.

A nationwide publicity campaign led to the formation of branches throughout the whole of the country. By July 1914, there were thirty "operational" branches. By 1915, this had grown to forty-three branches, with three in Dublin. The Dublin bases were at Central at 25 Parnell Square, Inghinidhe na hEireann at Harcourt Street, and Columcill in Blackhall Place. Until Cumann na mBan, branches were founded in local areas, and women joined with, or worked alongside, the Volunteers.

It was as if women everywhere in Ireland began to wake up to the notion that Ireland should be independent. Eilis ni Chorra recorded her emergence from her dreamlike state:

> Up to then life for me had been very pleasant, if ordinary. I was one of a "long" family and had many friends. Books, music and the theatre I loved, and I had just got a most congenial post—in the public library. Then came the 1914 war and life was changed. Before that time I had not given much thought to Ireland and Irish affairs. Of course I was proud to be Irish, and proud of all the men who had fought and died for Ireland, but I never dreamed that Irishmen would again take up arms against the English.... I knew nothing of the Irish movement and the tradition of nationality which had been kept alive by the "faithful few," the children and grand-children of the Fenians. The war-mongering and flag-waving in Belfast disgusted me. I felt mad when I heard Irish girls talking about "our" soldiers, saw them hob-nobbing with Khaki-clad men and selling flags to provide comforts for the troops. Then I felt fiercely Irish, and went around with a chip on my shoulder.[12]

Up in Belfast, James Connolly's daughter, Nora, was instrumental in forming a branch of Cumann na mBan:

> I sent a letter to all the nationalist newspapers, and had a meeting, and got Cumann na mBan started in Belfast. The trouble was that they all overlapped. There was only a small body to call on. We got quite a good branch of Cumann na mBan started. I was in charge of it. I remember then I was busy on something else; and I can't remember the name of the Secretary after me. The Secretary was the person in charge. Roisin Walsh was teaching in Belfast at the time; and Una Ryan—Dinny McCullough's wife—she was teaching, and she joined; and there was quite a few that we had not touched with, in our other meetings. We were glad to have them. Of course, there was not much to do at that time., beyond propaganda and general training; we had first aid, teaching history and the usual things like that.[13]

Her account is perhaps a little vague. So, too, are the movement's records. By October 1914, Cumann were claiming that there were "upwards of 60" branches. The imprecise figure may be reflecting the existence of regional branches in name only. In the early days there was some confusion.

In Dublin, Molly Reynolds in her witness statement to the Bureau of Military History wrote:

> I joined this Branch [at 6, Harcourt Street] and we learned first aid and signaling (semaphore and morse). Shortly after the formation of the Branch at Harcourt Street it was decided that we should learn drill and marching. As no room in Harcourt Street was large enough for this purpose Madame [Markievicz] gave us permission to use the Fianna Hall at 34, Lower Camden Street on one or two nights a week. I cannot remember the date we started these activities, but it was probably April or May 1914, because in June of that year we took part in the Wolf Tone Pilgrimage to Bodenstown as a branch of Cumann na mBan.
>
> The Inghinidhe na hEireann was the first branch of Cumann na mBan to get down to the work set out for the organization. After we had been working for some time, the Committee which was still meeting in Pears Street formed another Branch at 25, Parnell Square which was called the Central Branch.[14]

Margaret "Loo" Kennedy, likewise a member of the Inghinidhe branch, recalled:

> In Camden Street we were trained and exercised in drill, figure marching, stretcher-drill, signaling and rifle practice with a little rook rifle. We also went on route marches regularly on our own initiative in order to train the girls in marching and in taking control. We had two instructors from the Fianna for drill, signaling and rifle practice—Seamus Pounch and a man named [Michael] Devereaux.[15]

In his witness statement, Seamus Pounch goes into detail:

> The first meeting of women and girls I attended was held at Holohan Wickerworks Factory on Merchant's quay, and numbered over 200. I sorted them out and gave them the first drill instructions. I continued and took the work seriously. I completely organized and trained them, directed their training and wrote training notes.... I included signaling, semaphore and morse in my instructions, and stretcher drill. Special lectures were given by doctors and nurses in first aid and Hygiene. They were fully organized, trained and equipped for the 1916 Rising and proved their worth, and turned out in large numbers at almost every outpost.[16]

Pounch instructed his trainees to appoint officers in order to put the movement on a more military basis. Kennedy wrote:

> Seamus Pouch insisted that we should be put on a military basis instead of being governed solely by a committee, and that the officers should therefore be elected. Ours was the first Dublin Branch to have officers. The two officers were Eily Walsh as commandant, and Miss Rose McNamara as vice-commandant. The secretary was Miss Josephine Walsh and the treasurer Miss Marcella Cosgrave.

Eileen "Eily" Walsh in her own witness statement recalled:

> Simon Donnelly often came to the hall in Camden Street and drilled us also. We drilled twice a week. We did route marching and flag signaling. I do not remember any rifle practice, but we were shown how to load and unload and clean a gun. We learned first aid in our own branch under Dr. Kathleen Lynn and other doctors, but we went occasionally to the Purveyors Hall in Essex Street to lectures given by Dr. Curtin. We also went to No. 2, Dawson Street to make field-dressings so as to provide a store for any emergency that might arise.[17]

Aine Heron recorded that her branch of Cumann in Parnell Square spent one night on drill and the other on first aid. As 1916 approached, the Cumann, based in Dublin, would march out after dark with Nora Foley carrying the flag. This attracted some interest, for the public had not yet got used to the idea of women marching in step like soldiers.

In Limerick, there was equal enthusiasm, as Madge Daly relates in her witness statement to the Bureau of Military History:

> Soon after the formation of the Volunteers, a branch of Cumann na mBan was started in Limerick City. The first meeting was held in the Gaelic League Rooms, and the majority of those in attendance were members of the Gaelic League, or girls

belonging to families who had carried on the Fenian tradition. A provisional Committee was elected, and I had the honor of being made President.... Following the inauguration, Mrs. Dermot O'Donovan was Vice-President; Miss Mollie Kileen, Honorary Secretary; Miss Annie O'Dwyer, Honorary Treasurer.... From its inception, ours was a large and active branch, and I can recall over seventy girls who were active members to the end. Classes were immediately started for First Aid, Home Nursing, Drill, signaling and for instruction in the care and use of arms. For military matters we had the services of Captain Monteith and other Volunteer Officers, whilst we had four city doctors and two nurses.

The branch met in a Fianna Hall at the rear of 15 Barrington Street:

> It was a lovely little hall complete with stage and seating accommodation. We arranged lectures, Irish dances and concerts.... Terry McSwiney, Sean McDermott, Mary McSwiney, P.H. Pearse, Roger Casement, and many others gave lectures.

At the first annual convention of Cumann na mBan, held in Dublin on 31st October 1915, given that there were allegedly forty-three branches, attendance was low. The Dublin branches of course attended, it was easier for them, but nationwide the representation was minimal. There were delegates from Ardpatrick, Athenry, Belfast, Ballylanders, Castlebar, Cork, Drumcondra, Limerick, Liverpool, Lusk, and Tralee. Of course, not everybody could get away to attend. Many were working women. All the same, the lack of attendance was disappointing.

In the order of business, the ad hoc committee stood down for the election of officers. Jennie Wyse Power was elected first president. Nancy O'Rahilly was appointed vice president. In attendance was Constance Markievicz, but since she had earlier criticized the movement for its servility toward the Volunteers, no position was found for her in the popular vote. The question of increasing membership was raised. What was needed was an attention-grabber; a means by which the women could easily be identified as members of Cumann na mBan. This, in its turn, would attract new members. One way of addressing this problem was the adoption of a uniform:

> It was resolved that the use of a uniform be optional, but that none other be adopted by branches. It consists of a coat and skirt of Volunteer tweed and hat of same. Four pockets in coat, skirt at least seven inches off the ground, tweed or leather belt, haversack with first aid outfit. A gray or green felt hat and a haversack are recommended where uniform is not possible. Members of Cumann na mBan are in honor bound to give preference when purchasing, to goods of Irish manufacture.

While the women were looking for a sense of identity, events were overtaking them. On the night of 24–25 April 1914, the Ulster Volunteer Force, reputedly ninety thousand in number, succeeded in smuggling in almost twenty-five thousand rifles and five million rounds of ammunition from Germany. This gave them the military impetus to resist the implementation of Home Rule.

29.

IRISH VOLUNTEERS.

THE WOMEN'S SECTION OF THE VOLUNTEER MOVEMENT.

Cumann na mBan
(THE IRISHWOMEN'S COUNCIL),
Headquarters :—206 Great Brunswick St.

IRISHWOMEN, JOIN THE
VOLUNTEER MOVEMENT
AND BECOME MEMBERS OF THE ABOVE ORGANISATION.

First Aid and Ambulance Classes. Reserve Corps of Trained Nurses. Drill, and Rifle Practice.

Contribute to our Equipment Fund, which has already bought Rifles for the Volunteers.

Intending Members, join the nearest Branch, or communicate with the Hon. Secretary, Cumann na mBan, 206 Great Brunswick Street, Dublin.

BRANCHES IN EVERY COUNTY IN IRELAND.
Devereux, Newth and Co., Printers, Dublin.

Cumann na mBan recruitment poster

In Dublin, the reaction was mixed. Some admired their gumption; others became concerned. The Ulstermen who opposed Home Rule were now armed, and the British Army in Ireland had refused to move against them. Only an armed Irish Volunteer army in opposition could now enforce the democratic wishes of the majority. Following a meeting of senior Volunteer leaders, Sir Roger Casement, Darrell Figgis, and Erskine Childers met with the London agent of a Belgian arms dealer, who referred them to a dealer in Hamburg. He arranged the sale of fifteen thousand secondhand Mauser rifles and forty-nine thousand rounds of ammunition. The Mausers dated from the Franco-Prussian War of 1870. Though dated, they were still very effective.

To divert attention, as arms dealing was closely watched by spies, the arms dealer was informed that the rifles were destined for Mexico. Childers offered the use of his yacht, the *Asgard,* for transportation.

Erskine Childers, the son of oriental scholar Robert Caesar Childers, was raised by his mother's family, the Bartons of Glendalough near Annamore, County Wicklow. After graduating from Cambridge, he became a clerk in the House of Commons. He developed a keen interest in sailing, and his sailing experience gave him the background material for his now-famous novel *The Riddle of the Sands,* published in 1903. Childers became disillusioned with Britain over the Boer War, and he and his American wife, Molly, spent more and more of their time in Ireland, where they became fervent Irish Home Rulers.

Childers sailed aboard the *Asgard* with his wife, Molly, nee Osgood, Mary Spring Rice, and three Donegal sailors from Gola Island. Accompanying them was a second yacht, the *Kelpie,* owned by Conor O'Brien (a cousin of Mary Spring Rice), and his crew. The two boats rendezvoused at the Ruytingen buoy, just off the Belgian coast, where they met a tugboat that had carried the arms from Hamburg. To confuse British Naval Intelligence, a rumor was spread that an Irish trawler was transporting the cargo to Ireland. British warships were sent out to intercept all Irish trawlers in the North Sea. The two yachts sailed on untroubled. The *Asgard* landed her cargo at Howth on 26th July 1914. The *Kelpie* anchored off the Welsh coast, where she transferred her cargo to another yacht, the *Chotah,* skip-

Molly Childers and Mary Spring Rice on board the *Asgard,* **smuggling guns into Howth.**

pered by Sir Thomas Myles, a Dublin surgeon. The *Chotah's* cargo was landed at Kilcoole in County Wicklow.

Mary Spring Rice, despite the plethora of books by feminist authors, has largely been ignored. She was extremely influential, though in a quiet way, in Ireland's struggle for independence in the early twentieth century. She was born in London to Protestant parents in September 1880, into a wealthy aristocratic Anglo-Irish family. Mary was the daughter of Thomas Spring Rice, Second Baron Monteagle of Brandon, and great-granddaughter of the British chancellor of the exchequer, Thomas Spring Rice. Mary was brought up on the family's Irish estate at Mount Trenchard, overlooking the River Shannon. The children of the family were inculcated in Gaelic culture, and they were fluent Irish speakers, leading to membership of the Gaelic League and, she later, in Cumann na mBan. Close to the center of Irish nationalism and a wealthy woman in her own right, she financed to a considerable degree the purchase of the "Howth guns." During the War of Independence, she trained up nurses, sheltered men on the run, and acted as an IRA messenger. Mary Spring Rice died in Wales of tuberculosis in 1924 and was buried in Ireland with full military honors.

Cumann na mBan now faced a crisis following the split in the Volunteer movement. Irish Parliamentary leader John Redmond had called upon the Volunteers to join the British Army and fight for Britain in the First World War. Home Rule was an accomplished fact. Now was the time for Ireland's young men to show their appreciation, he maintained. Though Cumann originally announced its neutrality, a number of its members gave their support to Redmond. Eily O'Hanrahan recorded one such group at her Dublin branch of the movement:

> I joined Cumann na mBan at the instigation of my brother in 1914.... The loan of the hall at the back of the Catholic Commercial Club in O'Connell Street was given to us on the understanding that we were working for England as Red Cross workers.
>
> After the split the Cumann na mBan were asked which side they would follow. They divided into parties on both sides of the room. Not quite half remained faithful to MacNeill. The Redmondite Cumann na mBan left the building and the others kept possession, but when it was discovered what sort of politics we held we were told to clear out.[18]

With the danger of polarization within the movement, an attempt to reinforce the position of Cumann's neutrality was proposed. It was seconded, but it received no support when put to the vote. This led to the resignation of Agnes O'Farrelly, a founding member of the organization, as well as a number of other leading figures. A proposal was then put forward, and accepted, that Cumann na mBan would give its full support to the Irish Volunteers.

Outside of Dublin, some of the branches gave their support to Redmond,

Cumann na mBan marching through Dublin.

which led to further splits. In Limerick, supporters of John Redmond joined in numbers, with a view to taking over the local branch. Madge Daly recorded:

Soon after this development an election for a new committee was held, and some of these new members made an all-out effort to secure election; a few succeeded. A short time prior to this, we had made over £130 from a Fete in aid of the Arms' Fund. At our first committee meeting following the election, the Redmonite members enquired about our funds. They were informed that our collections were for the Volunteers' Arms Fund, and that we had handed over all the money to the Irish Volunteers for that purpose. The new members were very disappointed. We had the big majority on the Committee, however … so that we had full control. Following a few meetings, the opposition became dispirited by the course of events, and resigned in a body.

South of Dublin, at Ballon in County Carlow, there was also support for Redmond. He was, after all, the man who had succeeded in gaining Home Rule. Nan Nolan tells of the support that he was given:

Ballon, in the summer of 1915, knew there was a war on and believed it was being fought so that small nations like Ireland would be safe. Quite a lot of young boys, including one of my brothers, had joined the British Army to fight for what they thought was their King and country and the freedom of small nations. Every bit of news that could be got concerning the Allies' victories was hailed with delight. Often on those summer evenings as I learned my lessons, the sound of marching men was heard near the village, We would run up to see them carrying their wooden guns. They were called John Redmond's Volunteers, and while the boys at the Front sang "It's a long way to Tipperary," these used to sing "Keep the home fires burning." Older people believed all that, and brought us home flags. They were green with a gold harp in the center and a Union Jack in the corner.[19]

Previously, in September 1914, following the outbreak of the Great War, it was decided by the British Parliament that the Home Rule Act would not come into operation until an Amendment Act was passed including partition at the end of the war. At his tobacconist shop in Great Britain Street, Tom Clarke announced to fellow IRB man Sean O'Kelly his intention to call a meeting "of persons representative of advanced national opinion." His intention was to discuss what action Ireland should take now that England was engaged in the Great War:

We must see to it that we avail ourselves of this great opportunity to the full. He invited me [O'Kelly wrote] to attend this meeting. Before leaving him I asked him for the names of the others he proposed to invite. Among them were Griffith, Padraig Pearse and James Connolly. This historic meeting was held in the library in the Gaelic League headquarters, 25, Parnell Square. Tom Clarke presided and began by telling us why he had called us together. There was a full, free and candid exchange of views. Out of this meeting came the decision to arrange for the Insurrection of Easter 1916.[20]

Now it became important to convert the people to support such an idea. At harvest time 1915, an IRB man driving a horse and wagonette entered Ballon. As a stranger, he was a curiosity and he drew an audience. From the back of his vehicle, he addressed them:

Young men of Ballon and the surrounding places, you are listening to a lot of big talk these days. You are told to drill and fight for your country, but I say to you, drill by all means, but if you have to fight, fight in your own land. Never leave the shores of Ireland to fight for a foreign king. The day may soon come and you will remember my advice.

The day he was speaking of was still some six months in the future. For now, as Nan related, "The old policy of Redmond died hard."

The country was split in its loyalties. The Volunteers were split. Those who opposed Redmond's perception of the path of nationalism now found themselves more closely linked with Cumann na mBan, whose original credo was to support and assist the Volunteers in their defense of Ireland. The women now, in turn, developed a more militaristic approach to the search for a Republican Ireland. On 4th December 1915, using the pages of the *Irish Volunteer,* its leadership advocated:

Branches should be formed into squads of 6, including squad leader. Six of the best signalers should form a special signaling squad. The rest of the squads should be comprised of First Aid and Home Nursing only. The squad leader should be chosen for having the best knowledge of the work in which the squad is engaged in. Two squads form a section, which is supervised by a Section Commander, who is also selected on merit only. The Branch Commandant will direct and supervise generally.

MOBILIZATION

The Squad Commander should have the names and addresses of her squad, and the Section Commander should also have the names and addresses of the whole section.

The Commandant issues orders to the Section Commanders, whose duty it is to call up the members of their squads. When mobilization orders are expected members should leave word at home as to where they can be found, if they are going away

Constance Markievicz, suffragette, socialist, and soldier

from home. Quick mobilization is most impressive, and should be practiced often and at all hours, until you can bring out your Branch on parade at the shortest possible notice.

By the beginning of 1916, Cumann na mBan, though smaller now in numbers, had become a tightknit, well-organized, quasi-military organization, developing closer ties to the Irish Volunteers in the process. In April 1916, Constance Markievicz, an officer in the ICA, was appointed president of Cumann na mBan. This was important in that through her, James Connolly was able now to coordinate action within the various women's groups in Dublin; the Irish Citizen Army, Cumann na mBan, the IWWU, and the IWFL. How effective they would be, would be tested by the Easter Rising.

4

1916

Three into One

At a meeting of the Supreme Council of the Irish Republican Brotherhood held on 5th September 1914, it had been decided that an insurrection should take place before the end of the Great War between Britain and Germany. Now that day was upon them. The Rising was set for Easter Sunday 1916. Only those who needed to know were informed of the date. For the rank and file, the day was disguised as general maneuvers. Director of organization at Volunteer Headquarters Padraig Pearse issued the following directive in the official publication, *The Irish Volunteer*, for 8th April 1916:

GENERAL ORDERS

1. Following the lines of last year, every unit of the Irish Volunteers will hold maneuvers during the Easter Holidays. The object of the maneuvers is to test mobilization with equipment.

2. In Brigade Districts the maneuvers will be carried out under the Orders of the Brigade Commandants. In the case of the Dublin Brigade, the maneuvers will, as last year be carried out under the direction of the Headquarters General Staff.

3. Each Brigade, Battalion or Company Commander as the case may be, will on or before 1st May next, send to the Director of Organization a detailed report of the Maneuvers carried out by his unit.

Headquarters: 2, Dawson St. P.H. Pearse, Commandant
Dublin 3rd April 1916 Director of Organization.

As a member of the Supreme Council, James Connolly briefed his CIA commandants. Likewise, the instructions, though not the details, were passed on to Cumann na mBan through their local Volunteer units. Many of the women of Cumann na mBan were excited at the forthcoming big Irish Volunteer march through the city at Easter and that they would be part of it. Eilis Ni Riain reflected the expectancy in her witness statement to the Bureau of Military History:

On the Tuesday of Holy Week at our meeting we were told that there would be a special meeting on Friday night and as well as this instruction, arrangements were made for a special mobilization of all enrolled members for Friday night.

Although I was not officially a mobilizer, I helped a member at this work on Holy Thursday. There was a magnificent response to this appeal. The usual routine took place on Friday. We were ordered to report for duty for a march on Sunday morning at 12 o'clock. As far as I remember the rendezvous was Parnell Square. No uniforms or brooches were to be worn but rations were to be brought for twenty-four hours. Indication of something very special was apparent.

All the Dublin churches were filled to capacity by the different participating organizations on Saturday night, waiting for confession and on Sunday morning the number at Holy Communion was most impressive.

On Sunday morning on our way home from early Mass, we heard a newsboy shouting, "Stop Press!" and to our amazement learned of Eoin O'Neill's order countermanding maneuvers.[1]

The forthcoming parade produced a likewise expectancy, and disappointment, from Bridget Diskin:

I knew there were maneuvers coming on at Easter, and I came on Good Friday, I think in the morning, to help make the First-Aid kits.... I think it was on Saturday evening that Nora Foley gave us—my younger sister and myself—our mobilization order for Easter Sunday.... On Sunday morning the cancellation order appeared in the paper, and also Nora Foley called to the house to notify me of the position.[2]

The notice in the newspaper began with an emphatic, "NO PARADES!" It went on:

Irish Volunteer Marches cancelled. The Easter maneuvers of the Irish Volunteers, which were announced to begin today, and which were to have taken part in by all the branches of the organization in the city and country, were unexpectedly cancelled last night. The following is the announcement communicated to the Press last evening by the Staff of the Volunteers—

April 22, 1916.

Owing to the very critical position, all orders given to Irish Volunteers for tomorrow, Easter Sunday, are hereby rescinded, and no parades, marches, or other movements of Irish Volunteers will take place. Each individual Volunteer will obey this order strictly in every particular.

EOIN MACNEILL,
Chief of Staff,
Irish Volunteers

So the maneuvers were off, but behind the scenes, the atmosphere was charged with electricity. Early in the morning hours of Good Friday, Eoin MacNeill, chief of staff of the Irish Volunteers, but a man ignorant of what the IRB was planning, came to realize the full significance of the proposed "maneuvers." He discovered that the Volunteer units throughout the country had received orders from the IRB to take part in a Rising timed for Easter Sunday. Believing Pearse to be behind the intended Rising, he confronted him. Angry words were exchanged. "There will be no waste of lives for which I am directly responsible," MacNeill threatened. "I will not allow a half-armed force to be called out. I can promise you this, I'll do everything I can to stop a Rising—everything, that is short of ringing up Dublin Castle." Returning home, MacNeill immediately cancelled "all orders issued by Commandant Pearse, or by any other person heretofore." Later that morning Sean McDermott, Thomas MacDonagh, and Pearse called on MacNeill and revealed that an arms ship was expected from Germany. Very bluntly, they told MacNeill that the Volunteers were now under the control of the IRB. They convinced him that the landing of the arms meant that it was inevitable that a Rising would take place. While MacNeill was still not happy at the situation, he agreed not to interfere further and withdrew his former order. So, the mobilization and "exercises" that had been planned for Easter Sunday, 23rd April, could go ahead.

On Good Friday, Pearse went to Liberty Hall to inform Connolly of the situation with MacNeill. With a degree of uncertainty remaining, a meeting of the military council was held in the rear room of Mrs. Houlihan's shop in Amiens Street. With reassurances that MacNeill would not interfere, Connolly returned to Liberty Hall. That evening, mobilization orders and officers' commissions were made out. Constance Markievicz was appointed an officer. Among the other leading women present were Dr. Kathleen Lynn (medical officer), Helena Molony, Marie Perolz, Madeleine ffrench-Mullen, and Maeve Cavanagh. Markievicz reintroduced three more women to Connolly, whom she believed would be of use: Elizabeth O'Farrell, Julia Grennan, and Margaret Skinnider.

Elizabeth O'Farrell, born in Dublin in 1884, was a midwife and nurse by profession. A fluent Irish speaker, she was a member of the Gaelic League and Inghinidhe na h'Eireann, which she joined in 1906. During the Rising, she acted as a courier, and returning to Dublin, she joined the GPO garrison. Here, she cared for the wounded and attended to James Connolly after he was shot.

Julia Grennan was born in Dublin in 1883. By trade she became a dressmaker. Like O'Farrell, she was a member of the Irish Franchise League and a member of Inghinindhe na h'Eireann. During the lockout, she had worked in the soup kitchen at Liberty Hall. Now inducted into the ICA, she was sent to Dundalk and Carrickmacross with mobilization orders. Upon her return, she joined the General Post Office garrison and acted as a dispatch runner and later performed nursing duties.

Margaret Skinnider was born in 1893 to Irish parents at Coatbridge in Lanarkshire, Scotland. By profession, she was a math teacher. She was an active suffragist and later joined the Glasgow branch of Cumann na mBan. Skinnider also learned to shoot in a local rifle club. During one of her trips to Ireland, she met Constance Markievicz and thereafter took an active part in smuggling detonators and bombmaking equipment into Dublin, hidden under her hat. During the Rising, she acted as a courier, often dressed as a boy, and later she joined the garrison at the College of Surgeons, where she operated as a sniper.

Concerned that if the arms were landed too soon, the police might discover them, the Supreme Council of the IRB decided to delay their landing until the last possible moment. With all telegraphic ties to Germany cut off, they sent an indirect message to the German embassy in Washington for

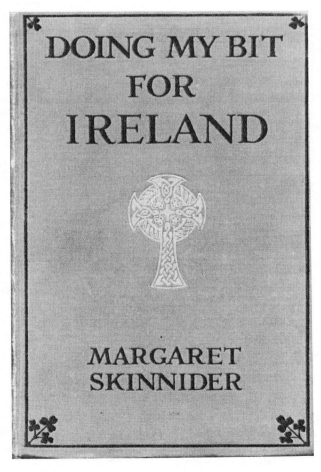

Doing My Bit for Ireland: Skinnider's account of Easter week

trans-shipment to Berlin. In February, British Naval Intelligence broke the German Code. They now became aware that a ship laden with arms was somewhere off the southwestern coast of Ireland. Lookouts were posted along the coast, and some twenty-nine auxiliary ships and boats of the Royal Navy began to look for the gunrunner. The German arms ship, the *Aud*, did not possess a radio, so the delaying message could not be sent to her. Approaching Tralee, she was sighted by the coastal watch station at Loop Head. They reported her presence as she continued along the coast. On Good Friday, she was intercepted by the armed trawler *Lord Heneage*, who reported her presence. Two Royal Navy sloops, *Zinnia and Bluebell*, intercepted her and ordered her into Cobh Harbor. At its entrance, the *Aud's* captain, Carl Spindler, scuttled her. Meanwhile, Sir Roger Casement, who had been in Germany seeking aid, had returned to Ireland aboard a submarine, the U19, captained by Kapitanleutnant Weissbach. Casement and two companions were sent ashore by a small boat, which unfortunately capsized as it approached the shore. Soaked, they scrambled ashore at Banna Strand. While his two companions, Robert Monteith and Joseph Dowling, alias Beverley, a former soldier, went off to look for aid, the exhausted Casement rested in the ruins of MacKenna's Fort. Monteith met up with a Volunteer from the Ballycellogott Company and was taken to the home of the McEllistrim family, whose daughter Hanna was a founding member of the local branch of Cumann na mBan. Fellow Cumann member Bessie Harrington related what happened next:

> When he arrived at McEllistrim's, Monteith was suffering from exposure and he was so bad that Lena McAllister (now Mrs. Brosnan,) had to massage his hands until circulation returned. She attended him during his stay there. Monteith was taken from McEllistrim's to John Byrne's house at Ballydwer Creamery, where Mrs. Byrne and her sister, Hanna McEllistrim, attended him. From Byrne's he was taken to Sean Tadhg Og and there his needs were attended to by other members of Cumann na mBan. This was the start of our work for men "on the run."[3]

Dowling meanwhile turned himself in to the police. He told them where to find Casement. The boat was discovered, a search was begun, and Casement was found. On Holy Saturday, the authorities at Dublin Castle knew everything. Here was clear proof of the tie-up with Casement, the Irish Volunteers, and the German enemy. Sir Matthew Nathan, assistant to the chief secretary in Ireland, went to see Lord Wimborne, the lord lieutenant. Wimborne was all in favor of raiding Liberty Hall, then known to be the headquarters of all the disparate Republican bodies. Such an attack could not be accomplished without the use of a field gun, but the nearest one available was at Athlone. Without it, there would be serious casualties on both sides. Nathan and Colonel H. V. Cowan, commissioner of police, suggested that the ringleaders should be arrested in a series of nighttime raids. As this would involve sixty to one hundred raids, it was not practical at such short notice. It would take a couple of days to arrange. That seemed to satisfy Wimborne.

MacNeill, having read the censored accounts in the morning newspapers of the arrest of a man at Ardfert, knew that it could only be Casement. There then following the news of the sinking of the *Aud*, MacNeill realized that an insurrection now would be suicidal. He wrote out a countermanding order to be delivered to all Battalion commanders in Dublin and throughout the country, canceling any instructions they might have received regarding the rising. Then he went to see Pearse. Confronted, Pearse told him, "We have used your name and influence for all their worth—now we don't need you any more. It's no use you trying to stop us. Our plans are laid and they will be carried out."[4] MacNeill warned Pearse that he intended to forbid any mobilization. He then proceeded to the offices of the *Irish Independent* and there followed the announcement inserted in the Sunday edition—"NO PARADES."

Sunday morning there was chaos and confusion among the Volunteer ranks throughout the country. At Liberty Hall, plans for the Rising were in complete disarray. Seamus Kavanagh of "C" Company, 3rd Battalion of the Volunteers in Dublin, sought clarification:

> On Easter Sunday morning I went to Camden Row about 12 o'clock. When I arrived there I saw a type-written notice on one of the huts to the effect that the maneuvers were written off, and that we were to keep in touch and keep ourselves in readiness for a possible immediate mobilization. I with my comrades were disappointed and dejected and we walked the city all day, calling back occasionally to Headquarters as we had been ordered to keep in touch.[5]

In the midst of the confusion, Cumann na mBan were left in limbo. They had planned for mobilization on Sunday, though they were not aware that it was to be a Rising. Now apparently the maneuvers were cancelled, and they had no explanation why.

Typical was Nancy, the daughter of Jennie Wyse Power. Following the confusion of MacNeill's order, she made her way to Liberty Hall:

> I went there and found the place in a commotion. The hallway, passages and stairs were packed with people coming and going so that I did not know where to turn.... At 6 p.m. I went to the mobilization point of Cumann na mBan, the Black Church, even though I realized that there would be nothing doing, and was sent away.[6]

In the hive of activity at Liberty Hall, those women present became aware that something was in the offing. "The atmosphere," Helena Molony recalled, "was like a simmering pot." Yet, as she remarked, there was also an air of despair:

> I saw Eoin MacNeill's countermanding order in the paper and heard the discussion in Liberty Hall. Connolly was there. They were all heartbroken, and when they were not crying, they were cursing. I kept thinking, "Does this mean that we are not

going out?" There were thousands like us. It was foolish of MacNeill and those to think they could call it off. They could not. Many of us thought we [the Citizen army] would go out single-handed, if necessary.[7]

There were comings and goings throughout the morning and into the early afternoon. In an upstairs room, the IRB executive thrashed out the problem. Tom Clarke wanted the Rising to go ahead as planned. Others, because of the chaos ensuing, urged postponement by one day so that new orders could be issued. By 1 p.m., the decision was reached that the Rising would take place at noon the following day. Now the women came into their own. They were dispatched throughout the country with the new orders. The following morning, Connolly summoned his own daughter, newly arrived from Belfast:

> "You are to take a message back to the North," said daddy.... "Pearse will sign it, so you must wait till he comes." [Taking her to one side, Connolly told her,] "We begin at twelve o'clock today. You will be safe enough till then. But afterwards I do not know.... Troops may be let loose over the country.... When you get to the North we will be fighting. See that there is no delay in delivering your message."[8]

Such was the secrecy involved that by the morning of Easter Monday, just one branch of Cumann na mBan, the Inghinidhe branch, was effectively mobilized. This was probably due to the presence of Jennie Wyse Power, president of Cumann na mBan, in whose home in the week prior, the leaders of the Rising had signed the proclamation of the Irish Republic. Divided into two groups, the branch was mobilized south of the Liffey at Cleaver Hall on Cork Street and at Dolphin's Barn. The members of the other branches in Dublin wandered around aimlessly, simply looking for clarification that did not come.

On Easter Monday morning at Liberty Hall, the headquarters of the Irish Citizen Army, Michael Mallin emerged from James Connolly's room and descended the stairs. On guard duty below was James O'Shea. "We will be fighting in a short time," Mallin informed him, "and we may have to fight alone." O'Shea asked if any of the Volunteers would fight. "There is no knowing," said Mallin, "but it will be short and sharp. We will all be dead in a short time." He then asked O'Shea how the lads were taking it, and O'Shea replied that the ICA would give a good account of themselves before they went down. Now the question was asked openly among the men: Would the Volunteers turn out to fight? Pearse assured all who asked that they would. The problem was, with the unexpected call to mobilize, and with it being Easter Monday and a public holiday, many of the Volunteers would have gone off for the day to the seaside with their families, or to the horseracing at Fairyhouse. Orders had been dispatched by girl messengers to mobilize, and in Dublin, those who remained were ordered to assemble before Liberty Hall.

In they came, and at 11.40 a.m., the disparate Republican groups, including some members of Cumann na mBan, were assembled along the road in front of Liberty Hall. There was terrific excitement. They knew that this was the day, the day that a generation had longed to see. Among the assembled Irish Republican Army as it was now designated, Matthew Connolly recalled years later, "As we lined up in front of the Hall, on the street, the sun was shining, and the Custom House clock told us it was twenty minutes to twelve." Bugler William Oman sounded the fall-in. The ICA and the Volunteers formed up. At this point, Countess Markievicz took up a copy of the first print run of one thousand copies proclaiming the establishment of the Irish Republic, and she read it out loud to the assembled soldiers. This was followed by loud cheers. About 11:50, Connolly barked out the order, "Column, attention—quick march!" Off they set. For Helena Molony this was a joyous occasion: "When we walked out that Easter Monday morning we felt in a very real sense that we were walking with Ireland into the sun," she exclaimed.

The total Citizen Army contingent was just 220, including twenty-eight women.[9] Under the command of Richard McCormack, a former British Army officer, a section of some forty-five men moved off at about 11:35 a.m., to seize Harcourt Street Railway Station. A second section, under the command of Sean Connolly, moved off in the direction of Dublin Castle and City Hall. This contingent included ten women—Bridget Brady, Mrs. Barrett, Bridget Davis, Bessie Lynch, Kathleen Lynn, Helena Molony, Annie Norgrove, Emily Norgrove, and Molly O'Reilly. Michael Mallin was dispatched to seize Stephen's Green. With him (though not as his second in command, as has so often been stated) was Constance Markievicz. Also included in the female contingent was Chris Caffrey, Mary Devereux, Madeleine ffrench-Mullen, Nellie Gifford, Bridget Gough, Rosie Hackett, Mary Hyland, Mrs. Joyce, Annie Kelly, Lily Kempson, Mrs. Norgrove, Margaret Ryan, and Kathleen Seery. The main force, under the command of James Connolly, proceeded to the GPO on Sackville Street. It included three women: Winifred Carney, Connolly's secretary; Julia Grennan; and Elizabeth O'Farrell. Later, women from Cumann na mBan joined this and some of the other garrisons. Lieutenant Ruaidhri Henderson later extrapolated the number of men and women initially available:

GPO area	approx. 135
Four Courts	320
Jacob's Factory	70
Boland's Mill	170
South Dublin Union	200
St. Stephen's Green	137
TOTAL:	1,132[10]

With just 1,132 available out of a possible 16,000 Volunteers and ICA soldiers, Connolly and Pearse could only hope that the remainder would rise in support—and sooner rather than later. British military forces in Dublin that Easter Monday stood at 111 officers and 2,316 other ranks. The numbers were as follows:

Marlborough Barracks, 6th Cavalry Regiment	35 officers	851 other ranks
Portobello Barracks, 3rd Royal Irish Rifles	21 officers	650 other ranks
Richmond Barracks, 3rd Royal Irish Regiment	18 officers	385 other ranks
Royal Barracks, 10th Royal Dublin Fusiliers	37 officers	430 other ranks
TOTAL:	111	2,316

Though already outnumbered by two to one and with the probability of British reinforcements arriving from other parts of Ireland, at the time the British forces lacked leadership. The general officer commanding, Major General Sir Lovick Friend, was on leave in London, leading to a leadership delay in response in Dublin. Of the 2,316 officers and men scattered throughout the barracks, a large number were also on leave in England over the Easter holiday, while others on leave were at Fairyhouse Races in County Meath or at the seaside resorts of Greater Dublin. Others on duty were undergoing training in the countryside, out at the Curragh. Administrative staff aside, this left a mere four hundred available for immediate duty.

Under the command of Captain Richard McCormack, a section of ICA men and women left Liberty Hall at about 11:30 a.m. with instructions to cross the river and take possession of Harcourt Railway Station, down near the South Circular Road. The station was the northern terminus of the Dublin & South Eastern Railway. It was along this line that the British reinforcements from the Curragh might be expected to come. Nine men under the command of Sergeant Joe Doyle were detached from McCormack's men to seize Davy's public house at the bridge over the Grand Canal, to prevent British troops in Portobello Barracks from crossing the bridge and advancing toward the Republican position in St. Stephen's Green.

Just prior to the departure of the main body of men and women leaving from Liberty Hall to seize the General Post Office, a further detachment, mainly of ICA men and women, was dispatched under Captain Sean Connolly to take up positions before Dublin Castle in Dame Street. His instructions were to seize some of the buildings commanding the approaches to Dublin Castle to prevent or impede the progress of British troops in that area. Connolly commanded a mixed detachment of both men and women. Helena Molony was in this group. She recalled the names of a few of the young women who took part: "the two Nor groves [Annie and Emily], Jinny Shanahan, and, I think, Brigid Davis." Also included were Bridget Brady, Katie Barrett nee Connolly, Bessy Lynch, Dr. Kathleen Lynn, and Molly O'Reilly.

The ICA established a garrison at City Hall, Dublin.

With the Castle entrance under minimal guard, Connolly led an assault against it. After some initial success, but killing an unarmed policeman in the process, Connolly and his men withdrew to take up positions in City Hall, just across the road, and in the newspaper offices nearby. Failing to capture Dublin Castle grieved Molony. In her witness statement, she expressed her frustration: "It breaks my heart—and all our hearts—that we did not get in [the castle proper]. We would have captured the Under Secretary, who was having lunch in the Castle." Sir Matthew Nathan was indeed in the castle. He was in a meeting with Major Ivor Price, the military intelligence officer, and Mr. A.H. Norway, secretary of the post office. With City Hall secured, Sean Connolly divided up his men into two groups, placing half of them on the ground floor and the other half up onto the roof, sheltered by parapets. Down below, where most of the women were based, windows were smashed and sandbags of whatever came to hand were put in place. Sniping commenced almost at once, with British troops based in the Bermingham Tower of Dublin Castle firing upon the rebels up on the roof of the City Hall. They responded, killing Sergeant Frederick Burke of the 10th Royal Dublin Fusiliers, as well as Second-Lieutenant Guy Pinfield as he crossed the castle yard. A fellow British junior officer was then wounded, as were thirty of the ordinary ranks. The British took cover and began maneuvering, seeking outflanking positions. Helena Molony was sent to the GPO for reinforcements. Gradually, in her absence, British soldiers succeeded in outflanking the City Hall garrison. They placed a machine gun at the corner of Castle Street and Cork Hill, enabling them to concentrate fire onto the rear and the side of the building. Now under serious fire, up on the roof, Annie Norgrove recorded the onslaught:

> Bullets were hopping like hail off the chimney pots and smashing the slates on the roof and the dome.... The men's faces blackened from the fumes and smoke of their rifles, some of the men had their handkerchiefs tied around their hands, their rifles were hot, now and then one of them would cry out a warning—keep your head down, Annie.... I heard the warning, and just as I ducked, a chimney pot smashed in smithereens around me.[11]

The firing on both sides continued. While the machine gun was reloaded, the defenders were able to respond with sniper fire. At about 2 p.m. Sean Connolly, who was up on the roof of City Hall, was shot by a British sniper. Cumann na mBan First-Aider Bridget Dawson crawled over to the fallen ICA officer to help him, but it was too late; he was mortally wounded. Helena Molony, now returned from the GPO with the promise of reinforcements to follow, recounted:

> Dr. Lynn was still there. She came up to attend him. She said, "I'm afraid he is gone." He was bleeding very much from the stomach. I said an Act of Contrition into his ear. We had no priest. We were very distressed at Sean Connolly's death. I particularly, as I had known him for so long and acted with him [at the Abbey Theatre]. His younger brother, Matt, who was only 15, was also on the roof and cried bitterly when he saw his brother dying.
> Jack Reilly took over command. I did not know him very well. After Connolly's death, there was nothing to do, only sit. The men in the main positions fired desultory shots all day.[12]

Jack (or John Joe) O'Reilly and Dr. Kathleen Lynn took command of the City Hall garrison. Without detailed orders from the GPO, all they could do now was to hold their position as originally ordered. The British snipers were taking their toll. Volunteer Charles Darcy was shot and killed. He was just fifteen years old. Jack O'Reilly was killed, as were George Geoghan and Louis Byrne. Following O'Reilly's death, Dr. Lynn took over sole command. At around 5 p.m., the long-awaited reinforcements arrived in the shape of George Norgrove and just seven men. The little garrison now faced up to a further 180 British soldiers drawn from Portobello, Richmond, and the Royal Barracks, sent to prevent the capture of the Castle. At 4 p.m., the little garrison came under intense machine-gun fire. Helena Molony wrote of how she and Dr. Lynn approached a window in City Hall on Monday afternoon when they were considering possible evacuation of the building, and she saw what appeared to be rain or sleet outside. It was actually a rain of machine-gun bullets. The expected mass attack came at 5 p.m. A VAD nurse within Dublin Castle watched the assault upon the rebel outpost:

> In the evening (Monday) we watched the men in the Yard bombing the office of the *Evening Mail* [adjoining City Hall]. The noise was terrific but eventually the building was successfully stormed.[13]

From the other side, Helena Molony recorded:

> There was a sudden bombardment. It came suddenly on us. On the roof level, on which were glass windows. And through the windows on the ground floor of the City Hall, there were machine gun bullets pouring in. From the ceiling the plaster began to fall. It was dangerous.

Up on the roof, the defenders responded as best they could, but they were facing overwhelming odds and superior firepower. The British soldiers, covered by suppressing machine-gun fire, reached City Hall, opening indiscriminate fire through the ground-floor windows as they did so. As Dr. Kathleen Lynn, the women with her, and the wounded sheltered partially behind a column within the downstairs floor, the ICA men retreated to the upper floors to continue the fight. Helena Molony recalled what happened then: "A window was smashed at the back, and then we knew they were pouring in— and they did come in the back. A voice said; Surrender in the name of the King!" An officer crossed the room toward the group of Citizen Army women, revolver in hand. "Anyone here? Speak or I shoot!" he demanded. Dr. Lynn approached the officer and offered the surrender of the small group of women, which was accepted. The British soldiers cleared the rooms on the ground floor, then progressed up to the next level. Here, they found Jinnie Shanahan, one of the Citizen Army women. As she was not in uniform, the officer assumed that she was a civilian caught up in the fighting. "Are there many of them here?" he asked. "Have they treated you badly?" "Oh no, sir," Jinnie replied, falling swiftly into her new role of victim. "They treated me well enough, but there must be hundreds of them up there on the roof."[14] Believing her, the troops moved cautiously forward going from room to room, They engaged in fierce but brief firefights before reaching the roof. As

Dr. Kathleen Lyon, suffragette and socialist, became commandant at City Hall.

they reached the roof, George Geoghan opened fire on them before he was cut down. By midnight, the few smoke-blackened men who had defied them, just five in number, surrendered.

The women were taken into custody and removed to Ship Street Barracks. The wounded men were put on stretchers and removed to the hospital. Jinnie Shanahan, the "neutral civilian," went with the women, where her ruse was quickly uncovered. She was welcomed joyfully by the other women of the garrison, who feared that she had been killed. It was then that the officer discovered that he had been fooled. "Oh, so you are one of them, are you?" he said with a rueful smile. As Helena Molony was to explain, "It would never occur to them, of course, that they were women soldiers. Actually, the women in the Citizen Army were not first-aiders, but did military work, except where it suited them to be first aiders. Even before the Russian Army had women soldiers, the Citizen Army had them."

The 4th Battalion Irish Volunteers, consisting of approximately two hundred men under Commandant Eamonn Ceannt, were designated to occupy the South Dublin Union. In addition to the workhouse, they took over Marrowbone Distillery, Watkins' Brewery, and Roe's Distillery. In their progression, they were joined by a section of the Inghinindhe branch of Cumann na mBan. They had been mobilized on Dublin's south side and marched to Dolphin's Barn, where they joined A Company of the 4th Battalion of the Volunteers. As the 4th Battalion marched off, the women fell in behind them in formation. Volunteer James Coughlan of C. Company remembered:

> We were halted when we reached one of the entrances to Marrowbone Lane distillery. Here a fairly large detachment of our battalion, accompanied by some Cumann na mBan and supplies on carts moved into the distillery. The remainder of us then marched via Basin Lane and James's Street to the South Dublin Union.[15]

Annie O'Brien recalled the brief march:

> We halted head on Cork Street and fell in behind Seamus Murphy's Company (A), which was about to take over Marrowbone Lane Distillery. Con Colbert and Christy [Byrne] had led their Company to Watkins' Distillery in Ardee Street. We marched into Marrowbone Lane after the Volunteers just as the Angelus was ringing. Rose McNamara led us in. We were told off—one squad of us in which I was—to the front of the building and the rest to the rear of the building. We had a full view of the front gate and could see everything that was going on.[16]

Additionally numbered in the women of Cumann na mBan who served in the Distillery were Eileen, Katie, and May Byrne; Annie, Eileen, and Lilly Cooney; Marcella Cosgrove; Josie Green; Josephine Kelly; Margaret "Loo" Kennedy; Bridie Kenny; Catherine and Mary Liston; Rose McNamara; Agnes McNamee; Julia McCauley; Josephine McGowan; Jinny Millner; Lizzie Mulhall; Rosa Mullaly; Kathleen Murphy; Lily O'Brennan; Margaret "Cissie" O'Flaherty;

Sheila O'Hanlon; Bridget O'Hegarty; Emily and Josephine O'Keefe; Maria and Priscilla "Sheila" Quigley; Josephine Rafferty; and Eileen Walsh.

Volunteer Robert Holland, positioned in the top story of the distillery, remembered additional Cumann members:

> A few of their names are Josie and Emily O'Keeffe, Josie McGowan, two O'Flaherty girls, two O'Byrnes, the three Cooney sisters, and a Miss Cumiskey who was, I think, in charge together with the wife of Captain Seamus Murphy was in charge of the whole garrison. There were two Monaghan sisters.[17]

Up on the top story, Holland waited and watched. At about 5 p.m. that Monday evening, Josie O'Keefe brought him up some food and a mug of tea. Just then, he observed a group of British soldiers advancing toward their position in extended formation. Holland told Miss O'Keefe to go down and report what he had seen to Captain Murphy and also to warn those on the floors below; then she was to return. With no other Volunteer to assist him in his upper observation post, Holland quickly instructed Josie O'Keefe in how to load the two rifles he had with him, a Lee Enfield and a Mauser:

> She learned the job of loading them very quickly. As a matter of interest each cartridge for the "Howth" rifle was about 6 inches long and weighed about a quarter of a pound. It had a lead top about an ounce and a half in weight and made a large entrance and exit hole.

So large, in fact, was the entry wound caused that the British were later to claim that the Volunteers were using "dum-dum" bullets. Holland continued:

> The soldiers appeared to delay, and one seemed to walk up and down giving them orders as to what to do. I sighted this particular individual on my rifle but before I had time to press the trigger of my rifle I was taken by surprise myself. A volley of shots rang out both from over and under me and then I fired. The soldiers went down and returned the fire. The fire kept on until dark. Josie O'Keefe kept loading up the rifles for me and then Josie McGowan came along with another rifle. The two stayed with me until it was almost dark and they brought me a can of tea and some bread and a can of fresh water.... Through the hours of darkness I could hear all the distant firing which at times appeared heavy.

Earlier that day elsewhere, another section of the Inghinidhe branch paraded on

Lily O'Brennan was part of the Marrowbone Lane garrison during Easter week.

Merrion Square to join with Eamon de Valera's 3rd Battalion. To their dismay, a courier from the garrison in Boland's Mill told them that they were not required. Why deValera refused their assistance has been open to speculation. The simple reason seems to be the old-fashioned notion that he did not want them exposed to the horrors of war. DeValera had established his headquarters at Boland's Mill in order to prevent entry into the city from the east and to deny the enemy the use of the railway line to bring troops in from Kingstown (now Dun Laoghaire). Outposts were also established. Miss Aine O'Rahilly, sister of The O'Rahilly, witnessed the preparation of one of them:

> From our house in Northumberland Road we saw everything that happened during the week's fighting. We saw the Volunteers fortifying No. 25 on Monday. I was on the street during the morning when two girls came along carrying two heavy cases. They must have been Cumann na mBan as they recognized me, but I did not know them. They asked if I knew where Paddy Doyle was. They told me they had ham and other food in the cases for him and the other Volunteers.... I brought the girls over to the house and knocked. The door was not opened but a reply came through: "I am Lieutenant Malone." The girls made themselves known and were admitted. I did not see them coming out again.[18]

The girls were a sister of James Grace, who was in the house, and her friend May Cullen. The young women did not remain, leaving by a rear door, before the house was sealed up once more.

The other branches of Cumann had been allocated to positions on the north side of the city. Here again they received word that their services were not required, this time from Edward Daly's 1st Battalion. After hanging around for several hours waiting for instructions, they were dismissed and ordered to reassemble on Tuesday. The next day, with no definite order arriving, the women from the Inghinidhe branch were told to make their own way to any garrison, where help was needed.

Elsewhere, at noon on Easter Monday, the rebels seized the General Post Office on Sackville Street. It was to be the headquarters of the insurgents. The building was put into a state of defense. The glass in all the main windows onto the street were smashed, and ledgers, books, mail sacks, and other available materials were placed as sandbags at the windows. Of the women who entered the GPO alongside their male ICA colleagues were Winifred Carney, from the Belfast Cumann, acting as James Connolly's secretary; Julia Grennan; and Elizabeth O'Farrell. If the Rising had gone to plan, the Central branch of Cumann na mBan, attached to the 1st Battalion of the Dublin Brigade of Volunteers, would have accompanied the men into the GPO and the Four Courts and its outposts. As it was, using her initiative, Catherine Byrne was the first Cumann na mBan woman to enter the GPO. Returning home that afternoon, she discovered that her brother had been mobilized. Grabbing her equipment, she ran after the company:

I turned into O'Connell Street past Tom Clarke's shop and, glancing back on hearing the sound of marching men, I saw a company of Volunteers led by Captain Michael Staines who was Captain in my brother's company. One of them told me the scrap was starting and that they were going to the GPO. When they came down to Nelson Pillar Staines gave the order, "Right turn," so I did the "Right turn too...." I went over to the footpath outside the Post Office to speak to Michael Staines. I asked him to let me in but he said no, I was to go home. He added, "I'll tell Paddy on you" (that was my brother). I hung around and by this time men had been posted outside the Post Office. I spotted Frank Murtagh at the Prince's St. corner and he recognized me. The Volunteers had broken in the front windows of the office, but the side windows had not yet been broken. I asked Frank Murtagh to lift me up to the side window at the corner where the stamp machine is now. He did this with the aid of another Volunteer and I kicked in the glass of the window. I jumped in and landed on Joe Gahan, who was stooping down inside performing some task. He started swearing at me, asking "What the bloody hell are you doing there?"[19]

The reply to Gahan's expletive was soon answered, as Catherine herself confirms:

While we were talking and laughing, an explosion occurred. Joe [Gahan] looked behind him towards the front of the Post Office and the remark was passed to me, "Here is your first case." It was Liam Clarke who was carrying a home-made hand grenade, which exploded as he entered the Post Office. At this time he was lying on the ground and was bleeding profusely from the head. Joe Gahan brought me a can of cold water and I washed Liam's head and I discovered he had a very nasty wound at the side of his head, which I dressed. Afterwards his eye had to be removed and he suffered the consequence of his wound till the time he died. He was a very nice man and I often met him afterwards, although I had not known him before the incident in the Post Office.

Over the days that followed, disparate members of Cumann na mBan entered the GPO under their own volition. Those known of included Commanding Officer Molly Reynolds, Kathleen Fleming, Annie Higgins, Martha Kelly, Maggie McLoughlin, Catherine Treston, Gertie Colly, Esther Wisely, Matilda Simpson. Brigid Foley, and Kathleen Ryan.

The principal Irish Citizen Army garrison was established at St. Stephen's Green on the south side of the city. Strategically placing a garrison here in the park was ill thought out. The park was dominated by surrounding large buildings from which enemy fire could be directed, as the defenders were soon to discover. The man in charge was Michael Mallin, though his disposition had been ordered by others. His second in command was Christopher "Kit" Poole. Attached to his staff was the formidable Constance Markievicz. Women soldiers of the ICA based here were Chris Caffrey, Mary Devereux, Madeleine ffrench Mullen, Bridget Foley, Mary Gahan, Nellie Gifford, Bridget Goff [or Gough], Foley, Rosie Hackett, Mary Hyland, Maggie Joyce, Katie Kelly, Lily Kempson, Bridget Murtagh, Mrs. Norgrove, Margaret Ryan, and

Kathleen Seery. Later that afternoon and into the next day, they were joined by other members of Cumann who were looking for a garrison to join. They included Nora O'Daly, Bridget Murtagh, and May Moore. The new arrivals were sent to join the ICA women at the park's summer house, then acting as a first aid station.

At the Harcourt entrance of St. Stephen's Green, as the Citizen Army entered the park, they were confronted by a constable of the Dublin Metropolitan Police. He ordered them out of the park. Constance Markievicz, who was with this group, drew her automatic and pointed it at the policeman, as also did a number of the Volunteers. Three shots were fired, and the unarmed policeman fell, mortally wounded. District Nurse Geraldine Fitzgerald witnessed the unnecessary shooting:

> A lady in a green uniform the same as the men were wearing (breeches, slouch hat with green feathers etc.)—holding a revolver in one hand and a cigarette in the other was standing on the footpath giving orders to the men. We recognized her as the Countess Markievicz.... We had only been looking out a few minutes when we saw a policeman walking down the footpath ... he had only gone a short way when we heard a shot and then saw him fall forward on his face. The Countess ran triumphantly into the Green saying, "I got him" and some of the rebels shook her by the hand and seemed to congratulate her.[20]

The civilians were cleared from the park, and the gates were locked. Trenches were dug. A first aid station was established in a small lodge in the southwest corner of the Green. In this group was the diminutive but lion-hearted Rosie Hackett; her white coat, which originally trailed along the ground, had been shortened to suit. She had received instructions from her mentor, Dr. Lynn, that she "would be with Miss ffrench-Mullen. Wherever Miss ffrench-Mullen would go, I was to be next to her," as she recalled in her witness statement.

In the original plan for the Rising, Commandant Edward Daly was to occupy a line running from the Four Courts along the north bank of the Liffey (to include the Mendicity on the south bank) up to Cabra in the north by way of Brunswick Street, establishing a series of outposts in the process. In the original plan, Daly was to have one thousand men under his command. On the actual day, he had approximately 320. Included in this number were a number of women, later added to, including Ellen Ennis, Bridget (or Brigid) Lyons, Pauline Markham, Bridie and Kate Martin, Florence Mead, Caroline Mitchell, Mary and Louise O'Sullivan, and Maire Carron. Later arrivals from the GPO garrison were Caroline Mitchell and Pauline Morkan.

Another strategic point, Jacob's Factory, which had featured so heavily in the trade union struggle of 1913, was garrisoned by men of the 2nd Battalion under Commandant Thomas McDonagh. His second in command was Captain Tom Hunter, and Major John McBride, veteran of the Boer War, acted as a military advisor. McDonagh was a known feminist and supporter of the women's franchise. Once the garrison was established, he sent out word for the women of Cumann na mBan assigned to him to take up their duties. His garrison then numbered 178 men, women, and youth (from Na Fianna na h'Eireann). Details of the women included are vague, though Abbey actress Maire Nic Shiubhlaigh is known to have joined the garrison during the week. At the garrison's surrender, five members of the Fairview branch of Cumann were arrested.

Tuesday morning dawned. In the early hours, troops from the 25th (Irish) Reserve Infantry Brigade began arriving in the capital. Brigadier General William Lowe took over command of British forces in Dublin. Kingsbridge Railway Station, the principal railway station to the south, was taken over to facilitate the arrival of reinforcements. Lowe set up a line of posts, effectively establishing a wedge between the principal rebel positions, cutting the rebel forces in two. At 3:20 a.m., one hundred men, including a machine-gun team under Captain Elliotson of the Curragh Mobile Column, occupied the Shelbourne Hotel and the adjacent Royal Services Club on the north side of St. Stephen's Green. The capture of these buildings broke the connection of the rebel headquarters at the GPO, with the rebels around St. Stephen's Green. At 2 p.m. additional British reinforcements began to arrive, including the 4th Dublin Fusiliers from Templemore, the Reserve Artillery from Athlone, and an Ulster Composite Battalion from Belfast.

Throughout Monday night and into Tuesday morning, the GPO garrison had extended outposts, across the road, and right down to the bridge over the Liffey. Upon her arrival, Aoife de Burca of Cumann na mBan was sent across the road to Reis's Building, where an outpost had been established. Up on the roof, a radio transmission station had been reactivated, and messages were sent out to the world that the Irish Republic had been proclaimed:

> The Volunteers were in possession when I arrived, accompanied by the doctor [Dr. Tuohy of North Frederick Street] Having been introduced to the Captain in command [Thomas Weafer] I was directed to the upper portion of the building. Here there were about eight members of Cumann na mBan, all of whom were Red Cross workers for the Republican army. [They were Maire Mapother, Chrissie Stafford, Maire McElroy, Lene Walshe, Bridie Richards and Mrs Barrett; at the adjoining Hibernian Bank were Mrs English and Mrs Quinn].
>
> Some were quite young, only in their teens. I never met a braver or more intelligent lot of girls: they were ready for duty, no matter how dangerous. Some of them even carried dispatches under fire, or took the place of wounded Volunteers [one of these was Maire Mapother].
>
> Commandant Thomas Weafer was the Captain over the battalion in Reis's and the Hibernian Bank. He was a tall, fine looking man, about 27 or 28 years of age, and seemed one fitted in every way for the position he held; his energy and zeal were untiring; his courage and kindness of heart unsurpassed.[21]

Having received no food supplies since the previous evening, Weafer asked for a volunteer to cross over to the GPO and ask the commissariat for rations. First aider Catherine Byrne agreed to go:

> I volunteered. Captain Weafer said, "Don't worry, I'll signal that you are going across so that you will have a safe passage." I reached the Post Office safely and, knowing well where the kitchen was, I went right up to it. It was then I saw Desmond Fitzgerald. I had not seen him on my previous visits to the kitchen. At the time I was not sure who he was. I asked a Volunteer for rations saying I had been sent for them by Captain Weafer. It was then Desmond Fitzgerald spoke, saying, "I'll give no rations until I know how many men he has." I said "There are a few women there too and am I to go back under fire and give that message to Captain Weafer?" He said, "Yes, and tell him Desmond Fitzgerald sent that message. I am Desmond Fitzgerald." I returned and Captain Weafer gave me a written message. I rolled up the piece of paper he gave me, put it in my mouth and went back across the street. I went straight up to the kitchen and gave the paper to Desmond Fitzgerald, who said, "That's all right. I'll see to that."[22]

Fitzgerald's actions might have seemed harsh, but he was responsible for serving all the garrisons with food, and he did not know how long the struggle would last. So, he was doing his best to eke out the rations for as long as possible. Nonetheless, his actions had endangered Catherine Byrne, who must have come under sniper fire.

Tuesday morning, a force of one hundred British soldiers with four machine-gun teams were positioned at the upper windows of the Shelbourne Hotel overlooking St Stephen's Green. At 5:30 a.m., the signal was given, and the machine guns opened up. "The Green was occupied by many Rebels," as British Army Captain Elliotson recalled. "There were women there, but no exception was made as women had already been found using rifles and taking part in the rebellion. Campfires and trenches were in the Green.... It was a cheerful but sad sight to see the campers scattering and running out of the far side of the Green." The action was quite ruthless, as those on the receiving end testified. Frank Robbins wrote of the episode:

> The British flagrantly ignored the Red Cross shelter from which a large Red Cross flag was flown. I take the opportunity of putting on record the utter disregard on the part of the British Military, who were in occupation of the Shelbourne Hotel, for the Red Cross, in order to remove any doubts that may exist in the minds of some people as to the supposed chivalry of that Army.[23]

Glasgow Cumann na mBan member Margaret Skinnider put the flesh on to Robbin's bare statement:

> Once that day I saw them shooting at our first aid girls, who made excellent targets in their white dresses with large red crosses on them. It was a miracle that none of them were wounded. Bullets passed through one girl's skirt, and another had the heel of her shoe shot off. If I had not seen this happen, I could not have

believed that British soldiers would disobey the rules of war concerning the Red Cross.[24]

More shots came from the nearby United Services Club, now occupied by British snipers. Commandant Mallin ordered a withdrawal to the safety of the College of Surgeons' building.

The fleeing garrison was given intense covering fire, from the IRA outpost at Little's public house, as they ran across the road. Once within the building and the doors barricaded, the Volunteers returned fire. Up within the roof space of the college, Margaret Skinnider took up a sniping position:

> I climbed up astride the rafters, and was assigned a loophole through which to shoot. It was dark there, full of smoke and the din of firing, but it was good to be in action. I could look across the tops of the trees and see the British soldiers on the roof of the Shelbourne. I could also hear the shot railing against the roof and wall of the fortress, for in truth this building was just that. More than once I saw the man I aimed at fall.[25]

Within the college, the first aid station was reestablished in the large and protected College Hall.

Nora O'Daly described it:

> The large blind upon which lantern slides were shown (to illustrate lectures in the College) was drawn down and that end of the lecture room was sectioned off for Red Cross work only, no one but First Aid assistants being allowed past the barrier.

The ICA established a garrison at the College of Surgeons.

These consisted of Miss Rosie Hackett, Miss B. Murtagh, and myself.[26]

The garrison settled down for a prolonged duel with the British. Following one sustained barrage of gunfire, little Rosie Hackett came very close to death. She:

> was lying down on one of the beds…. The men were trying out some rifles they had found in the College. The people upstairs sent for me to go for a cup of tea…. I had only left the bed, when a man, named Murray, casually threw himself down on it and, whatever way it happened, this bullet hit him in the face. We attended him there for the whole week. He was then brought to Vincent's Hospital where he died after a week. They remarked that had I not got up when told to go for the tea, I would have got it through the brain, judging by the way the bullet hit this man.[27]

Margaret Skinnider served as a sniper in the College of Surgeons garrison.

Though not stated, it would appear that Murray was shot by one of his own, in what is now euphemistically called "friendly fire."

Across the city at the GPO's outpost at Reis's Chambers, the garrison broke through into the Hibernian Bank. Burrowing continued through to Hoyte's the druggists at number 17, Lower Sackville Street, on the corner with Sackville Place. Within the bank, the women of Cumann na mBan established a first aid station. Two large Red Cross flags were hoisted through the windows overlooking Sackville Street. Aine Ryan was one of the women:

> Later that day most of the people in Reis's Chambers went into the Hibernian Bank and we with them. We got busy then filling baths of water and sterilizing it for First-Aid instruments, etc. They were afraid the water would be cut off. There was a huge bath of sterilized water and I was nearly killed by Mary Lawless for dipping a jug into it and destroying the whole lot. I was in terror of her afterwards. At this stage I met a very marvelous lady, Mrs English, with whom I got pally (I have to thank her for my certificates for service in Easter Week).
>
> Before nightfall two fellows came across from Reis's Chambers and asked for two girls to go back there to prepare meals, etc., as they had no girl at all. Mrs English immediately volunteered and I said I would go with her. When we had said that the fellow said, "Remember now, it is a death trap." My heart fell to my boots but I did not pretend anything. We went up and tidied up the place. Remember some of the

people. They were Captain Paddy McGrath, now dead, who was at one time Works Manager of the Irish Press: Captain Weafer and Sean McGarry. The wireless was in operation upstairs—John O'Connor (Blimey of the London-Irish) was at it all night with Fergus Kelly. I got to know Blimey well later.

There was a good lot of shooting that night and we were all taking cover. Mrs English was giving out the Rosary and we were answering it.

My memory tells me that some of the British occupied McBirney's roof during the night, because the boys were always looking over there. At daybreak things got quiet and Mrs English cooked a breakfast for the men. She gave them chops and we drank tea.[28]

Amid this domesticity, elsewhere the fight for Dublin went on in earnest. At the Mendicity on the south side of the Liffey, facing almost onto the Volunteer garrison at the Four Courts, this little outpost had come under serious assault. Concentrated British machine-gun fire was followed by sniping, the Volunteers returning fire when possible. Barely three hundred yards away, this little battle was being viewed by the ordinary citizens of Dublin, not all of whom appear to have been in sympathy with the rebels. Their daily life of Dublin's citizens had been disrupted. Crossing the city on her way home, Lilly Stokes came upon this fierce exchange:

I walked along the Quay past Guinness to the first bridge, where I joined a group of men at a Public House corner; it was all barred up. Its inmates knocking at me to go on, go on, into safety—they didn't ask me inside! They were shooting pretty fast now from the bathing house [at the Mendicity], I couldn't see at what, till I saw the soldiers coming out of the Royal Barracks—they were running for the shelter of the Quay wall and bending low running across the bridge. My group got excited: "The Military, The Military are comin' out, and their bayonets fixed. Lor' they'll take us for Volunteers, and the Officers laden with their revolvers!" And as they crossed the bridge, we all began to cheer and wave hats and shout orders to the soldiers: "Go round to the back, go round to the back, ye'll catch them there, kape in by the wall, ye'll be shot dead." We thought they were going to surround the bathing house but they evidently wanted to get to the Castle and thought they would get there by Parliament Street, but thought better of it as they neared the bathing house and came back by our side street. My crowd were greatly disgusted with them, having paid attention to their orders. "There now, d'ye see that? Such muddlin', it is aisy believing at the front."[29]

Earlier that morning, across the road at the main Four Courts garrison, Aine Heron and five Cumann na mBan women, dodging bullets, arrived to offer what help they could. She records:

When we arrived we got in without any difficulty.... Frank Fahy asked us where we would like to set up our hospital. As the windows of the rooms were all sandbagged and dark, we said we would use the room where the glass dome was and we would put out a Red Cross flag. Frank replied, "You may do so, but I greatly fear that the enemy we are fighting will have little respect for the Red Cross flag when it is ours."

We went down to the kitchen to clean up. We collected all the vessels we could find and filled them with water, as we were told the water might be cut off. While there, a Volunteer came in with a few big pieces of meat, and I took a cauldron and put the meat in it to cook, so as to have a good stew and plenty of soup. Up to this I think they had nothing but tea.[30]

Eilis O'Conell and a few other waifs and strays were directed to report to the Four Courts, as she herself narrates:

When we reached the Four Courts, after wending our way through high, narrow streets to avoid stray bullets, we were told to report to the Father Mathew Hall, Church Street, which had been handed over for a first-aid station to Commandant Daly by the Capuchin Fathers. On arrival at the Hall Father Augustine O.F.M. Cap., welcomed us. When we entered, several of our members were present, including Mrs. Fahy, Mrs. Conlon, Mrs. McGuinness, all of whose husbands were operating in the area. Miss Christina Hayes, Mrs Parker, Kathleen Kenny and Eileen Walsh, afterwards Mrs Murphy, a member of the *Inghini* Branch. Later in the day, Margaret Martin, Lily Murnane, Dora Hartford and Kathleen Martin arrived. The latter were members of the Columcille Branch and were introduced to us by Captain Dinny O'Callaghan.... Each member of Cumann na mBan was supplied with a white armlet and consequently became a member of the hospital staff.

For the first few days of the fighting, wounds treated were of a minor nature but as time went on the number of more seriously wounded patients increased and we carried them on stretchers into the hall and dressed their wounds.[31]

Not too far away, just behind the Four Courts, a team of about twenty Volunteers advanced upon Broadstone Railway Station with a view to establishing an outpost and preventing the arrival of British reinforcements by rail. Forward picket Eamon Martin was shot. The British had beaten them to it. The Volunteers made an orderly withdrawal and reported back to the Four Courts. Up at Phibsborough, the British had driven off a Volunteer outpost and established a battery of four 18-pounder guns. The position had been vital to the Volunteers in order to keep an avenue open for reinforcements of the 5th Battalion marching south under the command of Thomas Ashe. This was also a vital highway as a line of withdrawal out of the city should things not work out. The British had successfully sealed off Dublin from the north. By Tuesday evening, General Lowe had established a cordon, cutting Boland's Bakery, Jacob's Biscuit Factory, the South Dublin Union, and the College of Surgeons off from Volunteer headquarters at the GPO in Sackville Street. As darkness fell, the firing decreased into occasional sniping.

At dawn on Wednesday morning, while the majority stood on guard in the GPO, the women of Cumann na mBan were busy preparing breakfast. At about 9 a.m., the British began shelling the Hibernian Bank from the Ballast Office. Over at Reis's, Nurse Aoife deBurca remarked:

Our quiet time was at an end. At 10.30 a.m. or thereabouts, Commandant Weafer came into our center looking for a nurse to go to the Hibernian Bank, as they were expecting heavy casualties at any moment and would like some additional help. I gladly volunteered to go with him. I proceeded at once to get everything in readiness for the wounded, for judging by the tremendous firing, I knew I was in for a busy time. I was at work about half an hour when I heard a call from the upper landing, "First aid quickly." I hurried upstairs, two steps at a time. When I reached the top I found Commandant Weafer mortally wounded. Little I thought a short half hour before that this noble life was so near its tragic close; we did our best for him, but he only survived about fifteen minutes. He died as he had lived, brave to the last, and I'm sure he has his reward now where Peace and Joy abound. All his men seemed genuinely sorry for him, and some of them knelt by him till all was over.[32]

Volunteer William Daly was a little more graphic in his description:

At this time a message was signaled to us to get ready to evacuate the post [at Reis's] and retire to the Hibernian Bank of which Capt. Tom Weafer was O/C. At about 1 p.m. I saw Paddy Mitchell with a Red Cross armlet on the run round the corner from O'Connell Street into the Bank and he came out a few minutes later to us that Weafer was badly hit and he returned to the temporary hospital (which had been a mock auctioneer's shop) to get a stretcher and bearers to bring Weafer out, but owing to the intense firing, was unable to get back to the bank. We could hear Weafer yelling with pain and groaning in agony. The bullet struck through the liver and kidneys and the pain must have been terrible.[33]

Captain Liam Breen was sent over from the GPO to take Weafer's place. Following a bombardment, he was ordered to close the outpost and evacuate the people under his command. With the wounded on stretchers, and with a large Red Cross flag carried ahead of them, the evacuees waited until the gunfire subsided. It was about 12:30 p.m. when Cumann na mBan nurse Aine Ryan and another young woman braved crossing the road. Volunteer William Daly described what happened next:

The firing eased down considerably while the nurses and wounded made their way to H.Q. We who remained behind in the hospital gathered together all the mattresses and other materials of value in preparation for a rush across the road. There were nineteen of us left. Six of us took the grenades and the remainder took a mattress apiece. First of all a couple would rush out for about 3 yards and then run back and immediately we heard the burst of firing, seven or eight would rush across the road and, running in a zigzag fashion, made us difficult targets. The whole of us got into Princes Street. I had hobnailed boots on and halfway across I slipped and fell directly behind the statue of Sir John Grey with a mattress I was carrying on my shoulder. I got to my feet instantly and continued my rush while a cheer went up from the Post Office, but in my haste the rifle had slipped from the mattress and was lying in the center of O'Connell Street. Another man running behind me picked it up and continued on with it.[34]

With a surplus of nurses within the GPO, Aine Ryan was allocated to other duties;

> I went over finally to stay in the GPO with the other girls of the crowd. We were employed upstairs in the restaurant where there was a huge [cooking] range. I remember Desmond Fitzgerald who was in charge in charge of the cooking arrangements. I remember the British Tommy—a Dublin man—who was cooking all the time and joking with the girls. He was in great humor and he had a rosary beads round his neck. I don't know where all the religious objects that all the people in the GPO were wearing came from…. There were British prisoners there—some of them were officers—to whom we brought meals.

And all the time the shooting and bombardment continued, as the British tightened their grip. At the Four Courts, the British brought up an eighteen-pounder field gun. They placed it at the corner of Exchange Street and Wood Quay, on the south side of the river. Coming under intense Volunteer fire, however, they moved it back to Parliament Street. From there, they opened fire on the building. A couple of shells wrecked the room in which the defenders were returning small-arms fire, forcing them to withdraw. Across the road at the Mendicity, its small garrison was forced to surrender. Up behind the Four Courts in the North Brunswick Street sector, the Republicans were likewise experiencing a serious assault. Down at Mount Street, an outpost of Boland's Mills, the garrison was holding its own. Now they were confronted by British reinforcements, soldiers of the Sherwood Foresters Regiment recently landed at Kingstown. They had advanced on Mount Street, with its canal crossing into Dublin, in two columns.

Lily Stokes, who the previous day had witnessed the fighting along the Quays, recorded in her diary for Wednesday, 26th April:

> In the afternoon we went to Ballsbridge and watched the soldiers coming in—thousands of them. A Division had been sent over, it was ready to go to France on Monday. The men thought that they were in France when they arrived at Kingstown, calling out, "Bon Jour" to the people. They had a number of prisoners at Ballsbridge, amongst them some women; most of them looked the laboring classes.
>
> We heard the soldiers had had nothing to eat since they landed. They had a long march from Kingstown carrying heavy packs. They looked weary, so Maive, Pauline and I came back and Mother gave us two grand cans of tea, which we took to them by the Elgin Road lane, but alas! We could not give it to them, for they had just began advancing down Northumberland Road. They had cleared the Rebels out of Carrisbrooke House at the corner of Pembroke and Northumberland Roads—there were eight dead inside it. One soldier was killed. We saw the soldiers being sniped at, but none shot, the soldiers returning fire as they advanced.[35]

Then rather bizarrely, two women, one carrying a jug, came walking toward the bridge. They were nurses, Kathleen Price and Louisa Nolan. All shooting stopped as they started to attend to the wounded soldiers. Then two men in white coats appeared, their hands held up above their heads to show that they were unarmed. They were doctors, Myles Keogh and C.B. O'Brien. One of the nurses called out to the rebels and asked for a temporary truce while they assisted the wounded. It was given. A large number of nurses in white uniforms then emerged, as did two clergymen, Father McNevin and Father McCann. The doctors and nurses began carrying the wounded back across the bridge to Sir Patrick Dun's Hospital. With the wounded clear, the British assault resumed. The bridge was rushed again, but with the same devastating results. With some leadership restored, the British now began making inroads. They established exactly where their enemy was based and planned accordingly. With suppressing machine-gun fire, they advanced over the bridge. By 8 p.m. a one-pounder gun, firing incendiary shells, opened fire on the house. With more suppressing fire, the British advanced, throwing hand grenades into the fortified house. The rebels had suffered losses, with men being killed. With the house ablaze, the four remaining Volunteers evacuated their position, leaving their dead.

South Dublin Union was still holding out. Watkin's Brewery was vacated, its defenders crossing over to the distillery on Marrowbone Lane. Figures compiled at the time by Lt. Henry Murray of A. Company reveal the strength of the Marrowbone Lane defenders:

Battalion Staff	3
A. Company	25
B. Company	4
C. Company	43
D. Company	8
F. Company	30
Cumann na mBan	23
Fianna	7
C. Co. 3rd Battalion	1
Irish Citizen Army	1
TOTAL	145

With the coming of night, Rosie McNamara signed off the day at the distillery with the comment, "We emptied out the oats from the sacks and made the beds more comfortable; very cold. Miss Cosgrave or myself did not sleep and we envied the other girls, some of whom were snoring. We both keep watch while the guards gets a well-deserved sleep."

At St. Stephen's Green, the ICA had settled into the College of Surgeons, even contemplating taking the fight to the enemy. They burrowed through the connecting walls of buildings on the northwestern side of the Green in an effort to reach the South King Street corner. Finally, they breached the wall into the Alexandra Ladies' Club, a bastion of Anglo-Irish Unionism. There were women present there, totally unsympathetic to the rebel cause. R.M. Fox, in his history of the ICA, recorded what happened next:

> Two servant girls looked very frightened till one caught sight of some Rosary beads wrapped around the wrist of a Citizen Army man.

"Look!" cried the girl to her companion, pointing to the beads. "They're
Catholics!"

"What did you think we were?" demanded the Citizen Army man indignantly.

"Germans!" said the girl. "The lady told us you were Germans."

As the Republicans extended their positions on one side of the square,
British snipers were doing the same on the other side. They had established
themselves on the south side in the Russell Hotel and the University Church.
There was a danger of encirclement of the Republican positions. Commandant Mallin decided to set fire to the buildings over the other side of the
Square, hoping that the British positions would be affected. Margaret Skinnider, a rather remarkable woman, asked to be allowed to take part in the
raid. Given its danger, Mallin was reluctant but finally agreed. She headed
up one of the two teams. James Connolly's daughter Nora, who was there,
was in no doubt as to who led her team: "When they were going out to attack
the nest of snipers she was in charge of the squad. William Partridge, a very
famous man in the working-class movement was there and he and the other
members of the squad accepted she was in charge." On Wednesday night at
about 1:30 a.m., a party of fourteen men and women under the overall command of Lieutenant Thomas Donoghue slipped out of the College of Surgeons
with the intention of setting fire to an antique shop in Harcourt Street, just
around the corner from the Russell Hotel and the church, with the object of
the fire spreading to both buildings. Margaret Skinnider tells the tale of what
happened then:

> It took only a few moments to reach the buildings we were to set afire. Councilor
> Partridge smashed the glass door in the front of the shop that occupied the ground
> floor. He did it with the butt of his rifle and flash followed. It had been discharged. I
> rushed past him into the doorway of the shop, calling the others to come on. Behind
> me came the sound of a volley, and I fell. It was as I had on the instant divined. That
> flash had revealed us to the enemy.
> "It's all over," I muttered, as I felt myself falling. But a moment later, when I knew
> I was not dead, I was sure I should pull through. Before another volley could be
> fired, Mr. Partridge lifted and carried me into the street. There on the sidewalk lay a
> dark figure in a pool of blood. It was Fred Ryan, a mere lad of seventeen, who had
> wanted to come with us as one of the party of four.
> "We must take him along," I said.
> But it was no use; he was dead. With help I managed to walk to the corner. Then
> the other man who had stopped behind to set building afire caught up with us.
> Between them they succeeded in carrying me back to the College of Surgeons.[36]

On Thursday, 27th April, the northern approaches to the city were sealed
off. British troops north of the river began enforcing a cordon around the
rebel headquarters at the GPO in Sackville Street. By 10 a.m., they were within
one hundred yards of the post office. Then, under the cover of shelling and

suppressing machine-gun fire, they advanced as far as Middle Abbey Street, barely fifty yards away. Earlier the 2/5th and 2/6th Sherwood Foresters advanced upon the Four Courts, but instead of outflanking the rebel outposts, they inadvertently cut through them. In the darkness of the early morning, they became caught in crossfire, suffering heavy casualties.

South of the river Liffey, the 2/7th and 2/8th Sherwood Foresters approached the South Dublin Union. Throughout the day, they battled the defenders, eventually succeeding in gaining the workhouse grounds. Divided up to attack the many buildings that were being defended, as darkness descended chaos ensued, with the soldiers being caught up in friendly fire. Around 7 p.m., the Sherwood Foresters were withdrawn to prevent further loss of life. They left their casualties, six dead and nine wounded, to be taken care of by the Dublin Union medical staff.

At the GPO, firing grew more intense as the day got older. The impression among the garrison was that the British were getting the range of the GPO from the Parnell monument. Shells began to burst on the roof of the building, and a number of Volunteers stationed there received injuries. All were eventually ordered down to the lower floors. Connolly continued to visit the outposts. Sniping had intensified. The anticipated frontal attack had begun from the southeast from the junction of Marlborough and Lower Abbey streets. Each advance was thwarted by carefully positioned defenders. As the day passed into afternoon, a British attack was launched from the west on the rear and flank of the GPO. Connolly supervised the establishment of new outposts, but with dire consequences. On his way back to the GPO, he received a severe ankle wound. Molly Reynolds, a young Cumann na mBan woman acting as a Red Cross nurse in the GPO, wrote:

Another serious wounding was James Connolly. He got a bullet wound in the left leg which shattered, I would say, roughly from one and a half to two inches of his shin bone. There is a laneway running from Prince's Street to Middle Abbey Street [Williams Lane], and Connolly left the Post Office to visit some outposts in Abbey Street, using this laneway to reach them. After he had gone a short time, we heard a shout for a stretcher. Another girl and myself picked up a stretcher but we were not allowed to go out. We handed it to some men and they brought Connolly in. His leg was dressed, set in splints and a wastepaper basket was cut in two to make a cage for it. A bed was procured, and Connolly was placed on it. He refused to remain a patient in the Casualty Station and his bed was moved to the main hall where the headquarters were.[37]

Nurse Aoife de Burca gave the initial first aid:

I was not very long back when Seamus Connolly came in, slightly wounded in the lower part of the left leg; the bone was broken and the flesh very much lacerated. He seemed in great pain. I took off his boot and sock and helped dress his wound. We then got him to bed, where he was put under an anesthetic to have the bone set, which was performed by Lieutenant Mahony, R.A.M.C. (a prisoner), ably assisted by two of our own young doctors. I watched by him until he regained consciousness after the ether and felt honored by the duty. He was very brave and so grateful for the least attention. I well recollect praising the bravery of his men to him, saying what fine fellows they were and what spirit and courage they showed. "Oh" he said, "you needn't tell me. I know well their worth," and the tears coursed down his cheeks. I could scarce keep back my own when I looked at this lion-hearted hero stricken down, just when his leadership was most needed.[38]

With Connolly incapacitated, command devolved down to Sean McDemott and Tom Clarke. While holding no formal military rank, by virtue of their membership within the provisional government and, by extension, their senior positions within the IRB, they now directed the continuation of the fight. The struggle within Dublin had become tense. Clarke needed to know if the rest of Ireland had risen, which hopefully would take the pressure off them. It was decided that a Volunteer should be sent to Cork to ascertain the true position. Clarke approached Nurse de Burca and asked that a priest be sent for to hear the confession of the young lad who was to be sent. DeBurca recalled:

A young girl [Leslie Price, who was later to marry Tom Barry] who happened to be standing near happened to hear his question; she at once volunteered to go for a priest to the Pro-Cathedral or elsewhere. In order to do this, she had to cross the street which was being swept at the time with machine gun fire, but she never hesitated; she was only in her teens, but the younger those girls were the braver they seemed. The priest she brought back with her said she was as cool as a cucumber when the door was opened to admit her, smiling away, as if the city had resumed its normal life, and that there was no such thing as bullets whistling through the streets in all directions. She even waited for Fr. Flanagan on their way back to the GPO whilst he paused to attend to a dying man. I may here mention that the good father remained in Headers, till we had to evacuate it. He gave untold joy and consolation to everyone, especially the wounded, and I am sure his kindness will never be forgotten by any one of us. He heard the confession of the dispatch rider and sent him off in good spirits for the fair city of Lee [Cork], where I hope he arrived in safety.[39]

By 10 p.m. that night, Sackville Street was ablaze. The GPO's outposts had to be abandoned. Across the road, the roof of the Imperial Hotel was hit with incendiary shells; its roof fell in, and glass windows exploded with the heat. The decision was made. They would break out, but they were unable to cross to the GPO because of the intense British firepower. Hopefully they could escape northward to rendezvous north of the county with the Fingal brigade, who, they had been told, were in the field. Seamus Daly vividly recalled their departure:

So we were moving out. The first problem was to get rid of the Cumann na mBan girls. We had about seven or eight of them. Miss Hoey was in charge of them. We put her in charge. She used to be Arthur Griffith's secretary in the early days of Sinn

Fein. She was a most efficient and hard working woman during the whole thing.
And there was Miss Connor, a rather elderly lady from Kerry. I don't know what
became of her. They looked after the meals for the men during the week. They
escaped by the back. We got out the men by the back. I had nothing to do with that,
but Frank Drennan told me that he was getting the women across out through the
buildings into Earl Street and from there brought across the street into the Presby-
tery in Marlborough Street.[40]

It was dark now. The shelling had ceased. There was just the occasional shot
of a sniper. In the stillness of the night Captain Frank Henderson of F. Company, 2nd Battalion, reflected:

As night approached, it was apparent that the fires which had been caused by the
enemy were increasing in volume, and were getting nearer to us. I went up on the
roof of the GPO in the darkness to get an idea of position, and found that we were
practically surrounded by fire.

At Jacob's biscuit factory, the garrison had been isolated. Nothing more
was needed to be done by the British until they were ready. By Thursday evening, every outpost of Boland's Mill, down to the Grand Canal, had fallen to
the British. Max Caulfield, who had spoken to many of the survivors of Easter
week, was to write in 1965:

If the 2/6th South Staffords had attacked deValera's headquarters at dawn, they
almost certainly would have scattered the rebels like children. Rebel nerves, after a
taut jittery night, had reached breaking point, and actual physical weariness was
such that when Volunteer Lyons attempted to report to Captain John McMahon, his
Company C.O. in the bakery, he found him stretched out across an orange box like a
carcass of dead meat. Several other officers and men lay on the cement floor, utterly
exhausted.[41]

In the streets behind the Four Courts, there had been close-quarters fighting.
Out of humanity, the Irish called for a temporary truce to allow the British
to withdraw their dead and wounded, cut down in crossfire from so many
Republican positions. Against the Four Courts itself, the British had made
advances. They had succeeded in crossing the river, and they held the surrounding streets to the east of the Courts. Catherine Byrne, a member of
Cumann na mBan, bringing in a message from Pearse on Wednesday, discovered that there was no one looking after the needs of the Volunteers in
the Four Courts' outposts, and she was given permission to return the following day to administer to them:

As soon as it got bright in the morning I cleared out and reached King Street. Luck-
ily I recognized two Volunteers at the barricade there. I spent the rest of the week
there attending to the wants of the men. We had really no casualties. I paid a visit to
Fr. Matthew Hall twice. On one of those occasions, as I have already said, I saw
Liam Clarke lying on a stretcher. I bought ammunition to the men at the barricade
from the house where it was dumped.[42]

Within Marrowbone Lane Distillery, early that Thursday morning, the men of the garrison looked out from their posts. They discovered that the South Dublin Union garrison was completely surrounded by British troops and that a "battle royal" was under way. As the day progressed, sniper fire gave way to an all-out fight at the distillery. The Volunteers manned their stations, with the young women of Cumann na mBan by their sides loading rifles. Each Volunteer had three rifles. The British forces, estimated at three battalions, attacked in extended formation across the fields from the south and west. As they approached, a number of them broke ranks and made a dash for the boundary wall and safety. By 2 p.m., the garrison reasoned that there would be an intensive assault. In preparation, all the women were moved into the main hall for their own safety. The men were issued with hand grenades. As the British moved forward, they came into view of the Volunteers on the upper floors of the Distillery, who opened fire on them, causing more casualties. Under the cover of darkness, the British were able to bypass the distillery and gained access to the South Dublin Union grounds, only to be involved in friendly fire before retiring. That night, from the upper stories of the distillery, the Volunteers watched as Dublin burned.

Friday, 28th April, at 2 a.m., General Sir John Maxwell arrived in Dublin and assumed command of the British forces in the city. The newly arrived 2/4th Lincolnshire Regiment relieved the 2/6th South Staffordshire Regiment. A close cordon was established along the line of the Grand Union Canal, effectively sealing the south side of the city. The 2/5th and 2/6th South Staffordshire Regiments were sent to reinforce the British forces in the Four Courts area. The 2/6th Sherwood Foresters and the 3rd Royal Irish Regiment were moved west, against the GPO in Sackville Street. The 5th Leinsters moved against the GPO from the east in a pincer movement. Throughout the morning, the British troops closed in on the rebel positions, greatly assisted by a battery of field artillery.

Friday morning dawned. It was a beautiful spring morning. In the GPO, anticipating that a barrage of artillery fire would come at daylight, all explosives were moved from the roof down to the cellars of the building for greater safety. Orders went out to recall the men in the Liffey-Abbey Street outposts. Up on the roof, during the previous night, teams of men had been doing their best to prevent the roof from catching fire. The inevitable barrage began. Using spotters, the British gunners soon found the range, and shell after shell rained down on the GPO. The incendiary shells melted the lead on the roof, setting the building on fire. It began on the corner of the roof nearest O'Connell Bridge and burned from the top down. By about 4 p.m., the whole portico at the entrance to the building was a mass of flames. Down on the ground floor, the Republican leaders realized that they had no choice but to evacuate the building. At 6:30 p.m. or thereabouts, Commandant Joseph

Plunkett instructed the medical staff to get the wounded men and nurses ready to evacuate headquarters immediately. Some eight Volunteers were instructed by Pearse to act as their escort. Lined up to leave, Pearse addressed the women, thanking them for what they had done. Aine Ryan was one of the women Pearse praised for their bravery. In later life, she vividly remembered:

> On Friday Patrick Pearse sent for all of us girls and made a very nice speech to us. He compared us to the women of Limerick. I often regret I did not take down the speech in shorthand. He said he wished that everyone of us who was not qualified in first aid should leave, as the fighting would get very severe and it would probably come to using bayonets to fight their way out.
>
> Leslie Price took charge of those of us who were to leave. She carried a Red Cross flag. There were quite a number who remained.... We came out through the wall of a building in Henry Street. Sean McDermott and Patrick Pearse were standing inside the wall of the building and shook hands with each one of us as we passed out. I think the building was the Coliseum Cinema. Leslie brought us down Henry Street to Jervis Street Hospital on the suggestion of Father Flanagan, who had been down there already. It was full to overflowing. We were not admitted, but a nun spoke to Leslie and we marched on the Capel Street after Leslie and the flag. We turned right from Capel Street into Parnell Street. When we arrived at the junction with O'Connell Street-Cavendish Row, the military stopped Leslie and interrogated her but let us pass on.[43]

Aoife de Burca was also in the evacuee party, and she recalled (with some slight variance) the same sequence of events:

> It was now about 7 p.m. when all was ready and the order given to march, so off we started, accompanied by Fr. Flanagan, who carried the Red Cross flag. Each of us was laden with stores, some carrying First Aid requisites, others food, for, of course we did not know what fate would overtake us before we reached our destination which was Jervis Street Hospital. Our way lay through the Waxworks and on through passages which had been blasted for the purpose of retreat into the Coliseum Theatre. We had to proceed very slowly and cautiously on account of the wounded. It took us a considerable time to get through; part of the time we were in danger of bullets from the enemy, and the least little stumble over debris might have revealed our whereabouts. As long as I live I shall never forget that night; the suspense was awful.

Eventually they arrived at the refreshment bar of the coliseum. Here they waited in the dark while a door was forced into a back street. While they waited, the building was showered with machine-gun fire. DeBurca confessed that she had tried to pray:

> I tried to make an act of fervent contrition, but the situation was bordering on the comical as well as tragedy, so I burst out laughing instead. Another girl did likewise, and very soon we were all at it. I remember one Volunteer saying, 'That's right, let's keep our spirits up though we are facing death." Anyway, that laugh did us good and I recollect wishing not to die so that I could relate it all someday.

At last, after about three quarters of an hour, the firing stopped. Off they set again, through the upper balcony of the theater and down the wide staircase, and out through a side entrance into the street. Eventually they reached a lane that led to the back entrance of the Jervis Street Hospital. To their horror, they discovered that the buildings on either side of the lane were ablaze. Father Flanagan seized the initiative and shouted to the others, "We'll rush the flames, it's our only chance. Follow me!" With that he dashed through the flames, carrying the Red Cross flag. The others followed him in single file, the girls holding up their skirts. On the other side, they were almost at their destination when a voice called out, "Halt or I fire!" They stopped as ordered and Father Flanagan called back, "Wounded men and nurses for Jervis Street Hospital." Father Flanagan and captured British Army doctor Lt. Mehony stepped forward to be recognized. The party was then allowed to proceed. At the hospital, the men were separated from the women and led away. With their patients taken into care, the women were dismissed.

Back in the GPO, things were desperate. An attempt to create an escape route for the remainder of the garrison was thwarted by superior British firepower. At 8 p.m., Pearse told the remaining garrison that they would have to vacate the building. It was 8:40 p.m. when the withdrawal from the GPO began. A van was dragged across the lane outside to give some shelter to the departing insurgents. Connolly was carried out on a stretcher. There were three women with him: Winifred Carney, Julia Grennan, and Elizabeth O'Farrell. Pearse brought up the rear. The escapees all reached the Moore Street end of Henry Place and temporary safety.

After the withdrawal of the British troops from the South Dublin Union, everything was quiet until Friday afternoon, when troops were spotted around the Rialto Bridge over the canal. The Volunteers at the Union and Marrowbone Lane settled down in their positions, alert now to a probable assault. It began about 4 p.m., with the Volunteers returning fire. As it grew dark, the firing subsided. Both Republican garrisons were now isolated. The British had only to wait. At the Four Courts and beyond, fighting had become intense. Gradually the British were forcing the defenders back into an area tight around the Courts. In the process, the British were taking heavy losses. Boland's Mill had been isolated and surrounded. Surrender was inevitable.

By 11 a.m. on Saturday morning, General Maxwell, commander-in-chief of the British forces in Dublin, was preparing for the final assault. From Great Britain street, an eighteen-pounder began to shell the post office and its adjoining buildings. Across the river, at the junction of D'Olier and Westmorland streets, artillery also began shelling rebel positions along Sackville Street. The 3rd Royal Irish Regiment and 100 men from the Sherwood Foresters waited to assault the rebel GHQ. Elsewhere the 2/5th and 2/6th South Staffordshire Regiment crossed the river to reinforce the final engagement against the rebels in the Four Courts. Obtaining the surrender of the Volunteer Executive in the GPO became the priority. Their surrender would bring about a general ceasefire.

Early on Saturday morning, from their new headquarters, the Volunteers saw a group of civilians leaving Moore Street, just behind the burning GPO building. The party was led by a man carrying an improvised white flag. An order was shouted from the British barricade: "Females advance, and males stand." The women moved off, leaving the men. Then there was a burst of gunfire.

The Republican command decided to break through the British lines and link up with the Four Courts garrison, not realizing that it was not now possible. They began burrowing holes in walls from one house to the next. Supplies were first taken through, then the wounded. The advance party was forced to stop burrowing. The British were everywhere. Pearse recognized the futility of continuing. If only to prevent the deaths of more innocent civilians, the madness had to stop. He consulted with the other members of the provisional government, and together they agreed to open negotiations for a surrender. Sean McDermott approached Elizabeth O'Farrell and asked her to provide a white flag. This was hung out from one of the houses. She then received instructions from Pearse regarding the surrender. With some trepidation she emerged from 15 Moore Street waving a small white flag. The firing stopped, and Miss O'Farrell was beckoned forward toward a British barrier across the top of Moore Street and Parnell Street. At the barrier, she gave her message to an officer. He appointed another officer to escort her up Parnell Street toward the Parnell statue. At 70 Parnell Street the officer commanding the area came out to her. Miss O'Farrell gave her own account of the exchange:

> I said, "The Commandant of the Irish Republican Army wishes to treat with the Commandant of the British Forces in Ireland."
> Officer: "The Irish Republican Army?—the Sinn Feiners you mean."
> I replied, "The Irish Republican Army they call themselves and I think that a very good name too."
> Officer: "Will Pearse be able to be moved on a stretcher?"
> I said: "Commandant Pearse doesn't need a stretcher."
> Officer: "Pearse does need a stretcher, madam."
> I again answered: "Commandant Pears doesn't need a stretcher."
> To the other officer: "Take that Red Cross off her and bring her over there and search her—she is a spy."[44]

The red crosses were cut off of Miss O'Farrell's sleeve and the front of her apron. She was then taken over to the hall of the National Bank on the corner of Parnell Street and Cavendish Row, where she was searched. Satisfied that she was not armed, Miss O'Farrell was then taken to Tom Clarke's shop as a prisoner. Here she waited for the best part of an hour before General Lowe appeared. Unlike his junior officers, he was most courteous to her. She gave him Pearse's message. Lowe listened, then the two of them got into Lowe's staff car and were driven to the top of Moore Street. Lowe instructed her to go back to Pearse and tell him that "General Lowe would not treat at all until he (Mr. Pearse) would surrender unconditionally." He gave her half an hour to return with Pearse's response. In the meantime, the fighting would continue. It was then 2:25 p.m. At Volunteer temporary headquarters, 16 Moore Street, she gave Lowe's message to Pearse. The letter was read out loud for all to hear. The senior officers discussed the matter, and coming to an agreement, Pearse gave Miss O'Farrell a written message for Lowe. Returning up Moore Street, she found Lowe waiting in his car. He quibbled that she was a minute late, but not one to be bullied, she proclaimed that she was on time according to her watch. Lowe's aide-de-camp set his watch by hers to avoid any further complications. Lowe read Pearse's message; it was not one of unconditional surrender. Lowe made his demands clear—he would not treat at all unless Pearse agreed to unconditional surrender, and added, "and that Mr. Connolly follows on a stretcher." He gave her another half hour to appear before him with Pearse. If that did not happen, then hostilities would resume. She took the message back. There was a brief discussion, and Pearse agreed to accompany her back to General Lowe. The two of them walked up Moore Street to the junction with Parnell Street, and at 3:30 p.m., Pearse handed his sword to General Lowe. Lowe ordered that Pearse should be detained overnight. Miss O'Farrell was also detained temporarily with a view to having her take Commandant Pearse's order for surrender to the other commandants.

Connolly was carried out onto Parnell Street on a stretcher by four Volunteers and accompanied by three officers. The stretcher party was searched for weapons, then Connolly was ordered to be taken to Dublin Castle. Looking down from a window in the castle's hospital, a Voluntary Aid Detachment (VAD) nurse saw the arrival of the stretcher party:

> The arrival of James Connolly caused an unusual stir. From the window I could see him lying on the stretcher, his hands crossed, his head hidden from view by the archway. The stretcher was on the ground, and at either side stood three of his officers dressed in National Volunteers uniforms; a guard of about thirty soldiers stood around. The scene did not change for about ten minutes or more; somebody gruesomely suggested that they were discussing whether he should be brought in, or if it would be better to shoot him at once. It is more likely they were discussing whether he should be brought in and a small ward in the Officers' Quarters where he could be carefully guarded, was decided upon.
>
> The nurses in charge of him acknowledged, without exception, that he was entirely different from their expectations: no one could have been more considerate, or have been less trouble. About a week after his arrival he had an operation on his

leg. He was strongly opposed to this himself, but until he had been tried, he had to be treated entirely from a medical point of view.[45]

Following his operation, the VAD nurse observed:

> When he was coming round after the ether, the sentry changed, and he turned to the nurse who was minding him and asked, "Have they come to take me away? Must I really die so soon?" All through his behavior was that of an idealist. He was calm and composed during the court-martial, and said, "You can shoot me if you like, but I am dying for my country." He showed no sign of weakness till his wife was brought to say goodbye to him, the night he was shot, and about 3 a.m. he was carried down on a stretcher to the ambulance that was to bring him to kilmainham.

The GPO garrison assembled out on Sackville Street for the surrender. They were searched then marched away under guard. From a porch on the first floor of the Gresham Hotel, Gaelic League member Eileen Costello watched the surrender:

> I saw the Volunteers march out with their arms from the GPO by Henry Street. I also saw a couple of nurses and two or three men wearing Red Cross armlets. Many of the Volunteers at the end of the line spread out from the Rotunda were young boys under twenty. I think these belonged to the Citizen Army. They were not all in uniform but all had rifles. I thought the British soldiers spoke to them very brutally, shouting, "put down your arms." The Volunteers were spread out from the Rotunda past the Gresham Hotel to Cathedral Street.
>
> I heard the clatter of the rifles as they fell on the cobbles. I knew some of the men—Patrick and Willie Pears, McDonagh, McDermott and Kent. I had been meeting them continually at Gaelic League functions. I began to think what fate was in store for them and I began to weep. "Turn out your pockets," shouted an English officer. I saw many sets of rosary beads, envelopes and photographs being left on the ground. Then I heard "Take off these armlets. You have no right to them anyhow."
>
> I was gazing down at this sorrowful scene when I felt a tap on my shoulder and a voice saying, "Will you retire to your room, Madam?" It was one of two snipers [who had been on the roof of the hotel]. "Now," said the sniper. "we know more about you than you think." I was not frightened. "You have been signaling from the back windows," he accused. I told him that if I had been a Sinn Feiner I would have been outside with my friends and not signaling from back windows. "You're a whole-hogger," he said. "Yes I am." "When I see you weep I thought you was one of them," he said. I told him that I knew many of their young men and that I was anxious about them. "You have a mother's heart," he said.[46]

At the British Army temporary headquarters, General Lowe presented Elizabeth O'Farrell with five typewritten copies of Pearse's order to surrender; one of them was signed by Connolly for his own ICA men in the GPO area and in St. Stephen's Green. Miss O'Farrell was directed to deliver them. From Moore Street she proceeded toward the Four Courts with a guard:

> The guard left me at a barricade at Little Mary Street, after which I crossed the barricade and proceeded up East Arran Street.... I met Fr. Columbus of Church Street:

I had a little white flag with me and I told him where I was going, so he took the flag and offered to accompany me. We passed Charles Street, and went over into the side entrance of the Four Courts. We called in for some volunteers and saw Captain ——. We told him we had a message for Commandant Daly. He told us we would have to go round the quays to the corner of Church Street; this we did and found Commandant Daly strongly entrenched there. I gave him the order and told him of the Headquarters surrender. He was very much cut up about it but accepted his orders as a soldier should.[47]

Commandant Daly addressed his officers, informing them of the order to surrender. There was a protest. The Four Courts garrison was holding off the British. Why should they surrender? Daly was emphatic; the men must obey the Commander-in-Chief's order and lay down their arms. News of the surrender was quickly spread throughout the garrison. On an upper floor Volunteer Sean Kennedy recalled what happened next:

Some time about 4 p.m. on Saturday afternoon I heard a shout from the ground floor to my post, which I manned in company with Bob Leggett, to vacate our position and report down to the courtyard as the fight was over, or words to that effect.

I cannot say who gave us the message but myself and Leggett came down as directed and when we reached the courtyard I noticed other members of the garrison had fallen in—We fell in. We were told by Commandant Daly when we reached the courtyard, to hand our rifles out through the railings to British troops who were outside. The British troops were accompanied by a Capuchin Father from Church Street.[48]

It was about 7:45 p.m. that Saturday night when the Republican troops from the Four Courts marched up O'Connell Street and lined up.

Miss O'Farrell, her work done for the day, was found a room for the night overlooking Parnell Street. The next morning:

About 6 o'clock on Sunday morning I arose. On looking out of the window I saw about 300 or 400 Volunteers, and Miss Grenan and Miss Carney, who had left the Post Office with me, lying on the little plot of grass at Parnell Street in front of the Rotunda Hospital, where they had spent the night in the cold and damp. All their arms and ammunition were piled up at the foot of the Parnell statue. I had only just finished dressing when I was told I was wanted downstairs by Captain Wheeler to take round the orders to the other Commandants.

Wheeler, who was married to Constance Markievicz's cousin, drove her by car halfway up Grafton Street. Here, he halted, and she proceeded up to the College of Surgeons on her own, carrying a white flag. It was about 11 a.m., when up on the roof of the college a sniper saw a woman approach. It was Nurse Elizabeth O'Farrell, carrying her small white flag. She was recognized and instructed to go around to the side entrance in York Street. Here, she was admitted. She asked to speak to Commandant Mallin. As Mallin was sleeping, O'Farrell was taken to see Constance Markievicz. With Pearce's note, countersigned by Connolly, in her hand, Markievicz woke Mallin and told him of the order to surrender. Mallin merely acknowledged that he had received the note but did not comment. Miss O'Farrell withdrew and retraced her steps to find Captain Wheeler.

Mallin summoned the men in the various outposts to report back to the college. A number of his officers were opposed to surrendering and proposed that they should break out and make for the hills, fighting as guerrillas. Mallin rejected their proposal: "As soldiers we came into this fight obeying orders. I will now obey this order by James Connolly to surrender."

From Grafton Street by a circuitous route, Wheeler and Nurse O'Farrell drove to Boland's Mill. At Butt Bridge, O'Farrell dismounted and continued on foot, trusting the white flag that she carried. She was directed by a group of Volunteers to the Grand Canal Street Dispensary. Here she was directed to the rear of the building and admitted through a small window into a small room. De Valera at first thought it was some British hoax, but when other Volunteers verified who Miss O'Farrell was, he realized that she was to be trusted. However, he refused to surrender unless he had a direct order from Commandant McDonagh. O'Farrell returned to Captain Wheeler, and from there they progressed toward Jacob's factory. Here Nurse O'Farrell delivered the order from Pearse to McDonagh to surrender. McDonagh refused to obey. O'Farrell relayed what was discussed:

> He brought me into a small room and told me he would not take orders from a prisoner, that he, himself, was next in command and he would have nothing to say to the surrender until he would confer with General Lowe, the members of the Provisional Government already prisoners, and the officers under his command. An interview was then arranged by Fr. Augustine for Commander McDonagh with General Lowe. This took place outside St. Patrick's Park at about 3 o'clock.
>
> Commandant McDonagh then went to Marrowbone Lane Distillery to consult Commandant Ceannt, and after this consultation agreed to surrender also.

Constance Markievicz was an officer in the College of Surgeons garrison.

Earlier that Sunday morning in Marrowbone Lane, the girls of Cumann na mBan cooked breakfast for the men. About midday, the garrison was summoned to fall in. Rose McNamara recalled:

> Captain calls all the men together about 12 o'clock p.m. in the back yard; we all assemble too. He addresses us all in the most soul-stirring manner. He asked if there were any complaints about food or sleep. All answer "No," and if they were prepared to fight to the last, even tho' the old enemy whom we are fighting, played her old game and starved us out. They all shouted "Yes."[49]

They all returned to their posts. Save for the occasional rifle shot, all was quiet. Around 4 p.m., others in the garrison heard the men at the gate cheering. It announced the arrival of Commandant MacDonagh of the 2nd Battalion and the Reverend Father Augustine. He brought news of the surrender. McDonagh addressed his men, "Boys, it is not my wish to surrender, but after consultation with Commandant Ceannt and other officers, we think it is the best thing to do—if we do not surrender now they will show no mercy to the leaders already prisoners." He gave the orders to file in and prepare to march. Rose McNamara remembered the telling of the sad news, and "McDonagh leaves crying." Soon after, a British officer, Captain Rotherham, arrived to take the surrender. The men of the garrison were brought to attention and numbered off. They totaled slightly over one hundred. Commander Con Colbert addressed the men and women under his command. He informed them that he had received a dispatch from Commandant Ceannt to cease fire. The order had come from Supreme Command Headquarters. Ceannt and his men were waiting outside. Colbert announced that anyone wishing to escape should do so now. A few took up the option. Colbert then re-formed the people under his command, and with sloped arms they marched out of the distillery. Rose McNamara remembered:

> We (Cumann na mBan) all collected in front of the fort and shake hands of all the men and gave them all "God Speed," and told them to cheer up. Some of them were sad and some trying to be cheerful. After command from Captain to form fours all marched out the front gate through the city to St. Patrick's Park (Ross Road), all the girls marching behind, singing: one of our girls picked up a rifle in the street, carried it on her shoulder. We all (22 of us) gave ourselves up and marched down between two lines of our brave men.

Down Ross Road they marched, more like victors than the defeated, where at 6 p.m., Ceannt surrendered his men and also the women of Cumann na mBan attached to his command. Rose McNamara continues:

> We waited until all the arms were taken away. The men gave each of us their small arms to do as we liked with, thinking we were going to go home, but we were not going to leave the men we were with all the week to their fate; we decided to go along with them to the end whatever Our fate might be. Some of the girls had as many as three revolvers; some had more.

They were marched to Richmond Barracks. Annie Cooney takes up the story:

> We marched right into the big square where we were halted. There we were separated from the men who were put into a separate building. We were all—22 of us—brought into a large building up the stairs and we were first put into a rather small room, where we were divided up for the night, eleven of us in each of two rooms. A British military sergeant had charge of us and brought us tea in a bucket and some hard biscuits which we called dog biscuits. We ate and drank, what we got, as we were hungry. The sergeant apologized for the sort of food he had to give us.[50]

Later that day, the women from the other garrisons joined them. Little Rosie Hackett wrote of the hostile crowd they had to pass from the Four Courts to the Richmond Barracks. These were mostly the women of the slums whose husbands were soldiers in the British Army. Labor leader William Partridge told them to ignore the taunts and swearing, as Rosie relates:

> Mr Partridge was very good to us. He felt for us very much, because the crowds outside were terribly hostile. You could not imagine how they could be so terrible. He kept telling us: "Now girls, heads erect."[51]

Captain Wheeler and Miss O'Farrell returned to Trinity College to inquire whether they should try again to get the Boland's Mill garrison to surrender. In the meantime, however, deValera had surrendered. Diarist Lilly Stokes saw deValera and his men as they marched along the road and into captivity:

> Maive, Captain Ellis, the pretty girl and I nipped back and were just in time to see 70 prisoners from Bolands march past, fine looking fellows, swinging along in good step. Of course they looked shabby and dirty, they had been fighting for seven days. Until I saw them I thought they ought to be shot, but I don't know—it would be [a] terrible waste of material, if it was nothing else—it made me miserable to see them.
>
> The leader in Bolands was a fine looking man called the Mexican, he is educated and speaks like a gentleman.[52]

Nurse O'Farrell, having done General Lowe's bidding, was then shamefully treated:

Rosie Hackett served in the College of Surgeons garrison.

I asked if I was a prisoner, and he [an un-named British junior officer] replied,

"Very much a prisoner." I protested and said that I had General Lowe's word of honor that I should not be made a prisoner and he replied, "Oh, don't worry, you won't be lonely, as your friends, Dr. Lynn and Miss Molony, and all the rest, will be here in a few minutes—they are only taking exercise." I discovered the place was Ship Street Barracks. In the room there was a couple of tables and a plank affair, something like a bed on the floor. After some time Dr. Lynn, Miss Molony and nine others came in, and were quite surprised to see me—those eleven women had been lodged in this small room from the previous Tuesday. We then had dinner, consisting of bully-beef, biscuits and water provided by the military, and to this fare I contributed a barm-brack, an apple and a few sweets, which I had since I left the GPO on Friday night while we were at dinner another soldier came and took our names, and told us that when we had finished we were to be sent off somewhere else.... It was about 4 p.m. when we women were marched down to Kilmainham prison and delivered up to two other officers, counted and signed for.

Hearing of Miss O'Farrell's treatment, General Lowe immediately ordered her release. She in turn was complimentary to him and the other officers she had worked with: "I would like to say that I found General Lowe, Captain Wheeler and Lieutenant Royal most courteous."

Eilis O'Conell and a few companions who had avoided arrest now began to make their way back to their respective homes:

Every street corner was now lined with armed British Tommies and after zigzagging from one street to another in order to avoid the soldiers, we reached North Frederick Street in the evening, having passed another day without food—except the breakfast we got in the morning from Brother Pacificus.

Here we met two members of the Keating Branch who escorted us to the friendly restaurant of the Misses Molloy where we were treated to tea. They were more than kind and sympathetic. We then made our way to Fleming's Hotel, Gardiner's Place, where we met Miss McMahon, our secretary. We were welcomed back, and we told of our experiences during the week....[53]

The men of the Easter Rising, those perceived as having played only minor roles, were shipped over the English prisons, then later all gathered together at a former German prisoner-of-war camp at Frongoch in Wales. As the days passed, many wondered what might happen next. In New York, Mary Colum, an original founding member of Cumann na mBan, saw the newspaper billboards:

On a May morning, a fair sunny day, as I got off the subway at Grand Central on my way to see Mrs. Moody, who had come to New York, I saw the headlines of the early afternoon papers. Pearse, MacDonagh, and Clarke executed. I must have sat for long in the waiting room in a dream or a semi coma, for when I looked at the station clock it was late afternoon and I saw my husband standing in front of me. Day by day the roll of the executed continued, a few each day—Joseph Plunkett, Count Plunkett's son, a delicate idealistic poet boy, John McBride, Maud Gonne's husband, who had been in so many fights that when they wanted to bandage his eyes before he faced the firing squad he waved them aside with the remark, "I have looked down the barrel of a gun too long to bother about one now." There was the strong labor leader and organizer, James Connolly, who was shot seated because he could not stand on account of his wounds; there were the others, all those who had signed the proclamation or who had led battalions.[54]

London-based Patricia Lynch, having traveled back to Dublin days after the Rising had failed, was sitting down for lunch when the waitress approached her:

> In the restaurant where I had my lunch a waitress, pale-faced, haggard-eyed, told me that her sweetheart was a prisoner; she feared he would be shot. "They don't shoot German prisoners, although they call them 'Huns' and 'baby-killers'; they only shoot our brave Irish boys."[55]

Though the Volunteers had fought as a regular army, wearing a distinctive uniform, and had followed the rules of accepted warfare, they were not initially treated as prisoners of war, but rather as rebels and traitors.

Then there were the women prisoners: What to do with them? There were seventy-nine of them being held at Kilmainham or Richmond Barracks. Twenty-four of them were members of the women's section of the Irish Citizen Army. Some of them would have borne arms during the insurrection. The women from the lower ranks, some sixty-two of them, were treated as silly girls, and after a good talking to, they were released on 8th May. Emily Norgrove was one such young woman:

> Each of us was brought down and interrogated by Army Officers seated at a long table. We were asked … what we were doing in the garrisons, our answer was first aid when needed, some cooking if necessary, that was all that was asked of us, then we were brought back to our cells.[56]

Seventeen women, more prominent in the movement, including women who had not taken part in the Rising, were placed in the female wing of Mountjoy Prison while investigations against them continued. Five were then released, including Madeleine ffrench-Mullen. That left just eight. They were the fifty-eight-year-old Countess Plunkett, who was deported under the defense of the Realm Act to Oxford; Dr. Kathleen Lynn, deported to Bath; James Connolly's secretary, Winifred Carney; Marie Perolz; Helena Molony; Breda Foley; and Ellen Ryan, all deported to Aylesbury in Buckinghamshire. They were obliged to live at specific addresses at their own expense and to report regularly to the local police station. Some, unable to keep themselves, were interned at Aylesbury Prison.

That left just one female prisoner: Constance Markievicz (née Gorez Booth), a senior officer under Michael Mallin at the College of Surgeons. She was charged on 4th May 1916, in that she "did an act, to wit did take part in an armed rebellion and in waging war against His Majesty the King, such an act being of such a nature as to be calculated to be prejudicial to the Defence of the Realm and being done with the intention and purpose of assisting the enemy." In short, she was charged with treason—which carried the death penalty.

A subdued Markievicz stood before the court. Prosecutor William Wylie recorded the event:

> I saw the general getting out his revolver and putting it on the table beside him. But he need not have troubled for she curled up completely: "I am only a woman," she cried, "and you cannot shoot a woman, you must not shoot a woman." She never stopped moaning the whole time she was in the courtroom.... She crumpled up.... I think we all felt slightly disgusted [at a person who] had been preaching to a lot of silly boys, death and glory, die for your country, etc., and yet she was literally crawling. I won't say anymore; it revolts me still.[57]

It has to be said that Wylie had no reason to lie. Markievicz for her part was undoubtedly suffering from post-traumatic shock and struggling mentally with what was going on. The verdict of the court was "Guilty. Death by being shot." Having been briefed as to the inevitable verdict, Prime Minister Herbert Asquith had decreed that no woman was to be executed. He wished to retain the moral high ground. In the previous year, English nurse Edith Cavall had been shot by the Germans for spying. Her death became a powerful anti-German propaganda tool. Shooting Markievicz would have produced cries of hypocrisy from around the world. Accordingly, the court recom-

Suffragettes Hanna and Francis Sheehy Skeffington. Francis was shot by British forces at the start of Easter week, 1916.

mended that the prisoner be shown mercy, "solely, and only, on account of her sex." The death sentence was commuted to life imprisonment. Markievicz was temporarily moved to Kilmainham Prison to await transportation to England. She was later sent to Aylesbury Prison in Buckinghamshire, and there she joined fellow prisoners Winifred Carney, Helena Molony, and Ellen O'Ryan.

With the execution of the leaders of the Rising, the British created martyrs. Attitudes changed, and apathy among the people of Ireland now turned to sympathy and then to anger. Hanna Sheehy Skeffington, who had been so opposed to the armed cause, now expressed her sorrow for the men and women killed, which included the murder of her own husband. She wrote in the suffragette newspaper *The Irish Citizen* in September 1916:

> The ranks of the suffragists have been sadly depleted by the events of Easter week: the Irish Volunteers and the Citizens' Army were suffragists almost to a man, the women prominent in the movement were all convinced and practical exponents of the doctrine of equality of the sexes.... Of the dead leaders James Connolly stands foremost as a friend of suffrage, and of many a progressive cause an unfailing and courageous champion ... never a jibe at womanhood fell from his lips—with the wisdom of true statesmanship, that ought to have something of the seer, he recognized that the cause of Women and Labor was twin, and this gospel he preached unfailingly to his followers. James Connolly deserves a shrine in the heart of every suffragist.

5

1916–1919
Marking Time

Many of the families of those killed or interned after the Rising now found themselves in dire economic straits, without any source of income. Over twenty-five hundred men either directly, or indirectly, involved in the Rising had been imprisoned. As in the days of the Ladies' Land League, in the absence of the men, it was the women who stepped forward to fill the void and offer assistance. The women of Cumann na mBan, whose doctrine included the raising of funds for the Volunteers, were the first to come to the aid of the dependents. In Dublin, their meager funds of some £200 was quickly spent in answering the immediate needs of the Volunteers' families. What was needed was a properly organized fund-raising association. This was to be the Irish Volunteers Dependent Fund (IVDF), founded by Cathleen Clarke, Aine Ceannt, and Sorcha McMahon, and drew upon the membership of Cumann and others for organizational and clerical assistance. It advertised its formation, and its aims, in newspapers throughout Ireland:

IRISH VOLUNTEER DEPENDENTS' FUND

The Committee of the above Fund, consisting as it does of the near relatives of the execute leaders of the Insurrection of Easter Week, confident of the sympathy of their compatriots, earnestly appeal for adequate supplies for the carrying on of the work they have undertaken in the full assurance that they are acting as their dead husbands, sons, and brothers would wish.

The members of the Committee are convinced that the Irish people are desirous of succoring the dependents of those who suffered by the Rebellion, and we, the undersigned, feel assured that it is only necessary to indicate the extent of the assistance required to secure it in generous measure. The families of the men executed, killed in fighting, imprisoned or deported for their participation in the Rising are a charge on the nation.

Trustees—Mrs Tom Clarke, S. Nic Mhathghamha and E. MacRaghnaill.
Offices: 1, College Street, Dublin
Mrs Tom Clarke, President; Mrs Eamonn Ceantt, Vice-President:
S. Nic Mhathgamha, Hon. Treasurer; E. MacRaghnaill, Hon. Secretary.[1]

The fund dealt solely with the relatives and dependents of the executed and imprisoned Volunteers. At more or less the same time, a separate organization, the Irish National Aid Association, was also founded. It was established by members of the old Parliamentary Party and influential nationalist men and women in Ireland. It worked on broader lines than the IDVF. Not being connected to extreme and violent republicanism, it had the backing of the Catholic Church. The INAA announced its formation in the following terms:

> Other Associations have charge of the question of general distress and meet its special and urgent claims. Our Association appeals for immediate and national aid on behalf of another class not included there—the destitute families of some 300 men slain during the Insurrection, of 15 executed by court-martial, of 134 condemned to penal servitude, of 2,650 deported without trial, and of about 400 awaiting sentence of court-martial.[2]

Common sense prevailed and saw the amalgamation of the two organizations in August 1916, at the Gresham Hotel in Dublin. The new organization was known as the Irish National Aid Association and Volunteer Dependents Fund (INAAVDF), rather a mouthful. It established offices at 10 Exchequer Street, Dublin. There were strong objections by the IVD members to the presence of certain Irish Party members, in particular representatives from the Ancient Order of Hibernians. The objection was noted, and a committee was formed comprising twelve members of each of the former committees. Five labor members were also included, reflecting the part that the ICA had played. Father Bowden from the pro-Cathedral, a nominee of Archbishop Walsh, was appointed as administrator. Parish committees were established all over Ireland to raise money. There were door-to-door and parish door collections, meetings, and lantern shows. Thousands of photographs of the leaders of the Rising were produced and sold. In the process, the populace was politicized. Home Rule was no longer an option. The people began calling for a republic. To a considerable extent, this motivation was brought about by the successful takeover of the amalgamated committee by the Republican widows, Kathleen Clarke; Nancy, the American-born widow of Michael O'Rahilly; and Padraig Pearse's mother, Margaret. In its first national parish collection that same August, the INAAVDF raised £968. Later, money started coming in from America, as well as from Irish people living in England, Scotland, Canada, and Australia. It was noted that people living in poverty-stricken areas in London and Glasgow also contributed to the fund. One example was the O'Donovan-Rossa Club of 17 Defoe Road, Tooting, London, who sent £10.

The money raised in that first year enabled the committee to send Hanna Sheehy Skeffington, Nora Connolly, and Margaret Skinnider to undertake further fund-raising in the United States. Upon her return to Ireland, stopping off at Liverpool, Mrs. Sheehy Skeffington was presented with a Notice under the Defence of the Realm Act, issued by the secretary of state, denying her entry into Ireland. It was to prove but a temporary setback. Hanna went on a hunger strike. Not wishing for the death of a second Sheehy Skeffington, the government gave way after a few days, and she continued on her way to Dublin.

Throughout its life as an institution, the INAAVDF distributed some £138,000 to the dependents. Upon their return, former prisoners each received a lump sum—£40 for married men, and £20 for single men. Later, married men received £250, and single men £150, or the equivalent of a year's salary. The majority of the money raised was distributed through a series of subcommittees known as the Ladies' Distribution Committee, to the dependent families. By and large, these committee women were from Cumann. In September, the INAAVDF set aside £20,000 for the widows and mothers of the men who had been executed. All of this was organized while the soldiers of the Rising were still interned or in prison.

What was not revealed at the time, for obvious reasons, was that the women of Cumann na mBan were also rearming the Volunteers. At the time of the fiftieth anniversary of the Easter Rising, 1966, Eilis Bean Ui Chonail wrote in the *Capuchin Annual*:

> Selected members were quietly at work in a room at number 2, Dawson Street, making Red Cross packages of bandages and iodine—in preparation for the "Go" order. Members were also busy organizing *Ceilidhe,* concerts and other fund-raising functions, but many of the women did Herculean work in transferring guns, saving them from the British group. For some time "small arms" were being transferred from Sheffield as cutlery. The officious eye made the discovery, and rushed the news to Dublin Castle. Cumann na mBan were not beaten because the news was flashed to the headquarters of the Volunteers who, in turn, appealed for Volunteers who, in turn appealed for Volunteers to save the cargo of guns which was in grave danger. Three members of Cumann na mBan rushed to the scene and saved the cargo—one hundred and ten revolvers with ammunition.

As a consequence of such actions, Cathal Brugha observed that "it was the women who kept alive ... and the flag flying."

In England, following a political crisis over the conduct of the war in Europe, Herbert Asquith was ousted as prime minister to be replaced by David Lloyd George. He introduced into his war cabinet Edward Carson, a man whom he had previously given a pledge of a permanent six-county exclusion from Home Rule. Also included were Walter Long, a staunch Ulster Unionist supporter who became colonial secretary, Lord Curzon, Alfred, Viscount Milner, and Andrew Bonar Law, all of whom had urged Ulster's resistance to Home Rule. There was no place for Irish nationalist M.P.s. At the end of May 1916, John Redmond, leader of the Irish Parliamentary Party, and

Edward Carson met with Lloyd George to receive proposals for Home Rule whereby the postponed 1914 Home Rule Act was to be brought into operation immediately for twenty-six of the thirty-two counties of Ireland. The six northeastern counties of Antrim, Down, Armagh, Derry, Fermanagh, and Tyrone were to be excluded during the continuance of the war and for a period of twelve months after. Redmond interpreted this as meaning that after the war, negotiations would continue for the inclusion of the six counties into a united Ireland. But he had been fooled, for the duplicitous "Welsh Wizard" had written to Carson:

> Whitehall Place
> May 29th 1916
>
> Dear Carson,
>
> I enclose Greer's draft propositions.
> We must make it clear that at the end of the provisional period Ulster does not, whether she wills it or not, merge in the rest of Ireland.
>
> Ever sincerely,
> D. Lloyd George.
> P.S. Will you show it to Craig?[3]

When Redmond discovered what was happening, he withdrew his support for the proposal. Later in the year, the wily Lloyd George, in a bid to encourage America to enter the war, released the 560 prisoners in Frongoch, men who had not been specifically sentenced by court martial, but who were being held in Britain without trial. It was portrayed to the Americans as a Christmas gesture of goodwill. The men, and a few women, were all back in Ireland by Christmas morning. The release of the men from Frongoch had previously begun in stages. The first batch arrived at Kingstown (Dun Laoghaire) in August. They included Charles Saurin, Leo Henderson, Arthur Shields (later to become a Hollywood actor), and Seamus Daly. Daly sensed the change that had come about:

> At the time we left [after the failure of the Easter Rising] there was no mistake, the people of Dublin were definitely hostile to us, to the whole thing. But now we sensed change. There was one particularly dour little tram conductor who would never be civil to us before the time. When I got on the tram, he had been chatting on the front platform with the driver. The driver and he came round and shook hands with us heartily, and gave us a welcome home. When we got to Clontarf, there was quite a number of people there, and each shouting to the other, "The boys are coming home." They gave us a friendly reception.[4]

Then, in the days before Christmas 1916, the order came for the release of all the men. The camp was emptied on the day before Christmas Eve. A special train traveled during the night up to Holyhead for embarkation by boat. The first forty of the prisoners arrived on a cattle boat at the North

Wall. Many of them wore Sinn Fein badges, and they marched in military formation along the quays. Another 130 arrived at Westland Row Station by the morning train. Later that day, over three hundred arrived at the North Wall by steamer. On Christmas morning, a further twenty-eight landed at Carlisle Pier, and twenty more traveled through Dublin by train. They were back. News quickly spread around the city, and a breakfast was arranged for the men at Fleming's Hotel.

Things had changed in Ireland with the execution of so many of the leaders of the Rising. Margaret Skinnider, formerly of the St. Stephen's Green garrison, who was herself wounded during the Rising, observed the change:

> When I went back to Dublin in August [1916], it was to find that almost every one on the streets was wearing republican colors. The feeling was bitter too—so bitter that the British soldiers had orders to go about in fives and sixes, but never singly. They were not allowed by their officers to leave the main thoroughfares, and had to be back in barracks before dark—that is, all except the patrol. The city was still under martial law, but it seemed to me the military authorities were really nervous persons. Much of this bitterness came from the fact that people remembered how, after the war in South Africa which had lasted three years instead of five days, only one man had been executed. After our rising sixteen men had been put to death.[5]

In the months after the failure of the Rising, at a time of massive disruption, it was the women who brought together the disparate nationalists under the Sinn Fein umbrella. The women of Cumann na mBan spread the concept of republicanism throughout the country. As for the returning men, they discovered that plans were already under way for the raising of a new army. Recruiting and training had already begun by Christmas 1916, as Sean O'Duffy recalled:

> A movement was set on foot early in October of that year (1916) to reorganize the Volunteers, and A. Company met at Columcillle Hall, Blackhall Place. There the oath of loyalty to the IRA was administered by Dick McKee and Diarmuid O'Hegarty.[6]

Those Volunteers who had taken part in the Rising, but had escaped or evaded capture, had gone to earth. Then, barely three months later, they resurfaced. They were joined by the Volunteer prisoners given early release from Frongoch. Some fifty men, others say eighty, gathered in the summer of 1916 at a house in Rathmines, Dublin, the home of Cathal Brugha, a hero of the Easter Rising. He had fought in the South Dublin, where he was so badly wounded with twenty-five bullet and shrapnel wounds that he was released into the care of his family to die. But he did not. He survived but was forever lame in one leg. Brugha instructed them to get in touch with other members of their companies and battalions and to organize them into units and keep them together until all of their comrades had been released from British prisons. Over the months, the early released prisoners joined them, adding to their numbers. By August 1916, elements of the 2nd Battalion secured premises adjoining Clonliffe College. Meetings were held under the guise of a dancing class, as Seamus Daly was surprised to discover:

> I was a few days home when I got word that the Company had secured premises up in Clonliffe Road in a garage adjoining Clonliffe College wall, and that they were carrying it under the guise of a dancing class. I went up there on one night with several other chaps, and to our surprise we found the place packed out with boys and girls dancing away; but there wasn't more than half a dozen faces I recognized.[7]

At Easter 1917, preparations were made to celebrate the anniversary of the Rising. Tricolor flags and buntings were made. Replicas of the 1916 proclamation were printed and posted around Dublin. On Easter Monday, crowds gathered in O'Connell Street near the ruins of the General Post Office. At midday, a young man, risking life and limb, moved along the upper parapet and draped a large tricolor from a horizontal pole projecting out onto the street. After some trepidation, the police removed the flag, the flying of which was, after all, still illegal. At Liberty Hall, a banner was strewn across the upper floor above the entrance. It read: "James Connolly Murdered, May 12, 1916." The police, who were there in numbers to prevent such a thing, quickly tore it down. That was not to be the last of it. Some of the more resolute of the ICA women—in particular Helen Molony, Rosie Hackett, Jenny Shanahan, and Bridget Davis—grabbed another piece of calico and scrawled upon it the original message. Up through the building to the roof they climbed, barricading the door behind them, and from the roof they unfurled the new banner. A senior police officer ordered the caretaker to remove the banner. He refused, telling them that if they wanted it removed, they would have to do it themselves. More police reinforcements were sent for, and in the meantime, news of the incident drew large crowds. Eventually a group of policemen rushed the building and made their way up to the roof. They broke down the door after much labor and hauled in the offending banner, chastising the women in the process.

There were now incidents that, when viewed in isolation, did not amount to much at the time. Analysis shows that they were acts of defiance, and they were conducted by the ordinary people. Rose Murphy of Dolphin's Barn, Dublin, was arrested and fined ten shillings for displaying a ballad called "The Tool of England" in her shop window. A Miss Holmes of North Main Street, Youghal, who had expressed Republican sentiments had her house raided, and two shotguns were taken away. At Edinburgh, three men and four women—Mary Fullerton, Bridget and Roseann Healey, and Chrissie Little—were arrested for trying to smuggle arms and ammunition into Ireland. Two teenage girls, Maureen Durgan and Evelyn O'Brien of Mount Pleasant,

Ranelagh, Dublin, were prosecuted for displaying a Sinn Fein poster. In November 1918, Susan Walsh, Nora Murphy, Mary Flynn, and Josephine O'Sullivan were arrested in Cork for taking up an illegal collection for the Volunteer Dependents' Fund. In Dublin, Maisie O'Loughlin was charged with selling tricolors outside the church at Rathmines. Also at Rathmines, a Miss Judge refused to give her name in English when approached by two policemen. Finally, in Killarney, a Miss Gleeson's shop was raided and the police seized a number of books: "Handbook for Rebels" and "Ireland's Case Restated."[8]

For the men who returned from Internment in Frongoch, there were also dark days. Many of the men who returned found themselves unemployed or were victimized. The socialists set up the Connolly Co-operative Society, which provided work for those activists who were unemployed following their release. The National Aid Association also helped them out. It supplied them with money and services to get them back on their feet. The fund provided money to buy clothes, boots, railway fares, rent, tools, and medical treatment. They also gave the rank-and-file Volunteers a grant of £20 upon their return so they could have a holiday. Some men who could not return to their old jobs were given grants to set up small businesses, including fruit and vegetable shops, tobacconists and newspaper shops, bootmaking and hairdressing establishments, and market gardens. The INAAVDE also gave grants to the families of men who had been killed in the Rising, usually with a one-off payment and then £1–£2 a week. All of this work was instigated by the largely female members of the organization.

Poster for Sinn Fein in the general election of 1918.

The position of secretary to the INAAVDU became vacant just at the time when the Frongoch internees were released at Christmas 1916. Michael Collins, who had emerged as a leader among the internees thanks to his IRB connection, managed to secure the position of secretary upon his return to Ireland. His work within the INAAVDF gave him access to the network of parish committees throughout the country. Thus, he was able to build up connections and create an intelligence network. Kathleen Clarke, the widow of the executed Tom Clarke, saw his potential as a leader, and she gave him her support to become her husband's successor as chairman of the Supreme Council of the IRB. With that, Collins now had access to the records of that movement, too, and—or but—this enabled him to establish a parallel IRB government, working within the provisional Sinn Fein government. While Eamon deValera was seen as the political leader of republicanism, Collins was seen as the shadowy successor of Padraig Pearse, the "first" president of the Irish Republic. Collins progressively began to secure control of the republican movement for the IRB. Through charm and charisma, he put his plans into action. In this, he was assisted, knowingly or unknowingly, by a number of women. Linda Kearns was one such person:

> The next thing I remember was that Mick Collins and Diarmuid O'Hegarty called to see me early in 1917. They asked me to carry messages to a man called White who lived at a place called Ballinabole about three miles from Collooney, Co. Sligo. The messages were transmitted by White to Alec McCabe, who was on the run at the time. Afterwards, I found out that these messages were connected with the IRB organization. I also was sent to Kilroy's at Newport, Co. Mayo. On some occasions I brought back little bags of bullets that were sent up from Sligo by Alec McCabe.[9]

There was one woman in particular who helped the republican cause as no other. She was Lily Mernin. She was employed as a shorthand typist in the heart of the British administration in Ireland; the adjutant's office in Dublin Castle. Lily's cousin was Piaras Beaslai, later to become director of propaganda in the Irish government. Upon discovering where she worked, he informed Michael Collins. In her brief seven-page witness statement to the Bureau of Military History, she wrote:

> Apparently Beaslai spoke to Michael Collins about me, because some time in 1918, Michael Collins asked to meet me and Piaras Beaslai brought him to my home and introduced him to me as a Mr. Brennan. I did not know he was Collins at the time. He asked me would I be willing to pass out to him any information that might be of value which I would come across in my ordinary day's work. I remember he produced letters that he had intercepted concerning some of the typists and officers in the Castle, and things that are happening generally.... I promised to give him all the assistance that I possibly could.... Each week I prepared a carbon or a typed copy, whichever I was able to get. Sometimes I would bring these to the office placed at my disposal at Captain Moynihan's house, Clonliffe Road.[10]

Captain Jack White, who had trained the ICA under Connolly and later the Volunteers, had escaped retribution following the Rising. No doubt this was due to the fact that he was not directly involved in the Rising. He also had connections within the British Establishment, who traditionally looked after their own. From this position, to give him his due, he now actively badgered the authorities to secure the release of Constance Markievicz. He and other lobbyists were successful, and she was released on 17th June 1917, along with the other prominent imprisoned Republicans. Upon her return to Ireland, the INAAVDF awarded her £500, the amount awarded to the more prominent leaders of the Rising, including Eamon deValera and William Cosgrave. Upon her return to Dublin, Markievicz received a rousing welcome. Headed by James O'Neill, some two hundred men of the ICA, carrying hurlies, marched in military formation to Westland Row Station to meet her train. There they were confronted by a strong police presence. Their orders were to prevent such a demonstration. O'Neill was informed that the police had been given strict orders not to allow anyone onto the platform. O'Neill refused to accept any orders issued from Dublin Castle and called their bluff. He told them what he intended to do. He and a small group were going to meet the train. Then they were going to march in formation back to Liberty Hall. Reluctantly, the senior police officer, not wanting a violent confrontation, stepped to one side. His excuse, thus saving face, was that the ICA men were acting in an orderly fashion. Markievicz was greeted at the platform and escorted into the city aboard a wagonette to much cheering from the crowds. Behind her marched the ICA men in triumph.

Quite extraordinarily, upon her release, Markievicz was treated to strawberries and cream on "the terrace of the House of Commons, with Eva [Gore-Booth, her sister], Esther Roper [Eva's lover], Mr [Alfred] Byrne [Later Mayor of Dublin] and Captain Jimmy White resplendent in top hat and spats."[11] The Establishment had forgiven her, or at least it was prepared to tolerate her. In the autumn of 1917, Markievicz was reelected president of Cumann na mBan. She had been the most prominent female figure in the Rising, and a cult had developed around her. She crucially had the active support of Kathleen Clarke, Margaret Pearse, Aine Ceannt, and Nancy O'Rahilly, otherwise known as "The Widows," who, for the moment, were very influential within the Republican movement.

The Plunkett Convention, named after Count Plunkett, father of the executed Joseph Mary Plunkett, was held on the first anniversary of the Easter Rising. It was held at the Mansion House in Dublin, and representatives from nearly six hundred branches of Cumann na mBan throughout Ireland, were present. In conclusion to his speech to the women, Count Plunkett asked them to stand and affirm their rededication to Ireland, as the Volunteers had recently done. They did so, repeating after Plunkett:

1. That we proclaim Ireland to be a separate nation.
2. That we assert Ireland's right to freedom from all foreign control,

denying the authority of any foreign Parliament to make laws for Ireland.

3. That we affirm the right of the Irish people to declare their will is law, and to enforce their decisions in their own land without let or hindrance from any other country.

4. That, maintaining the status of Ireland as a distinct nation, we demand representation at the coming Peace Conference.

5. That it is the duty of the nations taking part in the Peace Conference to guarantee the liberty of the nations calling for their intervention, releasing the small nations from the control of the greater Powers.

6. That our claim for complete independence is founded on human right ad the law of nations. We declare Ireland has never yielded, and has ever fought, against foreign rule, and we hereby bind ourselves to use every means in our power to obtain complete liberty for our country.

In conjunction, the first anniversary of the Rising saw the establishment of the League of Women Delegates, later renamed Cumann na dTeachtaire. This was a coming together of women from the Inghinidhe branch of Cumann na mBan, the Irish Women Workers' Union, and women from the Irish Citizen Army. Its function was to ensure that the women's voices were heard within the progression for Irish independence. The feminists James Connolly, Thomas McDonagh, and latterly Padraig Pearse were now all dead, and there was no assurance that the equality of women was uppermost in the minds of, or even being considered by, the new leaders of Sinn Fein. With persistence, Cumann na dTeachtaire succeeded in securing positions of four of its members onto the Sinn Fein executive. Constance Markievicz, Kathleen Clarke, Kathleen Lynn, and Grace Plunkett were voted onto the executive. Later, Aine Ceannt became the director of communications, and Hanna Sheehy Skeffington became the director of organization.

Now they had a voice, but were the men listening? The equality of women was not perhaps foremost in the minds of the male Sinn Fein committee members. Their concentration was on winning democratic control. All the rest would follow on later ... probably.

Sinn Fein needed some idea of how much support there was for its avowed aim of an Irish Republic. The opportunity came with a number of byelections. At Roscommon, Sinn Fein put up Count Plunkett, father of the executed Joseph Plunkett, as its candidate. The Parliamentary Party candidate received 1,708 votes; Plunkett received 3,022. A second byelection cropped up in South Longford. Sinn Fein put up Joseph McGuinness as its candidate. At the time, he was a convict in Lewes Prison. The Republican slogan was

"Put him in to get him out." Polling day was 9th May 1917. Eilis Na Riain, of Cumann na mBan, took an active part in McGuinness's campaign:

> I had a particular interest in this election, as the candidate Joe McGuinness, was a personal friend and, incidentally, this was my home constituency. In the early stages of the campaign I arranged a week's leave and set off for the country without delay. I made a personal canvas of my native parish and the surroundings and the fact that I knew the candidate was almost sufficient to convince the people to go to the polls. The candidate was in prison and the slogan, "Put him in to get him out" was ringing in everybody's ears. I was obliged to return at the end of the week. I continued to return at the end of the week. I continued to work in McGuinness's house and at the election office and feverishly awaited the result.... Our joy was great when we heard of the victory and I think we walked the streets all night in our excitement.[12]

Eilis Ni Chorra also worked on the McGuinness campaign:

> The Longford election has become part of our history, and I shall always be glad that I took part in it. How well I remember the tension on the morning after voting day when from the windows of a house opposite the courthouse we waited for the result, and the awful disappointment when it was announced that our opponent, McKenna, was in by a majority of thirteen. There were half a dozen other people, including Count and Countess Plunkett, with us, and we had drawn back from the windows to discuss the matter, when we heard a deep rousing cheer and on looking out saw a big Tricolor being waved from the courtroom window by the brother of our candidate—we knew then that we had won.... Afterwards we learned that our majority was thirty-seven.[13]

The largely unknown McGuinness had won—but by only thirty-seven votes after a recount. It was but a tiny majority, but the English liberal newspaper *The Manchester Guardian* realized the significance of this Sinn Fein victory. It was, it declared, "the equivalent of a serious British defeat in the field." The continued imprisonment of political prisoners had been highlighted by the election. To mitigate against any further demands, Britain now released all the remaining Irish political prisoners.

Early in June 1917, Major Willie Redmond, member of Parliament for East Clare, was killed at Messine in France. Eamon deValera was chosen by his party to stand in the forthcoming byelection. The Parliamentary Party candidate was a popular local man and barrister, Patrick Lynch, K.C. He put forward the argument for continuing the struggle for Home Rule through parliamentary procedure. Uncompromising, deValera declared that he stood for an independent Irish Republic. Nothing else would do. The people of Clare agreed. DeValera received twice as many votes as Lynch: 5,010 against 2,035. Sinn Fein now had three members of Parliament, but members who insisted that they would only sit in an Irish Parliament, Dail Eireann.

On 5th August 1917, Thomas Ashe, hero of the skirmish at Ashbourne in 1916, and a senior member of the IRB, gave an oration to the executed

Roger Casement at Ardfert. Between ten and twelve thousand people gathered to hear him. Three thousand men, many in Volunteer uniform, marched there. There were also three hundred horsemen, five hundred cyclists, and a number of pipe bands who attended. Ashe, now supreme head of the IRB and commandant of the Dublin Brigade, was later arrested for making a seditious speech and sent to Mountjoy Prison. Denied political status, he followed the suffragette tradition and went on a hunger strike. He was force-fed, and in the process his lungs were flooded, and he developed pneumonia, from which he died on 25th September. His funeral was attended by nine thousand uniformed Volunteers. At the graveside, a firing party gave a final salute. Michael Collins stepped forward to give the funeral oration. It was short and to the point: "Nothing additional remains to be said. That volley which we have just heard is the only speech which is proper to make over the grave of a dead Fenian." Such a show of strength at Ashe's funeral alarmed the British authorities so shortly after the rebel defeat of Easter 1916, when it was believed that militant republicanism had been destroyed. An order was issued prohibiting parades, drilling, the carrying of arms, and the wearing of unauthorized uniforms in public. The response of the Volunteer leadership was to challenge this prohibition. On Sunday, 21st October 1917, a series of public parades were held throughout the country. Outnumbered, the forces of law and order could only stand by and watch. They did take note, though, of the names and addresses of those who took part, with a view to making arrests in the future. As a consequence, a number of Volunteers were forced to go "on the run," in order to avoid arrest.

At the end of October 1917, Sinn Fein called a political convention to look at the way forward toward Ireland's independence. It drew about two thousand delegates, including members from over one thousand Sinn Fein clubs in Ireland and Britain. A committee was formed to run the campaign. It was thought that there would be a contest for the presidency, but both Count Plunkett and Arthur Griffith, the two leading contenders, stood down by agreement, in favor of Eamon deValera. In accepting the nomination, deValera sought to placate the moderates in the movement by declaring that Sinn Fein aimed "at seeing the international recognition of Ireland as an independent republic, and, having achieved that status, the people might by referendum, choose their own form of Government, when they would deny the right of the British, or other foreign Government to legislate for Ireland." With no suggestion of violence, Sinn Fein won the backing of the Roman Catholic Church in Ireland.

Like a number of others appointed to the new Sinn Fein Council, Cathal Brugha no longer saw a need for the IRB. Sinn Fein, the Democratic alternative, was now the driving force for Irish independence. From a religious point of view, deValera, who had briefly been an IRB man, always had scruples about being a member. It was a secret society, and secret societies were condemned by the Roman Catholic Church. DeValera tried unsuccessfully to persuade Harry Boland and Austin Stack to leave the organization. For the moment, though, he was prepared to allow the IRB and its very active new leader, Michael Collins, to prepare the Volunteers for any eventuality. Even Brugha, now at odds with Collins, believed that at the proper time, physical force to assert Ireland's sovereign independence could be justified.

Under the guise of the Sinn Fein conference, the Volunteers held a secret convention on 27th October 1917, at the Gaelic Athletic Association's ground at Jones Road, Drumcondra. Most of the delegates had also attended the Sinn Fein convention as members. The Volunteers met to elect a national executive to oversee the movement. Eamon deValera was voted in as president, thus bringing the two main thrusts of Irish Republicanism—political and military—under the control of one man. Cathal Brugha, who had done so much to keep alive the Volunteers following the defeat of the Rising, was appointed chief of staff. To give balance, appointees were selected from the four provinces. In addition, specialist directors were appointed. Richard Mulcahy was made director of training, and Michael Collins became director of organization. Two other senior IRB men, Diarmuid Lynch and Sean MacGarry, were elected to the posts of director of communications and general secretary respectively. Six of the twenty members elected onto the Volunteer national executive were also members of the Sinn Fein executive, thus establishing a greater military-political relationship. By the end of the year, in order to coordinate the work of the various Volunteer units throughout the country, it was decided to establish a general headquarters staff, based in Dublin. The members of the executive met to select its staff. When it came to appointing a chief of staff, the two principal candidates were Michael Collins and Richard Mulcahy. Being the better known of the two, Mulcahy, a hero of the Battle of Ashbourne, was selected over Collins. Collins, however, was appointed director of organization and adjutant-general. The role was undefined, allowing Collins to engage in a myriad of activities, including intelligence. Sean MacMahon was appointed quartermaster-general; Rory O'Connor, director of engineering; and Dick McKee, director of training and Mulcahy's successor as O/C of the Dublin Brigade. Regarding policy, it was decided that it would not order the Volunteers to take the field unless there was a considered possibility of waging war with a reasonable expectation of success. In the meantime, the Volunteers would continue to train and to search for arms. Initially, Mulcahy began reorganizing the Volunteers along the lines of the British Army, with companies, battalions, and brigades. This suited the British, for they knew that in fighting a conventional war, they could defeat the Volunteers. At this time, there was no suggestion in Mulcahy's mind of fighting an alternative guerrilla war.

Away from Ireland, in the stalemate of the Great War, the Germans now seized the initiative, and in a new campaign—*Blitzkrieg*, or lightning war— they drove the Allies back several miles. British Prime Minister Lloyd George called for conscription in Ireland. The intention to levy conscription, while postponing the establishment of Home Rule, enraged nearly everyone. The Irish no longer trusted Britain to keep its word. Home Rule had been put off indefinitely, and yet Britain expected Irishmen to go off and fight for "small nations." To the majority of Irish people, citizens of a "small nation," it was incredible hypocrisy. When the proposal was presented in the House of Commons, even the Irish Party, who had persuaded a large section of the Volunteers to fight for Britain, voted against the levying of conscription in Ireland. Nevertheless, the bill passed into law on 16th April, by 301 votes to 103. John Dillon and the Irish Party M.P.s left the Commons in protest and returned home to organize opposition to the Act. On 18th April, the lord mayor of Dublin convened a meeting at the mansion house to debate the issue. In the face of this national threat, all parties—the Irish Parliamentary Party, Sinn Fein, and the Irish Labor Party—became as one in their opposition. There was little disagreement, and at the end of the meeting, Eamon deValera drew up the words of the Anti-Conscription Pledge: "Denying the right of the British Government to enforce compulsory service in this country, we pledge ourselves solemnly to one another to resist Conscription by the most effective means at our disposal." For international consumption, the following declaration, also drawn up by deValera, was passed unanimously by the conference:

> Taking our stand on Ireland's separate and distinct nationhood and affirming the principle of liberty that the governments of nations derive their just powers from the consent of the governed, we deny the right of the British Government or any external authority to impose compulsory military service in Ireland against the clearly expressed will of the Irish people. The passing of the Conscription Bill by the British House of Commons must be regarded as a declaration of war on the Irish nation.
>
> The alternative to accepting it as such is to surrender our liberties and to acknowledge ourselves slaves.
>
> It is in direct violation of the rights of small nationalities to self-determination, which even the Prime Minister of England—now preparing to employ naked militarism and force his Act upon Ireland—himself officially announced as an essential condition for peace at the Peace Congress. The attempt to enforce it will be an unwarrantable aggression, which we cal upon all Irishmen to resist by the most effective means at our disposal.

A delegation from the Mansion House Conference, with representatives from all of the political parties, sought the support of the Catholic Church, and sanction resistance to conscription. In that again it did not mention violence, the bishops had no qualms in accepting deValera's motion. The bishops came out in support, declaring, "We consider that Conscription forced in this way upon Ireland is an oppressive and inhuman law which the Irish people have a right to resist by every means that are consonant with the law of God."

Days later, the Irish Trades Union Conference convened in Dublin to decide what form of protest Labor would take. Fifteen hundred delegates attended the congress. The unanimous decision was that a twenty-four-hour general strike should be called. The Women Workers' Union organized a march through Dublin in support, bringing the city to a halt. Gone were the days when the police could break up such a march. That Sunday, 21st April, the Anti-Conscription Pledge was signed at church doorways and in other places across Ireland by thousands of people. On 23rd April, a one-day general strike was held nationwide. Cities and towns, with the exception of Loyalist Belfast, came to a halt. Trains, trams, and taxis did not run; banks, factories, and shops closed for the day. No newspapers appeared throughout much of the country. Ships were left unloaded along the quays. People came out onto the streets, in orderly protest, against conscription. The British Government was shocked by the response, but more so by the organization behind it. The British response was predictable. It put in place measures to replace civil rule by military dictate. Field Marshal Lord French was appointed governor general of Ireland. His response was typical of the military mind: "Home Rule will be offered and declined, then conscription will be enforced. If they [the Government] will leave me alone I can do what is necessary. I shall notify a date before which recruits must offer themselves in various districts. If they do not come, we will fetch them."[14]

By a series of rallies and marches and speeches, the women of Ireland highlighted the opposition to conscription right across the country. Concerned that they might be proscribed, they worked under a number of pseudonyms, most especially "Women's Clubs." One such member, Mollie Cunningham, revealed in her witness statement 1681 to Bureau of Military History:

> Women's Clubs or Societies have been formed in places, and women are unfortunately the most active supporters, if not openly, by their home influence, of Sinn Fein, viz., they hate the idea of enforced military service for their male friends.

These clubs followed the direction by a Women's Day Convention, drawn from women who had attended the earlier Mansion House Conference. Its chairwoman was Alice Stopford Green, who had financed the purchase of the Howth guns. Alongside her as secretary was Agnes O'Farrelly, M.A., a founding member of Cumann na mBan and later a professor in the National University. On 9th June 1918, Cumann na mBan organized "An Ireland Women's Day" (La na mBan) as part of the continuing anticonscription campaign. Some forty thousand women in Dublin signed the anti-conscription pledge, led by the seven hundred members of the Dublin Cumann. Elsewhere around the country, women in the thousands paraded around its cities and towns. At Waterford, about fifteen hundred women paraded through the city carrying banners with the inscription: "The Women of Waterford will not have Conscription." They were accompanied by five marching bands. In Tipperary, three thousand women marched, then afterward signed the national anticonscription pledge:

> Because the enforcement of conscription on any people without their consent is tyranny, we are resolved to resist the conscription of Irishmen.
> We will not fill the places of men deprived of their work through refusing enforced military service.
> We will do all in our power to help the families of men who suffer through refusing enforced military service.

What would have undoubtedly led to bloodshed, had French attempted to impose conscription on Ireland, was averted when the last German offensive of World War I was checked and forced back. Within months, Germany

Clann na Gael Republican Girl Scouts marching through Dublin

sued for peace. The conscription crisis was over, and the women had played no small part in the resistance to conscription. Cumann na mBan, whose efforts to support the Volunteers during the Rising had been thwarted, had now come into their own.

Alongside the conscription crisis was the so-called German plot. On 12th May 1918, Anglo-Irishman Lord John French took up his appointment as the new viceroy of Ireland. Within five days of his arrival, he declared that there was a "German Plot" and that Sinn Fein had been in treasonable communication with the German enemy. The evidence was dubious, to say the least. It was more German intention than reality, speculative messages among the German High Command picked up in intercepted transmissions. Nevertheless, it gave Britain the excuse it needed to make arrests and, in the process, destroy the anticonscription movement. As a consequence, seventy-three of Sinn Fein's leading activists, including deValera and Griffith, were arrested. Michael Collins, who became aware of the intended arrests on 15th May through his intelligence contacts within the Dublin Metropolitan Police, warned deValera, but he, realizing the impact on world opinion, made no attempt to evade his arrest. A number of women from Sinn Fein and Cumann na mBan were also picked up. Constance Markievicz was arrested and interned in Holloway Prison in London. Dr. Kathleen Lynn was in Sinn Fein headquarters when it was raided in the search for those to be arrested. She escaped out of the back of the building and went on the run. Collins, Boland, Mulcahy, and Brugha avoided the roundup.

The arrest of so many Sinn Fein activists created a power vacuum, and into this void stepped the IRB in the shape of Michael Collins, and his close IRB friends, Harry Boland and Richard Mulcahy. Collins immediately set about establishing a system of communications throughout the country, with men answerable to him and him alone. In a short time, the whole Republican movement came under his control. The result was to create a more militant underground leadership under Collins, while the political movement, still following a line of passive resistance, remained in the hands of deValera and Griffith. In the absence of the leaders of Sinn Fein, Collins and Boland went through the list of nominated Sinn Fein candidates for the forthcoming general election. They redrafted the list to reflect only those who favored a "forward policy." Now in prison, with democracy thwarted by the British, deValera made it known to those outside that he would now support military action if it should come to it.

With the Republican movement apparently leaderless, the British authorities set about breaking the will of those remaining. Drilling by Volunteers was prohibited, as was the wearing of unauthorized military uniforms. On 21st June 1918, a further byelection was held in East Cavan, in Ulster. It was seen as a litmus test for the state of the country. The British expected it to be won by the Parliamentary nationalists, but to their consternation it was won by Arthur Griffith, the imprisoned Sinn Fein leader, with a majority of over 1,220 votes. Again, the British response was repression. Strong Republican districts were proclaimed special military areas. All public meetings, including fairs, were prohibited. On 4th July, Sinn Fein, the Volunteers, Cumann na mBan, and the Gaelic League were all proclaimed as dangerous associations, and meetings of these organizations were banned. In the following months, the police broke up meetings, sporting events, and concerts that they believed might be covert meetings of the proscribed organizations.

In December 1918, a month after the cessation of hostilities with Germany, a general election was called throughout the United Kingdom. This was what Sinn Fein had prepared for, the democratic legitimization of an Irish Republic by the will of the people. Their success in a number of previous byelections buoyed them up with the confidence that they could win. Even though the war was over, Sinn Fein was still subject to wartime restrictions. Their manifesto was heavily censored, and a number of their election agents were arrested for sedition. On the positive side, an enlarged electoral register—with a rise from 698,098 to 1,931,588—extended the vote to all men over the age of twenty-one, serving soldiers over the age of eighteen, and women over the age of thirty.

The women of Cumann na mBan campaigned tirelessly throughout Ireland to make sure that every nationalist woman voted for Sinn Fein. Instructions from central office were sent to each branch, and from there the women went out into the towns and villages and into the countryside to put the message across. Details of who was entitled to vote, and when and where, were prepared. These instructions were passed on, with local details added to by each branch:

> A woman of thirty years of age or over on 15th April 1918 is entitled to vote if she fulfils either of the following conditions—1. That for the six months prior to the 15th April she herself has occupied in the constituency either a dwelling house or else land or business premises value £5 or over. (If she occupied a dwelling house the question of value does not arise).—2. That she is the wife of a man who fulfils the conditions in paragraph 1.
>
> It is sufficient to occupy part of a dwelling house, provided that that part is occupied separately, independently of other people in the house. Lodgers are entitled to vote only if they rent unfurnished rooms.
>
> A woman who resides on premises by reason of her employment is entitled to be registered as a voter if her employer does not reside on the premises. The same applies to the wife of a man who resides on premises by reason of his employment.
>
> Secretaries are directed to prepare lists of all women in their districts who possess above qualifications and would be likely to vote for a Sinn Fein candidate.
>
> On or before June 15th the Clerk of the Crown and Peace will publish, either at his own office or at the local Post Office, lists of voters. Secretaries are directed to

compare their lists with these official ones, and if there are some names missing from the latter to see that the women claim their votes. Particulars as to making the claims will be published at the same time as the voters' lists. Secretaries must see to it that the claims are properly made.[15]

The increase in numbers was swelled by the number of young men prevented from emigrating by war. This was Sinn Fein's target electorate, and as a young positive party, they targeted the young who were looking for change and a better future. In the forthcoming election, a number of candidates holding dual positions in Sinn Fein and the Volunteers were selected to run under the Sinn Fein banner. Eleven of the twenty members of the Volunteer executive would be elected as members of the Irish Parliament. Included in that number was Mulcahy, who was selected for Clontarf; Boland for Roscommon; and Collins for South Cork.

At the general election, held on 14th December 1918, Sinn Fein triumphed at the polls. They won sixty-seven seats, the Irish nationalists won six, and the Unionists twenty-six. The people of Ireland as a whole had voted for a Republic by a majority of 73 percent. Twenty-four of the thirty-two counties returned only Sinn Fein candidates. Of the nine counties of Ulster, the Unionists had a majority in only four—Antrim, Derry, Down, and Armagh. They were in a minority in Tyrone and Fermanagh, while three of the Ulster counties—Donegal, Cavan, and Monaghan—returned no Unionists at all. Constance Markievicz and Winifred Carney had been put forward as Sinn Fein candidates for the election. As was widely predicted, Markievicz was elected, and in the process she made British Parliamentary history in being the first woman elected to the British Parliament. She polled 7,835 votes against William Field of the Irish Parliamentary Party, a man who had held the seat for twenty-six years, who gained 3,741 votes, and against Alderman J. J. Kelly, who gained just 312 votes. Winifred Carney, an Ulster woman, was not so successful. She was not as well-known, and she failed to get much support in the predominantly Unionist constituency of Central and East Belfast. The *London Times* reported in its edition of 17th January 1919: "The General Election in Ireland was treated by all parties as a plebiscite and admittedly Sinn Fein swept the country."

The people of Ireland as a whole had given Sinn Fein a mandate to pursue a policy of independence from the British Empire. Sinn Fein, the Irish Parliamentary Party, and Labor refused to sit in the Westminster Parliament, and instead they formed their own parliament, Dail Eireann (Assembly of Ireland). They met as T.D.s (Teachtai Dala) for the first time in the Round Room of the Dublin Mansion House on 21st January 1919, the day after the Paris Peace Conference had opened. All elected members in the Irish election regardless of political party, Unionists included, were invited to attend. Of the possible 105 members, thirty-three Republicans who would have been there were in prison, most without trial, since the previous 17th May 1918.[16] The thirty-fourth member, Pierce McCann of Tipperary East, was to die in prison, a victim of the influenza pandemic then sweeping the world. Edward Carson's name was called, but of course, he was not there. Nor, indeed, were the other Unionist M.P.s. Only Sir Robert Woods had the good grace to write and say that he would not attend. Michael Collins's name was answered, as was Harry Boland's—but not apparently by them. The two men had slipped quietly away over to England, and at the beginning of February, they assisted the escape of deValera and fellow prisoners of Lincoln Jail, Sean McGarry and Sean Milroy. Robert Barton was also rescued about this time from Mountjoy Prison in Dublin. On 7th March, in a face-saving gesture, the British Government made a general release of its untried prisoners—Arthur Griffith, Countess Markievicz, W.T. Cosgrave, Dr. Richard Hayes, Dr. Brian Cusack, and Joseph McGuinness.[17]

The ordinary women, if you will—the members of Cumann na mBan—proved their worth during the general election, a point perhaps not fully appreciated at the time. They escorted the elderly and infirm to and from the polls. They looked after other women's children so that their mothers might play a more active role. They distributed election materials and catered for the personnel engaged in the election. Where they had underscored in 1916—through no fault of their own, it should be admitted—they more than proved their worth in 1918.

At the first session of the Dail, the imprisoned Eamon deValera was elected president. Arthur Griffith, former leader of Sinn Fein, was appointed secretary for home affairs; Cathal Brugha, a known feminist, got defense; Count Plunkett became minister for finance; W.T. Cosgrave was given local government; and Constance Markievicz became secretary for labor. She became the first female cabinet minister to hold office in any European country. William Cosgrave was appointed to local government, and Michael Collins got finance. Collins's mission was now to organize a bond issue in the form of a national loan to help finance the administration of the Republican government and its army. The appointment of Brugha to defense automatically promoted his deputy, Richard Mulcahy, to be chief of staff of the Volunteers. The first session of the Irish Parliament opened with Cathal Brugha presiding. He read out a message to the free nations of the world. Britain's reaction was to censor all Irish newspapers to the events of the day. Not to be mentioned were any references to the democratic program, the declaration of independence, or any speeches of the proposer and seconder of the declaration of independence. While Britain denied its existence, the Dail began creating an alternative government to take over from the British. In response, seeing that the Irish were in earnest, Britain turned to her old tool of repression.

On 1st April 1919, deValera, amid strong security, was present at the opening of the second session of the Dail. He was formally appointed president. He, in turn, appointed Michael Collins as minister of finance and Richard Mulcahy as chief of staff of the Irish Republican Army. Collins was given full power to raise a national loan to be used in a campaign of national recognition, and for the promotion of trade and commerce. Also included in the brief was the financing of a Republican civil service and the establishment of arbitration courts. Collins was given power to raise a national loan "without further reference to the Dail," which permitted him to covertly divert money to armed resistance. By financing such institutions, the Dail had become more than just a government in name only; it had become an alternative government. It was a direct challenge to British authority. Up to this point, the British Government had been exclusively in control of Irish revenue and taxation. To maintain that monopoly, and to strangle the Dail at birth, they declared that the Loan Scheme was in itself illegal. The British Government then used every means in its power to suppress it. A special government task force raided banks and checked their accounts for any trace of the loan. Yet, despite this harassment, £379,000 was raised in Ireland and almost 45 million in the United States. In the following year, the Irish Government retaliated. The Dail declared the British collection of income tax in Ireland to be illegal and ordered Irish people to refuse to pay it. The British found it impossible to take effective action against the wholesale refusal to pay. Further, upon the instructions of the Dail, taxes forwarded by county councils to the British Local Government Board in Dublin were now stopped. Further financial dismantlement of the British administration followed.

Another blow to the British administration was the boycotting of British law courts and the setting up of Republican courts in their place. These new courts provided inexpensive justice. The judges, consisting of women as well as men, were rarely trained or qualified, but had an innate sense of justice and fair play. Naturally, the British proscribed them, with all involved liable for arrest. Alice Cashell of Galway was appointed as a Republican judge, as she herself testified:

> Meantime the Republic was getting under way. The courts were next tackled. At a convention in Galway, justices for the county were next tackled. On a poll I was elected … as Parish Justice for Connemara. John Cloherty was also elected for this area. So we proceeded to hold our "courts." Sometimes we held them openly—at other times secretly at midnight. I remember holding one openly with John Cloherty in Clifden. The matter at issue was land trouble. It was the case of the Clifden Castle estate. Some time before this a certain Toby Joyce of Clifden had bought the castle and lands which the tenants claimed should be divided amongst them. The case had been fought on behalf of the tenants by Canon McAlpine, a bitter opponent of Sinn Fein in the British courts but without success. There was very great bitterness over the matter; riots in the town were frequent. Joyce attended our court but

we failed to get him to give up the lands. Eventually the question was settled in the Galway (Sinn Fein) Court. [Compulsory purchase of the estate, for redistribution to the tenants, was decided upon.] The next step was to acquire the money for the purchase of the lands. I put my case and obtained the necessary thousands to buy the land from Joyce. We bought the estate, stripped the land, and transferred the land to the tenants.[18]

Money for the purchase was drawn from the Republican Land (Mortgage) Bank, established by the "Provisional Government." The owner, Joyce, received a full market price, as decided by an independent valuer, and the land was distributed to the tenants, which was Sinn Fein policy in the abolition of landlordism.

Alice Cashell also spoke of the secret midnight courts that she was sometimes obliged to preside at:

I got a message to meet certain Volunteers at Toombeola, about three miles distant, at midnight and that they would bring me to Roundstone where a court was to be held. I cycled to Toombeola and was met by Volunteers as arranged, and we went on to about a mile or so outside the village where we left our bicycles by the roadside. We climbed over walls into fields and so bye-passed the village where the police still lived.... At length we arrived at a small stone building apparently standing alone in a field, but actually in a graveyard as I learnt later.... Then the prisoners were brought in, blindfolded. They had been held on charges of larceny.

They were duly tried, and when found guilty, were banished from Ireland.

By 1920, Republican courts were established in twenty-one of thirty-two counties. Both solicitors and barristers eventually put their trust in this new form of justice. Even the *Irish Times*, an avowedly Unionist newspaper, freely confessed that the "the Sinn Fein courts are steadily extending their jurisdiction and dispensing justice, even-handedly between man and man, Catholic and Protestant ... landlord and tenant."[19] Not only were the British courts isolated, but so, too, was the police force, the Royal Irish Constabulary. The women of Cumann na mBan played an important part in this, as Margaret Sweeney relates:

We visited shops which supplied the R.I.C. with provisions, and instructed the shopkeepers that they were not to supply the R.I.C. with any goods. We kept watch on such shops to see that this instruction was carried out. Generally our instructions to the shopkeepers were carried out by them, and the R.I.C. were compelled to commandeer the goods they required, which, of course, at this time they paid for. Later on, when the Tans came, they often took goods without payment. We also persuaded the people not to associate with them and, in this way, made outcasts of them in society.[20]

The women of Cumann also took part in the boycott of Belfast goods, following clashes up in the north, and discrimination against Catholic nationalists, as Margaret Sweeney again relates:

A boycott of Belfast and Northern Ireland goods was also instituted at this time as a retaliation for the pogrom carried out by Unionists and Orangemen in the North against the Catholic residents there. At this time Belfast supplied most of the goods coming to Leitrim County. The Volunteers raided trains, shops, vans and so forth, and seized and destroyed all goods supplied by certain "black-listed" Northern firms. As well as going to the various shops and warning the owners not to stock Belfast goods supplied by the black-listed firms, the girls of Cumann na mBan did a big amount of intelligence work in this respect and were able to keep watch on all goods coming into the area.

At the local government level, Sinn Fein took over the running of towns and cities across Ireland. Jennie Wyse Power was elected as a member of the Dublin Corporation. To assert her role as a representative of the Republican movement, she insisted in signing the register as "Siobhan Bean an Phaoraigh." The council clerk took exception, stating that because her name was not in English, she was ineligible to take her seat. An out-and-out row took place in public, much to the amusement of many, for Jenny could be quite formidable when she set her mind to it. In the end, the clerk backed down, and Siobhan Bean an Phaoraigh took her seat.

In the Dail's appointment of ministers, it was appropriate that Constance Markievicz, a leading figure within the ICA, should be made minister for labor. She held the cabinet post from 1919 to 1922, becoming only the second government minister in Europe. What was increasingly obvious was that labor was being sidelined. The Rising was being manipulated into the manifestation of a Republican "triumph." The ICA's part in the Rising, along with the socialist ideals of Connolly, were being dissipated. Upon their return from internment, in view that they found themselves at odds with Sinn Fein over their socialist agenda, the men of the ICA decided that they should break away from the IRA and operate independently. They were reconstituted as a separate entity. Its council appointed James O'Neill as commandant of its army.

As a consequence, the Labor movement and its trade union, the ITGWU, were perceived as now being something separate to mainstream Republicanism. Much was made of the fact that when the ITGWU commemorated its members killed in the Easter Rising, it also commemorated the five thousand members of its union who had enlisted in the British Army during the Great War and had been killed. Those men, who had survived the war, upon their return were seen somehow by Republicans as traitors. They were denigrated and maligned. It took the best part of a century before these men were duly honored for their stand against German militarism.

The Socialists, for their part, saw the new Republicans as bourgeois, attempting to replace one capitalist society with another. Without the guidance and strength of Connolly, the ICA had become ineffectual. Once seen as a bastion of feminism, it became a misogynist organization in the eyes of its female members. Connolly's Women's Section became defunct after the Rising, nevermore to be revived. Women within the ICA were perceived, under the new post-Connolly structure, merely as support staff to the men. There were now also problems between the ITGWU and the ICA. Referring back to 1917, Helena Molony recorded the breach:

> At this time—1917—we were defeated; nobody thought we would rise up again. Liberty Hall was mainly a Trade Union Headquarters. They were not all patriotic. Some of the Dublin workers were ex-British soldiers. After the rebellion, the premises was largely in their hands. Also, there was a section—Larkin versus Connolly. Larkin stood for international working men's movements. Connolly's followers were mainly nationalists. There was that antagonism. The Union was in the hands of Larkin's section. The Hall was in their hands too. We knew we had unsympathetic members in the back, and enemies in the front.
>
> They did not want the Citizen Army there at all. They were only tolerated, they were there on sufferance. The Union men would have liked to tell them to go, but, on account of Connolly, they did not have the courage to do it.[21]

The trade union forbade the ICA to engage in military activities on the premises, for fear that the British would close down the hall. The singing of rebel songs within the hall was also discouraged. It would seem that the trade unions no longer felt that they needed the ICA. It had lost its relevance. In the coming War of Independence, the ICA was to play only a minor role, being sidelined by Michael Collins in favor of the Volunteers, or as we should now call them, the soldiers of the Irish Republican Army. As for the women, a number of them drifted away to join a more welcoming and feminist Cumann na mBan.

Cumann had failed to fulfill its full potential during the Rising; This was not through its own fault, it should be added. There had been a breakdown in communication. Individual members, as we have seen, had proved their worth. In the period that followed the Rising, this failure led to a degree of soul searching, followed by a rededication of purpose. A new executive of nine was established, breathing new life into the organization. They were a mixture of old and new members—Republican and feminist—Kathleen Clarke, Aine Ceannt, Margaret Pearse, Nancy Wise-Power, Mary McSwiney, Fiona Plunkett, Nancy O'Rahilly and her daughter, and Madge Daly. Membership increased as a consequence of their vitality, with new branches being formed and old ones being revitalized. Brighid O'Mullane was one of the organizers, starting up new branches of Cumann na mBan:

> It was my custom to contact the Volunteer O.C, who gave me the names of reliable girls. Having got the names, I convened a meeting, generally at the private house of one of the girls; occasionally it might be at a local hall or even a barn. I first lectured the girls on the aims and objects of the organization, and the work they would be

asked to do. I had a good deal of prejudice to overcome on the part of parents, who did not mind their boys taking part in a military movement, but who had never heard of, and were reluctant to accept, the idea of a body of gun-women. It was, of course, a rather startling innovation, and in that way Cumann na mBan can claim to have been the pioneers in establishing what was undoubtedly a women's auxiliary of an army. I fully understood this attitude and eventually, in most cases, succeeded in overcoming this prejudice.[22]

While the shooting at Soloheadbeg in January 1919 is generally credited with starting the War of Independence, there were at least two incidents in the Tralee area that preceded it. In both cases, the women of Cumann na mBan acted in support of the Volunteers, as Bessie Cahill (nee Harrington) relates:

In April 1918 Gortalea RIC Barracks was attacked and two Volunteers, John Brown and Richard Laide, two gallant soldiers were killed. The other men, who were on the attack, had to seek shelter and the Cumann na mBan were called upon to assist them in many ways, We were the first branch in Ireland after 1916 which had active Volunteer officers on the run after a barracks attack to look after.

About June 1918, two RIC men were fired at in Tralee by Thomas McEllistrim and the late John Cronin and intense police activity followed. The two men had to leave the area for some time, but this did not reduce the police activity.

The Cumann na mBan remained active despite police raids by organizing, training and organizing concerts and dances in aid of the funds.[23]

6

The Women's War

With the Dail proscribed by the British, the Irish Parliament was obliged to meet in secret—and not necessarily the full Dail. Its control over the Volunteers was, in the process, considerably weakened. This enabled Michael Collins and the now powerful IRB to implement a more militant policy, without recourse to the authority of the Irish Government. Some form of military confrontation with the British now seemed inevitable. It happened on 21st January 1919, at Soloheadbeg, in County Tipperary. Soloheadbeg is situated about two and a half miles from Tipperary town. Explosives for the local quarry were routinely taken by a horse and cart, escorted by about a half-dozen fully armed men of the paramilitary Royal Irish Constabulary. A company of local Volunteers from the South Tipperary Brigade, commanded by Seamus Robinson, resolved to ambush it and steal the gelignite. After a few days' delay, Robinson dismissed most of his company, leaving just nine men. On the fifth day of their stakeout, a lookout espied the horse and cart approaching. As luck would have it, there were only two guards. Entering the ambush zone, Robinson called out, "Hands up!" In response, as the Volunteers approached them, the policemen brought their rifles to bear. The Volunteers reacted first and opened fire, killing the two men, Constables James McDonnell and Patrick O'Connell. James Godfrey, the cart driver, and Patrick Flynn, his assistant, raised their arms in surrender. The police carbines and ammunition were gathered up, and the cart was seized and hastily driven away. Where this ambush differed from the previous raids was in the killing of the two policemen—both Roman Catholics. That made a considerable difference. The Catholic Church condemned the killings as murder. Most newspapers also took this line. Many in the provisional government also condemned the killings. There was a demand that those involved should be sent away. Plans were made to get them away to America. The ambush party, however, refused to go, believing that if they did, their exploit would be looked upon as the act of criminals or cowards. Instead they went on the run, determined to carry on the fight. As such, Michael Collins and the IRB realized that everything had now changed. There was no going back. Ireland was at war.

After several months on the run, remnants of the "Soloheadbeg Gang" were summoned to Dublin, there to be found in safehouses. One particular house was the shop of Harry Boland, a close friend of Michael Collins. Harry's sister, Kathleen, takes up the tale:

> I remember an interesting incident that took place in 1919, shortly after the Solo-headbeg affair. Joe O'Reilly came to our shop in 64, Middle Abbey Street. I should have mentioned that Harry opened a tailoring and outfitting business about October of 1917, and it became an important center for dispatches from all places, especially from Cork, Kerry and Tipperary. Joe said Mick Collins wanted to see me. I went to his office in Mary Street, just near Liffey Street. He said there were some very important men from Tipperary, mentioning the name of Sean Treacy, coming up to Dublin and he was going to send some of them out to me. He also asked me whether I knew any other safe houses where the people were not talkative and where these men could stay under assumed names. Incidentally, the name Sean Treacy had taken was Ryan. I sent Joe O'Reilly to Miss Eva Doherty, a quiet girl that I knew in Cumann na mBan, to get some safe houses, and she recommended to him Malone's house in Grantham Street and the Delaney's in Heytesbury Street.
>
> That evening, Seamus Robinson and Sean Treacy arrived at our house. I'll never forget my feelings when I saw the condition they were in. The soles were gone from their boots, and they were footsore, weary, wet through and hungry. We gave them a hot meal in the kitchen. They stayed with us a couple of nights and then moved on somewhere else. Sean Treacy, Seamus Robinson and their two companions came often to stay with us afterwards, bringing with them various Volunteers.[1]

From Boland's, Sean Treacy and Dan Breen were taken to another safe-house, Professor John Carolan's home, Fernside, at Drumcondra, then on the outskirts of Dublin. One day in the city, Breen was identified and confronted by two policemen from G. Division, the political department of the Dublin Metropolitan Police. Breen made them aware that he was armed, and they backed off, but one of them discreetly followed Breen to Drumcondra. That night, British agents and soldiers led by Major Gerald Smyth raided the house. After a brief firefight in which both Smyth and Captain A.P. White were killed, Treacy and Breen escaped out of an upstairs window. In the process, Breen was badly cut as he crashed through a glass conservatory below. Eventually he found a house where the people took him in. From there, he was taken to the Mater Hospital. Realizing that Breen would need treatment for his wounds, the British made a systematic raid on all of Dublin's hospitals. As they approached the Mater, Breen was removed to the greater safety of the home of Dr. Alice Barry at 8 Herbert Place, in Dublin, as she herself relates:

> About October 1920 when the British forces were raiding the Mater Hospital for Dan Breen and the danger of his capture was getting greater, he was brought in a car

or cab by Rory O'Connor and Gearoid O'Sullivan to the house in No. 8, Herbert Place where I lived with my mother.... Collins who knew we were sympathizers to the cause had previously asked us to dissociate ourselves with Sinn Fein public politics and to keep our house as a refuge for dangerously wounded IRA men. Our house was quiet and in a quiet street.

I attended to his wounds the first night he was with us, but Surgeon Barneville who had probably been attending him in the Mater came to see him next day and possibly once or twice after that. His wounds healed in a few weeks. He got clothes through Phil Shanahan who was his only visitor and then arrangements were made to transfer him to Dun Laoghaire to the house of another Mrs. Barry.[2]

Catherine Rooney recalled a tension-filled raid upon her Dublin family home:

The peculiar thing about our house was that although we always had stuff in our house we were only raided twice in a rather casual way. Nothing was got. In one raid at an early hour of the morning the Black and Tans, led by a British officer, came. [After an incident guns had been left at the house] When the knocking came my father went down to open the door after handing his gun to my mother. My mother had three of the guns, my father had one and I had one. They were not loaded. Some of the men were downstairs and demanded of my father to be brought upstairs. I had got a long stocking to tie the gun around my body and when they came to the room, they told me to get up, but I said I would not until they left the room, pretending to be frightened and shy. My two young sisters were in another bed in the room, but they slept on and were not disturbed. The raiders went to the door while I got up, putting a blanket around me. My mother hid two of the guns on her person in the same way and she put the third under the baby in the cot.[3]

Without women searchers, the women could not be properly searched. No guns were found, and the nighttime raiders departed.

Safehouses were also required for senior officials of the new Republican government. Michael Collins, with a price of £1,000 on his head, used a series of safehouses; some served as offices, while others provided a place to sleep. A number of women were involved in renting and purchasing these houses. Mary Flannery Woods was one such woman:

Batt [O'Connor] was to act as a go-between [for Collins]. Mick's chief purpose was to get safe houses for himself and for the men, to carry out espionage.... Following on from this I bought a house in Harcourt Terrace, the last house on the left-hand side facing the canal. It was owned by a Mr. Cantor, a Jew. Seumas O'Connor was the solicitor who completed the transaction. The price was £800. I was buying the house ostensibly for my nephew. Mick himself used the house up to and perhaps after the Truce. Batt built a secret cupboard in it for arms and ammunition, and a man could hide in it, as also under the flooring in the foundation. A trusted man called Byrne (?) did this sort of work for Batt who was a builder.[4]

Mary Rigney, a Sinn Fein worker, was housekeeper at one of the houses:

I was sent by order of Arthur Griffith during the months of November and December 1920 as a guard to Michael Collins' headquarters in Mespil Road, Dublin. My duties were to answer the door and cook for Michael Collins his lunch and his tea. It was Miss Hoey's house, No. 3 near the Leeson St. end of Mespil Road and he went under the name of Mr. O'Brien, if anybody inquired about him.

While he was there working—he did not sleep there although there was a bed-room at his disposal, which he furnished himself—his messengers visited him with dispatches at various hours during the day. I was told by Miss Hoey that I need not worry about these men coming and going, as each possessed his own latchkey in order to avoid any delay on the steps. They had instructions never to knock.

Collins worked in the front room and thus had a close view of anyone who might come in by the front gate. Should there be a knock at the hall door I was to answer it. In case of spies who might come as professional beggars etc. The door was never to be left open for one moment.

In the upstairs living room and downstairs kitchen of No. 3, Mespil Road, the late Batt O'Connor had made hiding places for papers, ammunition, guns, etc., in the paneling over the windows. There were sliding panels which were not perceptible except to someone who knew them. Coming in from the back garden facing you was a door leading into a cubby hole under the stairs. The back wall of this cubby hole had shelves on which were old tins, boxes, cleaning materials, etc., which are nor-mally kept in such places. This wall could be opened by pressing a spring and behind it was a large space which was capable of hiding an amount of important papers.[5]

Mary Flannery Woods was entrusted with the purchase and renting of other houses, as she herself tells:

> Another house I got was 9, St. Mary's Road which I rented for six months from Mrs Mary McCarthy, 9, St. Mary's Road, for Mick Collins and his men. Batt O'Connor instructed me to go to the house…. I pretended the house was for my delicate sister who wanted to be near the church and her doctor. I used to stay there to get Mick Collins' breakfast and my husband used to stay with me. Mick did not come there every night. After some time I got Mrs. Comerford to housekeep for Mick.[6]

Mary Flannery Woods secured other houses, and was persuasive in getting others to take in men on the run:

> In addition to these houses I was constantly searching for safe houses for other wanted men to spend a night or two in, and these men used to come to my house to leave or call for their arms. Cumiskey's private house in Marlboro' Road was one of them—he was a provision merchant in Donnybrook…. Mrs. Byrne of Home Villas, Donnybrook; my sister Mrs. B. Woods of Eglinton Terrace, kept any men I sent her. Mrs. Considine's house in Morehampton Road and Mrs Hand's house on the same road were always open to men "on the run" and always had a welcome for them. Mrs. Nolan of Wellington Road took in Sean Etchingham.

She lists in her witness statement a number of other people who took in men on the run, including Citizen Army couple, the McGlynns; Mrs. Cuffe in Glengarry; "Alfie White's mother," in Peter's Place; and Mrs. Humphreys of Aylesbury Road. Mrs. Pat Bolger of Morehampton Road stored arms, and Dr. Fleury of Portrane Asylum took in men who were injured.

Through their intelligence network and the use of "Touts," the British discovered the names and addresses of active participants and known sympathizers. Midnight raids followed in the search for men on the run and for documents deposited in the houses of known sympathizers. In frustration, and sometimes as an example to others, the houses were sometimes put to the torch, especially out in the countryside. Margaret "Peg" Broderick-Nicholson was an active member of the Galway branch of Cuman na mBan, so much so that she was singled out one night for a raid in an effort to frighten her:

> Some time afterwards another raid took place when they asked if I was in. I called out down from the top of the stairs and said: "Surely I am allowed to dress myself." They replied: "No, come down as you are." I went down and snatched a coat from the hall-stand. My mother shouted after me: "Be brave, Peg." I thought at first they were going to shoot me, but they took me out and closed the door, then grabbed my hair, saying, "What wonderful curls you've got" and then proceeded to cut off all my hair to the scalp with very blunt scissors. I might say they did not handle me too roughly, which is strange to say. There was no further comment until they finished, when they pushed me towards the door and said, "Goodnight," All spoke with English accents. I had to have my head shaved by a barber next day in order to have the hair grow properly. As I remembered it afterwards I should have gone 'on the run,' as I was reliably informed that at least one RIC man was seen to point me out to the Black and Tans.[7]

Margaret Sweeney's house was also raided in a search for guns or documents. She was a member of Cumann na mBan, and she lived at Cloone, County Leitrim:

> the enemy at this time were very active, raiding houses and staging hold-ups every day. One of the first of our members to come under their attention was Kate Healy. She was arrested and interned until after the Truce, being released in August 1921. They found some documents or records of the organization in her house. A few days later, the enemy raided our house and made a thorough search of the place. They had with them two female searchers, one of whom I believe was a man dressed as a woman. During the search of our house, they stole some articles, including a watch belonging to my brother. They found nothing in the house that could be used against us, although if they had been a little earlier, there would have been dispatches there, but my sister had just delivered them to the Brigade O/C, Sean Mitchell. There was also an amount of documents and other stuff concealed in a place at the back of the house, but they failed to find them.[8]

There was a similar raid at 131 Morehampton Road, Dublin, by an auxiliary officer–led party of soldiers in the search for documents. This was the secret residence of Liam Mellowes, the Republic's director of purchases. His housekeeper was the indomitable Mary Flannery Woods:

> About 12.30 one night there was a thundering knock at the door and my husband went to open it. Liam and Sean Etchingham were in the house, the latter in bed....

> Presently Liam came downstairs to the dining room, sat around the fire with us and whispering, inquired of me where was the document he had given me in the morning.... I had put it into a casket on the sideboard. I whispered to Liam who got up and lit a cigarette for the soldier who was on guard at the door while I got up and removed the paper from the casket.... I handed it to Liam who opened it and handed me back one paper which I passed to my daughter who put it into her stocking. Liam used up the other papers, one by one, lighting cigarettes which he gave the soldiers.... During this time the Auxiliary officer who was with the military had the contents of two or three bookcases on the floor and was systematically searching every book, evidently for some document. It was clearly not men they were looking for. They stayed from 12.30 till after 4 a.m. Before they left the Auxie officer and Andy [Mary's husband] went upstairs to Etchingham's room and found him in bed, with the Tommies sitting on the bed listening to the racing tips he was reading from the sporting papers he always had about him.

Erskine Childers, author of *Riddle of the Sands* and director of propaganda for the Republican cause, wrote a series of articles for the *Daily News*, later brought together as *Military Rule in Ireland*, published by the Talbot Press in Dublin. In it, he detailed a number of such raids. The pamphlet was widely circulated, leading to an investigation by representatives of the British Labor Party. Childers particularly highlighted the distress caused to women and children in these late-night raids.

Then there were the frightful raids, where men came in the night to murder. Early on the morning of 20th March 1920, Thomas McCurtain, lord mayor of Cork, was shot dead in front of his wife as he opened the door in response to a loud knocking. At the inquest into his death the following month, the jury, very bravely, found that he had been murdered by the RIC and brought in a verdict against the British Government and its agents, including District Inspector Oswald Swanzy. A meeting held at Union Quay Barracks, Cork, on the previous day included Swanzy, Divisional Commissioner Clayton, and County Inspector Maloney. Among the items for discussion was the part possibly played by McCurtain in a failed assassination attempt on the life of Viceroy Lord French. What seemed to clinch McCurtain's assassination was the murder a few hours earlier of RIC policeman Constable Murtagh of Shandon Barracks, who was shot near Pope's Quay. Swanzy was credited by Michael Collins with having given the order for the murder of McCurtain, and he was to pay for that by his own assassination the following August.

In Dublin, another British murder team was also operating. On 23rd September, members of the gang shot dead John Lynch in his bed in the Exchange Hotel in Dublin. Lynch was a Sinn Fein Loan organizer. Papers were taken from his room, and the information contained within them might have led to the death of shopkeeper Peter O'Carroll. This occurred at 1:50 a.m. on Saturday 16th October 1920. Peter O'Carroll and his wife, Annie, were awakened by a heavy and persistent knocking on the front door of their home at 92 Manor Street. This was strange, because there was a nighttime military curfew in Dublin. O'Carroll put on some clothing, then went down to investigate. Annie peered down from the front bedroom window. There were three men gathered around the front door of the shop. She saw the electric light in the shop being turned on as Peter proceeded to unlock the door. Above in the bedroom, Annie heard some movement below. There was the sound of a *thud*, then all was silent. The shop room light was switched off. After a few minutes, when Peter did not return to the bedroom, Annie went down to investigate and found her prostrate husband lying in a pool of his own blood. He had been shot in the side of the head. Curiously she had not heard the shot being fired. The gun must have had some sort of silencer. She fled back upstairs in terror, and from the open bedroom window screamed out, "Murder! murder!" A local man with a pass to be out during curfew came to her assistance, and both made their way around the corner into Aughrim Street to seek the administrations of a priest, Father Turley. He gave Peter the Last Rites. An ambulance was called, and the body of Peter O'Carroll was taken to Richmond Hospital, where he was pronounced dead. The British authorities in Dublin refused to allow a public inquest. Through embedded intelligence within the British system, Michael Collins was convinced that the principal murderer was Captain J.L. Hardy, attached to F. Company of the Auxiliaries. His companions were said to be Lieutenant Peter Ames, alias McMahon, and Captain G. T. Baggalley. Ames and Baggalley were later shot and killed on Bloody Sunday, 21st November 1920. Hardy was away at the time and escaped.

Five months after the murder of O'Carroll, on 7th March 1921, there were two more horrific murders. The victims were George Clancy, the mayor of Limerick, and Michael O'Callaghan, his predecessor. Both were shot in front of their wives. At Mayor Clancy's house, off the North Strand, there was a heavy knocking at the front door. Mrs. Clancy opened the hall door and was confronted by three men wearing overcoats with their collars turned up, caps pulled down over their eyes, and wearing goggles to hide their identities. Realizing the danger her husband was in, she attempted to close the door, but it was forced in. The men opened fire on her husband, who fell mortally wounded in the hallway. Mrs. Clancy herself was wounded in the wrist as she attempted to save her husband.

Years later, Mrs. Kate O'Callaghan gave a witness statement to the Bureau of Military History regarding the callous murder of her husband, Michael:

> On the night of Sunday, March 6th, Michael and I went to bed about 11 o'clock, having spent a very happy day together.... I fell asleep and was awakened by a loud knocking at the hall door. I got up and, throwing up the bed-room window, said: "Who's there?" It was a darkish night, and I could see nothing, but a voice from the

steps, a voice I recognized, replied: ""Who lives here?" I said, "Michael O'Callaghan." "We want him," came immediately, two voices this time. My mind stabbed me with the thought that this formula preceded murder in Ireland, and I felt faint with horror, but I said calmly enough: "Well, you can't see him at this hour of the night." The voice I knew said again: "We want him, and we're coming in anyhow." ... Turning to my husband who was getting out of bed, I said: "It's the usual thing...." I bent out again, "Is there an officer in charge?" "Oh yes," came the answer, "One officer." "Two officers," said the other voice. In spite of myself, while I put on my dressing-gown and shoes, I cried a little, and my husband said, "You're nervous, and I'll come down with you this time. 'Tis the usual thing. Don't be afraid, dear." ... He had lighted the candle and put on his gown and shoes, and we went down stairs together.... He lighted the hall gas, and put the candlestick on the hall table, and, as I went towards the door, I said: "Don't stand there in the middle of the hall. You never know what is going to happen." He said: "It's all right," and stood just behind me while I unlocked and unchained the door. I opened the door wide, and when I saw the two men with goggles, and hats pulled down, and coat collars up about their ears, my heart leaped in my breast. I knew it was murder. Both men said together, waving their revolvers at Michael: "You come out here. Come out." My mind worked like madness ... stretching out both my arms to cover Michael and pushing him back behind me, I shouted: "No. No. My God, not that."

I heard Michael say, "No, no," just twice, as the men advanced after us in the hall. I caught at their hands as they tried to get me out of the way; there was a struggle for a second, and the man on my right hand, the man with clear glasses and the blue eyes, freed his right arm and fired over my shoulder. I turned to see Michael stagger from the hall table, against which I had pushed him and fall on the mat at the foot of the stairs. In my agony, I relaxed my hold of the man, and that same devil slipped past me and emptied his revolver into my dear husband's body as he lay on the ground.

I screamed all the time. I knocked them twice as our feet slipped on the polished floor; my shoes fell off: I tore at their faces and heads instinctively; they never said a word, but beat me with their hands on the head, shoulders and arms. We fell against the umbrella stand, and at last with an effort, they threw me off, and I fell heavily on my hip on the floor. I shall never forget the agony I suffered as I lay there screaming and helpless while I watched them running down the grass in the shaft of light from the hall door.[9]

The man leading the assassination team is generally credited, or discredited, to have been Auxiliary Cadet Inspector George Nathan, formerly of the Royal Warwickshire Regiment.[10] His companion, it is claimed, was Auxiliary Cadet Lieutenant Leslie Ibbotson, formerly of the Manchester Regiment. There appears to have been a degree of collusion between the murder gang and some sections of the military and police. The murderers were given a free hand without interference to accomplish their mission. At the Military Court of Enquiry that followed on 10th March, one Private Lewis, the sentry on guard at the Strand Barracks, testified that he had seen three men passing the barracks going toward Clancy's house. He heard six shots being fired, which he reported to his NCO. A few minutes later, he saw three unidentified men returning and going toward Sarsfield Bridge. At no stage did he challenge the men, whom he took to be British soldiers. The NCO reported the matter to the officer in charge of the guard, Lieutenant Smythe, who did nothing for three-quarters of an hour, before investigating, thus giving the assassins time to withdraw. George Nathan was called to give evidence at the inquiry. He confirmed that he had led previous raids on both O'Callaghan's and Clancy's homes. The purpose given was that there was reason to believe that the two men were in possession of seditious material. In that there had been previous raids, Mrs. O'Callaghan was adamant that it was Nathan who called out for admission that night, as she recognized the voice from the previous raids. No charges were ever brought against him or Ibbotson.

This was to be the lot of many women, seeing their loved ones killed before their very eyes.[11] Many a woman in Ireland at the time, living alone or with her children, her husband away fighting in a flying column, was subject to nighttime raids, raids made in the hope of catching a returning husband, and when frustrated, the house would often be ransacked in anger.

The war was not to be a conventional war, with big battles in which the women could act as auxiliaries to the Volunteers in the field. There were to be no big battles. This was to be a guerrilla war. As such, it was a war that could be won, not overnight, but possibly over months, or even years. There was a saying, "Those who can endure the most will eventually succeed." The IRA, plus a successful propaganda campaign in Britain and America, would over three years wear down the British and force them to the negotiating table. This form of hit-and-run warfare harkened back to an address Major John MacBride had made prior to surrender at Easter 1916. MacBride had fought in the Irish Brigade alongside the Boers in the South African War against Britain. He advocated the approach taken by Christian de Wett, the Boer commander, who used irregular troops made up of farmers who, having successfully ambushed British troops, returned home to their farms the next day. MacBride warned the men that never again should they allow themselves to be cornered in a building, surrounded by superior men and firepower. Among the avid converts to MacBride's method of warfare was Michael Collins.

The key to a successful war against Britain was to remove the eyes and ears of its intelligence source in Ireland—the Royal Irish Constabulary, and in Dublin, the G. Department (the political section) of the Metropolitan Police. In Dublin, the G. Men were approached and told to desist in their activities or face the consequences. Their reaction was one of indignation that they should be so threatened. Assassination was the only path open to deal with the police threat. Collins formed the Squad, a team of assassins. They went after Detective Sergeant Patrick Smyth, perhaps the most aggressive of the DMP men. He was shot on 30th July 1919. Mortally wounded, he died a week later. Detective Daniel Hoey was next. He had led a raid in search of Michael Collins just a week before. He was shot on 13th September. In November, Squad members fired at Detective Thomas Wharton near St. Stephen's Green. Though wounded, he survived and retired from the force. Detective Sergeant John Barton, who was investigating the attack on Wharton, was himself killed on 30th November 1919. The next month, Detective Constable Walshe was fired on, but he escaped.

At the end of 1919, Detective Inspector W.C. Forbes Redmond was brought in from Belfast as assistant commissioner to reorganize the G. Division. Redmond was accompanied by his own team. On the night of 20th January 1920, he organized a raid on Cullenswood House, where Collins had a basement office. Richard Mulcahy. minister for defense and head of the IRA, was also living there with his wife. Barely warned in time, the couple escaped, but they left valuable papers behind to be discovered. Collins ordered Redmond's execution. On the evening of 21st January 1920, Squad member Joe Dolan put a bullet in Redmond's head as he walked from his lodgings in Harcourt Street toward the castle. Soon after, Redmond's team returned home.

In February 1920, Walshe and Constable Dunleavy were targeted as they walked through the city. Walshe was killed, and Dunleavy was wounded. Detective Constable Harry Kells was killed on 14th April, and a week later, on 20th April, Detective Constable Laurence Dalton was assassinated. For its own safety, the G. Division was moved into Dublin Castle, but on 8th May 1920, Detective Sergeant Richard Revell was shot seven times. Miraculously he escaped death, but he never returned to political work. By the summer of 1920, the G. Division had been effectively neutralized.

Out in the countryside, the attacks against the RIC police barracks began in January 1920. So successful were they that by April of that year, the RIC were withdrawn from all rural areas, leaving great swaths of the country tentatively in Republican hands. This permitted, to a great extent, the free movement of the IRA columns. Of the 1,299 RIC barracks throughout Ireland, 434 were abandoned. They were later burned by the Volunteers. By the summer of 1920, the IRA had successfully burnt over 351 vacated police barracks, along with fifteen occupied ones. Some twenty-two regional tax offices were also attacked and destroyed, thus denying revenue to Britain. In response, the British began fortifying the remaining barracks with steel shutters over windows, cutting loopholes and laying barbed-wire entanglements around the buildings. The police were then reinforced by ex-soldiers, recruited in Britain, who, because of their makeshift uniforms, half-police and half-army, became known as the Black and Tans. By 1921, they numbered seventeen thousand. In addition, a new force, 2,200 in number, known as the Auxiliary Cadets and comprising in the main of ex–British Army officers, had also been deployed throughout Ireland. Both forces acted with a brutality not seen in Ireland since the days of Oliver Cromwell. In April 1920, Sir Hamar Greenwood was appointed chief secretary in Ireland. General Sir Hugh Tudor became the chief of police. All intelligence gathering was placed under a single director of intelligence, Colonel Ormonde de l'Epee Winter. Using the auxiliaries and officers seconded from the British Army *"on special service"* as their entries in the *Army List* indicated, a more ruthless gathering of information and murder was embarked upon.

The fight for independence that began as small ambushes against the police to acquire arms had, by mid-1920, developed into small battles with permanent Flying Columns of about thirty men, coming together with other columns to comprise a small army of one hundred or more Volunteers. As such, they were able to take on the British, as at Kilmichael and later Crossbarry in open combat. At Crossbarry 140 Volunteers under the command of Tom Barry, took on and defeated a convoy of Auxiliaries, then later fought a rear-guard action against twelve hundred encircling British troops. So confident did the guerrillas become that the columns entered British-occupied towns at night, defying the soldiers to come out of their barracks and face them, as at Bandon. At Drishanebeg, they ambushed a military train in the railway station and, in a prolonged action, caused severe casualties.

The problem that these IRA columns faced, apart from a lack of arms and ammunition, was their dispersal after an action. Because of their size, they could not be accommodated in a single community. Therefore, they were split up into smaller units for dispersal over a fairly wide area when seeking food and sleeping accommodations. Thus broken up into smaller units, there was always the danger of being isolated and captured by raiding parties. To a degree, this problem was solved by local Volunteer companies in whose territory they moved. They, with the assistance of Cumann na mBan, provided accommodations and food and stood guard to protect the resting column. The women often acted as mobilizers, bringing the disparate groups back together again at a designated location for further actions. They also acted as spotters for the guerrilla groups, placing themselves in great danger of being shot. Margaret Sweeney of Leitrim relates:

> When the Volunteers were preparing ambush positions, such as placing mines in the road or blocking roads by felling trees across or cutting trenches through the road surface, the girls of the Cumann na mBan performed the duties of scouting the roads well in advance of the points at which the Volunteers had protection parties. In this way, we were able to give warning of the approach of enemy forces. In one or two instances where the girls were not on such duty, the Volunteers were surprised at their work. We kept watch on the enemy posts and observed their movements. When there was unusual activity, it was apparent that a raid or round-up was being contemplated, and we sent out warnings, as far as possible, to the Volunteers to be on the alert.[12]

But with each minor victory, each successful ambush, repercussions always followed, and invariably the homes of known guerrilla fighters were put to the torch and the women who remained suffered.

In the early days, and indeed in some of the latter days during the War of Independence, there was, as has been indicated, a shortage of arms. So, after a skirmish or an ambush, rifles collected from the dead, or surrendered police or army detachments, were collected up and delivered to other flying columns. A number of women were so engaged, not only in transporting arms but also IRA personnel. Perhaps the best account we have comes from the pen of Linda Kearns. In this part of her narrative, she is most circumspect and does not name her passenger:

> Another time I was driving a *very* much wanted man … and we were held up at Carrick-on-Shannon and questioned. My companion did not speak at all, and I showed my permit and professional card [she was a nurse], and explained that I was taking a patient to the country—whispering the word, "Drink! Very bad!" and touched my forehead significantly. The officer glanced sharply at my companion, who in response to the part I was acting, continued to stare straight in front of him, with dull, vacant look. We were then told that it was all right, and that we could pass on, but knowing as I did who my friend was, and how differently the military would have acted had they realized his identity, my nerves suddenly seemed to fail me, and my hands shook on the wheel. I was for driving full speed ahead, my only thought to get away from those questioning eyes and voices. But the man beside me whispered very softly: "Drive steadily—*not* quickly; we are not yet out of the wood." His voice steadied me, and we got away all right. Afterwards we could laugh over it, my friend remarking that while he had been "on the run" he had passed for many men, but never for an alcoholic lunatic before![13]

There was another time when Linda was not so lucky. This time, she was transporting men and arms:

> I was driving my car on the night of November 20th, 1920, at about 11.30 p.m. The car contained besides myself, three young men [Commandant Jim Devine, and Volunteers Eugene Gilbride and Andy Conway] and a certain amount of "stuff"—10 rifles, 4 revolvers, and 500 rounds of ammunition, to be exact. It was a very dark night, and we were going steadily along the quiet country road. My hands were on the wheel, my eyes looking ahead, intent only on my driving, when suddenly, like a thunder-clap, came the order to halt. How clearly it all comes back to me—the surrounding darkness, which our lights made more black, the men sitting tensely beside me, and then the silence broken by the sharp, quick word—"Halt!" and again—"Halt! Damn you, halt!"
>
> I stopped the car, and we were immediately surrounded by a crowd of the most savage and undisciplined men which it has ever been my misfortune to meet. They were all drunk, shouting and talking together, and no one seemed to be in command. They were a mixed lot, comprising military, police, and Black and Tans. My three companions were at once pulled violently out of the car and searched, and the automatic pistol which the Commandant had in his possession was taken from him

immediately. The three of them were badly used, and it was impossible not to admire them for their coolness and self-control.

After some brutality on the part of the British patrol, Kearns was separated from the men and driven to the British barracks in Sligo. Here she was reunited with her three companions:

> I shall never forget the scene in the day room of that barracks! The prisoners were just thrown in by force. Commandant [Devine] was terribly badly beaten, and bled profusely from the head; indeed all were more or less hurt.... My own leather overcoat, gloves, wristlet watch, and signet ring were taken forcibly from me, and never returned. In the center of the room was a table, on which was a strange mixture of rifles and ammunition, whiskey and porter! ... After a while the Head Constable's daughter came and searched me, and I was then taken to a lock-up—a tiny room, with hard bench and stone floor, and it was most bitterly cold on that November night.

The mistreatment that she received is not recorded in this published account. This is detailed in the witness statement (404) that she recorded with the Bureau of Military History under her later married name of Mrs. Linda McWhinney:

> The police recognized the rifles that we had captured. It was then they saw red; they beat us up, calling us murderers.... Eventually, an officer came in to me with an overcoat over his pajamas—he may have been an Auxiliary—and spoke very nice to me. He said if I told where I was going and whom I was to meet I would be allowed to go home and nobody would ever hear about the episode, adding that I was damned unlucky to have got myself into such a stew. I still refused to give any information.
>
> When he left, the RIC took me on again and one of them, a notorious fellow nicknamed Spud Murphy, gave me a bad time. He beat me about the head and chest and broke one of my front teeth. A real Cockney Black and Tan who was among them protested against this conduct. He said: "Leave 'er h-alone; she might be as h-innocent as the child h-unborn." After this, they put me in the only place they had available—the mortuary—and locked me up.

From Sligo, the four were taken by destroyer along the coast to Derry, and from there Linda was taken to Armagh Female Prison. After a brief imprisonment at Walton jail in Liverpool, she was returned to Ireland and Mountjoy Prison. From there, she, Mary Bourke, and Eithne Coyle escaped over the wall with outside help. From there, they were taken to safety at an IRA training camp in County Carlow until the truce was announced.

So, what of Cumann na mBan at this period? Previously, in late 1919, the executive published its military organizational objectives in *Leabhar na mBan*. They envisaged the forthcoming war as a conventional war, where they would provide nurses and ancillary staff on and off the battlefield. They had not considered a guerrilla war of hit-and-run. As such, much of the training they undertook was never put into practice. In 1916, it was the individual acts of bravery of members of Cumann and others that proved significant. Most of the women involved out in the countryside were related to, or were close friends of, members of the guerrilla units. Here they were used as nurses at times, providers of meals and accommodations for the fighting men, mobilizers, dispatch carriers, and transporters of weapons in areas where there was a shortage of arms. Contact was not necessarily through the chief officers of Cumann, but more often through sisters, cousins, and sweethearts. In the towns and cities, and in particular in Dublin, the women provided safehouses, as we have seen, and in one or two cases, they supplied high-grade intelligence to Michael Collins.

EithneNi Chumhall, May Burke, and Linda Kearns in Duckett's Grove, Carlow, 1921

For both sides, winning the war was dependent on good intelligence. The gathering of such takes many forms, from mere "tittle-tattle" to high-risk information gathering. Right in the lead, and largely unsuspected, was the information gathered by a number of special and, in some cases, unique women. No matter how inconsequential, when gathered and analyzed alongside other bits of information, a bigger picture may emerge. Women who worked in the public sector, such as maids, receptionists, and telephone and telegraph operators, could all be expected to pass on information. Peg Flanagan passed on little bits of gossip and unconsidered comments made by men of the Black and Tans when at their leisure:

> I was on the advice of Michael Collins that I took over a restaurant called the West End at 40, Parkgate Street, a few months after the arrival of the Black and Tans. He thought it would put me in a position to be of great use to the Volunteers as it was just beside Kingsbridge and on the direct road in from Kildare, and he knew that it was frequented by the British forces.... I was able to get a lot of information from

these men for the Volunteers. I also got quite a lot of guns (revolvers) and ammunition. They sometimes had no money and would leave their guns which I handed over to the Volunteers.... We were often able to get information from the soldiers on guard at the Military Barracks, Arbour Hill and the Royal—about where Volunteers prisoners were located and passed it on to Mick Collins' men.... Brian Houlihan who was a member of the Intelligence Branch, used to take messages for us down to Phil Shanahan's in Foley Street, Jim Kirwan's in Parnell Street and Vaughan's Hotel in Parnell Square. Barney Mellows used to come to us too. He used to get information from someone in the Castle about people who were to be arrested.[14]

Unknown member of Cumann na mBan, 1921

Then there was the interception of the post, telephone, and telegraph. Collins had his share of "wire taps," to use the modern parlance. Among those assisting Irish intelligence was Miss Annie Barrett of Killavullen, County Cork:

I entered the Post Office Service as a telephonist at Killarney in 1906. After about six months I was transferred to Mallow. Early in 1919 I was appointed Supervising Telephonist at Mallow.... My first contact with the Irish Volunteer Organization was made through my brother who was a wireless operator. This was early in 1918 when he put me in touch with Tom Hunter and Danny Shinnick who were the Volunteer leaders in the Castltownroche-Killavullen area.... I arranged with the latter to relay all military and police messages passing through Mallow during my spells of duty to the Mallow Intelligence section of the Irish Volunteers. At this time I made copies of all such messages and handed them in to the house of Bill Hayes, who was a railway porter.

At this time also I passed on details of a telephonic conversation between the British Headquarters at Cork and O/C British Forces, Mallow, in which instructions were given to erect a camp at Mallow to intern suspected persons, including women and children, and also to erect a series of blockhouses between Mallow and Shanballymore. I also learned at this time that the code word to be used if Conscription was to be enforced was "TURKEY."

In May 1919 I obtained particulars of a telephone message from Dublin to the British forces at Fermoy informing them that some men who had been wounded in the rescue of Sean Hogan at Knocklong, were being accommodated in a house in the Mitchelstown area. Instructions were issued to raid this house. I immediately passed this information by means of telegraph messenger to the local Intelligence Officer who relayed it to Battalion and Brigade Headquarters. The wounded men were removed before the British raided the house in Michelstown district.

> Sometime in the spring of 1921 I overheard a telephone message from Headquarters, British Military at Cork in which instructions were issued to surround a Cork Column which was "resting" in the East Kerry area. Arrange- ments were being made for troops from Limerick, Tralee, Killarney, Buttevant and Fermoy to surround the area. I immediately passed on this information. The Column withdrew from its billets and so avoided the round-up.[15]

Margaret O'Callaghan recorded another instance of a "phone tap," but right in the heart of the British Establishment in Ireland:

> There was a telephonist from Kerry, whom Dinny [who was later to marry Margaret] knew, in the Vice Regal Lodge and she was able to give him a lot of information which we passed on to Mick's agents. For instance, she knew about Lord French's departure from Roscommon on the day of the ambush in December 1919. Dinny had a place of business in Capel Street at the time and she would come down and give him whatever information she had.[16]

Michael Collins succeeded in infiltrating a number of women into Dublin Castle, the nerve center of the British administration in Ireland. Aine Ryan of Cumann na mBan knew of two such women:

> The Intelligence Branch of the IRA had got two women, an aunt and a niece, into employment in the Castle in the year 1920. Sarah McDonagh was the aunt's name. She was the parlor maid and the niece a learner in the household of Colonel Whiskard (?). I used to visit the aunt—the first time was with Molly Gleeson.... Sarah's job was to report anything of interest that she heard or overheard while she was working with Colonel Whiskard. I cannot say what means she used to send information out, or whether her information was of any importance.[17]

This appears to be a slightly distorted version of Aine's sister Eilis's account, but then, trying to remember the events of some thirty years previous and without the full details of what was happening at the time, this is only natural. Eilis was at the center of what happened:

> One morning about June 1920, when Lilly [a friend] arrived at North Frederick Street she exclaimed, "I have an urgent message from Mick. Could you get a reliable parlor-maid for Mr. Alfred Cope in Dublin Castle? She must be young and good looking; the matter is urgent." This request required deep consideration. We knew from the list of unemployed that we had no member available and were unable to locate anyone among our own crowd to suit the job. Maire Gleeson, one of our members, was an employee of the late Dr. Donnelly of Haddington Road and the parlor maid there—though not a member [of Cumann na mBan] was sympathetic. The Bishop had just died, and this girl had obtained employment in one of Maurice Collins' shops. We decided this girl would be more than suitable if only she would accept the offer. I immediately went to the shop and discussed the matter with her, stressing the importance of the opportunity. She there and then accepted the offer, providing her employer agreed. Before I left the shop Maurice arrived and I told him my mission. He said if Miss McDonagh agreed—this was the girl's name—he'd get in touch with Mick immediately. She was installed in her job in the Castle in a

few days. Arrangements were also made regarding her visitors. I was debarred from even recognizing her in the street, Maire Gleeson, who was staying with Mrs. McDonagh's married sister on Drumcondra Road, my sister, Aine, and Aine Malone were selected as suitable visitors. It was arranged—by the Intelligence Department— that her lady visitors would call on her at times which coincided with the exercising of prisoners in the Castle Yard and when they were on identification parades. At this time many Volunteers were captured and brought to unknown destinations and the visitors' job was to endeavor to identify them on parade together with general observation at the Castle.[18]

Perhaps a little more security-conscious, with Irish typists within the castle coming under suspicion, the authorities began recruiting in England. "Tudor's Typists," as they became known, named after General Hugh Tudor, chief of police, "became the rage, and the sight of large numbers in summery attire, more suited perhaps for tea at the Shelbourne or the Bonne Bouche than for office routine, trooping to the balcony when anything novel appeared in the Castle yard, lent a new flavor of romance to the scene."[19]

One of "Tudor's Typists" was Nancy O'Brien—Michael Collins's cousin. She had been working in the post office service in London and was brought over to Dublin as a cipher clerk to decode messages. It was an incredible lapse of security on the part of the British in not checking her background. With her help, Collins was getting messages even before the British secret service officers for whom they were intended.

Three women posing as if in ambush. In reality, women were not permitted to take part in the shooting.

Perhaps the most successful of Collins's agents within the Dublin Castle administration was Lily Mernin. Lily Mernin was born in Dungarvan, County Waterford, in November 1886. Her father was a baker and confectioner by trade. He died when his children were quite young. Lily went on to train as a shorthand typist, and she worked in a number of Dublin offices, before being appointed to the garrison adjutant's office in Dublin Castle.[20]

In Dublin, two murder gangs were now operating—Collins's Squad, and Colonel Winter's team, known to Irish Intelligence as "The Special Gang." The object of both was the elimination of the other, and of their leaders. With each murder by Winter's men, papers and information were gathered up, which it was hoped would lead to the capture or death of Collins and his men. Collins acted first, using the information supplied by Lily Mernin. In her brief seven-page witness statement to the Bureau of Military History, she records her part played in the destruction of Winter's "murder gang":

> I was employed as a shorthand typist in the Garrison Adjutant's office, Dublin District, Lower Castle Yard.... The Garrison Adjutant for Ship St. Barracks and Dublin District at the time was Major Stratford Burton. The work that he gave me to do was connected with Volunteer activities generally and, in addition, Court-martial proceedings.... Each week I prepared a carbon or a typed copy, whichever I was able to get. Sometimes I would bring these to the office placed at my disposal at

Lily Mernin and her cousin Piaris Beaslai. Lily was one of Collins's most successful spies in Dublin Castle.

> [IRA] Captain Moynihan's house, Clonliffe Road.... Before the 21st November 1920, it was part of my normal duty to type the names and addresses of British agents who were accommodated at private addresses and living as ordinary citizens in the city. These lists were typed weekly and amended whenever an address was changed. I passed them on each week either to the address at Moynihan's, Clonliffe Rd. or to Piaras Beasley [her cousin who had recruited her.]
>
> On various occasions I was requested by members of the Intelligence Squad to assist them in the identity of enemy agents. I remember the first occasion on which I took part in this work was with the late Tom Cullenin 1919. Piaras Beaslai asked me to meet a young man who would be waiting at O'Raghallaigh's bookshop in Dorset St. and to accompany him to Lansdowne Road. I met this man, whom I learnt later was Tom Cullen, and went with him to a football match at Lansdowne Road. He asked me to point out to him and give him the names of any British military officers who frequented Dublin Castle and GHQ. I was able to point out a few military officers to him whom I knew.[21]

In his private papers now housed in the Imperial War Museum in London, one of the men on that list, Captain R.D. Jeune, wrote, "In November, information was coming in well and we were beginning to get on top of the

IRA, who were becoming desperate. I happened to receive information from three different sources to the effect that something was going to happen, but there was nothing definite." Before the British could act, Collins acted first. The day of the assassination of these British agents was set for Sunday, 21st November 1920—Bloody Sunday. In a series of coordinated attacks set for 9 a.m., Collins's men and units from the Dublin Brigade of the IRA virtually wiped out British Intelligence in Ireland.

28, Pembroke St.: Major Dowling, Captain Leonard Price, Captain Kennylyside, Colonel Woodcock and Lt. Col. Montgomery, were all killed.

119, Morehampton Rd.: Lt. Donald Lewis McClean, McLean's brother-in-law John Caldow, and an informer, T.H.Smith, also killed.

92, Lower Baggott St.: Captain Newbury, killed.

38, Mount St.: Captain George Bennett and Lt. Peter Ashmun Ames, killed.

28, Earlsfoot Tce.: Sergeant John Fitzgerald, also known as Capt. Fitzgerald and Captain Fitzpatrick, killed.

22, Lower Mount Street: Lt. Anglis, alias McMahon, and Lt. Peel, attacked but survived.

119, Baggott St.: Captain G.T. Baggalley, killed.

Gresham Hotel, Sackville St.: Capt. McCormack and Capt. Wilde, killed.

Eastwood Hotel, Fitzwilliam Sq.: Major Callaghan and Col. Jennings, were away for the night and survived.

Harcourt St.: Major King, Captain Hardy and Captain Jeune were on duty elsewhere, and survived.

Incidental to the scene, Auxiliaries Garniss and Morris were killed when they went to investigate the shooting. It was a close-run thing. Given a few days more, the tables might well have been turned. The death of Captain McCormack was controversial. It was claimed at the time that he was in Ireland purchasing donkeys for the British Army in Egypt. His was an influential Irish family, with connections to the old Irish Parliamentary Party, so questions were raised. Nonetheless, he was on Lily Mernin's list of British agents.

Following the synchronized assassinations of the British agents, there was a quick response from the Auxiliaries and Black and Tans. Men were stopped along the streets and searched, perhaps understandably, in a sometimes-brutal fashion. With a lack of female searchers, women were not stopped. This is what Irish Intelligence had counted on. The guns used that day were passed on to trusted women from Cumann. Annie O'Brien, nee Cooney, and her sister Lily were two such women, as Annie's statement to the Bureau of Military History testifies:

We were at the [University] Church at the appointed time and, to avoid attracting attention, we went into the church in turns, two at a time, and attended Mass while the third remained in the porch and watched. We heard the shooting quite near, as the operations were in progress in that area, and after waiting during what seemed to us an eternity, the three fellows came along walking pretty smartly and handed their guns to us, one each, in a laneway between the church and Harcourt Street corner. We put the guns in our pockets and proceeded home via Cuffe Street and other lanes, avoiding main roads.

The dead agents were replaced by quickly trained, and briefed, MI5 men. A new department was established for them in the Upper Castle Yard. Initially, to Collins's disappointment, Lily Mernin had no direct contact with this new unit. From time to time, they did venture down to her office, though:

These Intelligence Officers used to come into our office. The three girls of the staff were curious to know who they were. Some of the girls would ask, "Who was so-and-so that came in?" In this way, we got to know the names of the various Intelligence Officers. Some of the girls in the office were very friendly with them and used to go around with them. General conversation would give a lot of information concerning their whereabouts, things that were said, etc. Any information obtained was immediately passed by me to IRA Intelligence.

The war had brought women into public life as never before. From 1916, and before, they were seen in the uniform of Cumann na mBan, marching like men, and on the hustings, working for the election of Sinn Fein candidates in 1918. They provided safehouses, fed and nursed the wounded, transferred arms, and supplied high-grade intelligence. Truly they had come into their own. They took the risks, they took the beatings and imprisonment, but in the writing of the history of the War of Independence, their names have been forgotten. They were whitewashed out of history, ironically among others, by Dorothy Mcardle, whom Eamon deValera appointed to write the official history of the Irish Republic.

7

The Women Betrayed

Coming under increased international pressure to stop the atrocities being carried out by Crown forces and to bring the war to an end, not to mention the cost of that war; more money was being pumped into the country than was coming out, British prime minister, David Lloyd George, wrote to Eamon deValera. After an exchange of notes, he wrote again on 30th August 1921:

> We send you herewith a fresh invitation to a Conference in London on Oct. 11, where we can meet your delegates as spokesmen of the people whom you represent, with a view to ascertaining how the association of Ireland with the Commonwealth of Nations known as the British Empire may best be reconciled with Irish National Aspirations.

And so the negotiations for peace in Ireland began. Mary MacSwiney begged deValera to be part of the delegation, but he turned her down. He considered her to be "too extreme." The negotiations lasted from October to December 1921, but they did not deliver on an Irish Republic. The Government of Ireland Act of 1920, based on the prewar Home Rule Bill, granted the establishment of a twenty-six-county Irish Free State and provided for a parliament in the north to govern six of the Ulster counties. In addition, members of the Free State Dail were required to take an Oath of Allegiance to King George V and his successors. Failure to accept this offer, Lloyd George threatened, would lead to the resumption of "immediate and terrible war."

Reluctantly, Michael Collins and his team signed off on this agreement, and the proposed treaty was brought before the Dail for ratification. After some lively discussion, the vote on the treaty was taken by calling the roll. The atmosphere was tense as each member of the Dail voted for or against. At the end, the totals were declared; it was close—sixty-four for ratifying the treaty, fifty-seven against. To the ordinary people of Ireland, the truce had brought a sudden return to normality, an end to the intolerable strain of British reprisals, and it had given them a sense of hope for the future. Amid the cheering that there would be peace, there was also despair. Dominion

Home Rule was not the Republic that the politicians had all voted for back in January 1919. There was a huge sense of betrayal, particularly among the Catholic population of Northern Ireland, soon to be trapped in a "Protestant State for a Protestant people." This was also the feeling among many of the women members present who had voted against acceptance. They included Mrs. Pearse, Mrs. Clarke, Madame Markievicz, Mrs. O'Callaghan, Miss Mac-Swiney, and Dr. Ada English. Pragmatically, Michael Collins portrayed the treaty as "a stepping-stone to the Republic." For many of the women of Cumann na mBan, it was a betrayal. Cumann had always resisted the strong pressure to amalgamate into Sinn Fein, for they knew that in the process they would have lost that independence. So, they developed alongside other organizations, but somehow, it would seem, they lost contact with the evolving situation. But then they were not alone; there were also hardliners in the Volunteer movement, and the women were prepared to be led by them.

The women called an extraordinary general meeting of the executive. Markievicz presided. After some discussion, in which the word *traitors* was used more than once, a resolution was proposed:

> This Executive of Cumann na mBan reaffirms their allegiance to the Irish Republic and therefore cannot support the Articles of the Treaty signed in London.

The resolution was adopted by twenty-four votes to two. The executive then summoned a convention of all the branches throughout the country and beyond. A few hundred delegates attended the meeting held in Dublin in early February. In many cases, they represented district councils that comprised six or more branches, as Brighid O'Mullane indicated in her witness statement. The proposal was put forth by the Cumann na mBan's president, Constance Markievicz, and argued in favor of by Eileen McGrane, Josephine Aherne, Kate Breen, and Brighid O'Mullane. Mrs. Wyse Power and Min Ryan spoke against it. After some discussion, a vote was taken, and the delegates voted in favor by a majority of 419 to 63 to ratify the proposal of opposition to

Catherine Daly Clarke, one of "the Widows." She refused to accept the treaty.

the treaty. This led to a split in Cumann na mBan. The wives of men who had taken a pro-treaty stance generally followed their husbands' views. These women included Min Ryan, the wife of Richard Mulcahy, now minister of defense, as well as the influential Jennie Wyse Power and her daughter Nancy, all members of the executive. Leaving the meeting, the pro-treaty members resigned from Cumann na mBan and formed a new organization called Cumann na Saoirse (Company of Freedom, or Freedom Group).

Down in Limerick, as in other Irish counties, Cumann na mBan was also split. Madge Daly recalled:

> When the Treaty was carried, Limerick Cumann na mBan lost some of its members, but the majority remained loyal to the Republic. During the Civil War, the Republican forces in the New Barracks were joined by Cumann na mBan who helped in many ways.[1]

In the Dail, Eamon deValera, who was totally opposed to the treaty, resigned his presidency. After his failure to get reelected on 10th January 1922, based on his opposition to the treaty, he and his supporters left the Dail. Those members of the IRA and others opposed to the treaty, including a number of women from Cumann na mBan, gathered at the Four Courts along the quays in Dublin. They issued a declaration refusing to recognize the provisional government. Likewise, around the country anti-treaty Republicans began taking over the former British garrisons. While there were some physical confrontations, by and large, opposition was still only vocal. Success in a general election in June 1922 confirmed the provisional government in power. Prominent Republican women opposed to the treaty—including Countess Markievicz, Kathleen Clarke, Margaret Pearse, and Dr. Ada English—all lost their seats in the Dail.

On 22nd June 1922, Field Marshal Sir Henry Wilson, military advisor to the Northern Ireland Government, was assassinated in London in reprisal for attacks on Catholics in Ulster. The British Government believed that the death was ordered by Republicans opposed to the treaty. General Macready, in charge of the remaining British forces in Dublin, was ordered to attack the Four Courts on the following day. To have done so would inevitably have led to the resumption of the Anglo-Irish war. Crisis talks followed between the British and the Irish Free State Governments. The British gave the Irish an ultimatum, demanding that the occupation of the Four Courts end or they would face the resumption of war. As the Free State Government procrastinated, the Republicans within the Four Courts kidnapped General J.J. O'Connell of the Free State Army. This was seen as a direct challenge to the legitimate government. At 3:40 a.m., on 28th June, the provisional government issued an ultimatum to the Four Courts garrison to release O'Connell and depart. This was refused, and an hour later an artillery assault on the

Four Courts was begun, using guns borrowed from the British Army. After forty-eight hours of bombardment, the Four Courts was a blazing ruin. Its garrison surrendered. Elsewhere throughout the city, other buildings had been seized by the "Irregulars," as they were now called. They took over Whelan's Hotel, Hamman's Hotel, and Moran's Hotel.

Moran's was occupied under the command of Oscar Traynor. He was joined, among others, by Countess Markievicz, who took up a position as a sniper. Coming under sustained fire, the Moran's Hotel garrison was evacuated and moved to the Gresham Hotel. At Hamman's Hotel, where deValera was based, just prior to its surrender Ernie O'Malley, in his colorful account of the war, *The Singing Flame* (pp. 130–31), recalled:

> The girls had refused to leave. They recited the proclamation of Easter Week: "The Irish Republic is entitled to, and hereby claims, the allegiance of every Irishman and Irishwoman. The Republic guarantees religious and civil liberty, equal rights and equal opportunities to all its citizens." Why, if men remained, should women leave? The question was debated with heat in rooms of burning buildings, under the noise of shells and the spatter of machine-guns. Cathal Brugha had to exert his personal influence to make them go.

The Republicans in the city held out until 5th July, but with much of O'Connell Street now ablaze, they were forced to abandon their positions

Those opposed to the treaty seized the Four Courts, Dublin.

and surrender or attempt to break out. C.S. Andrews, in his autobiography, *Dublin Made Me* (p. 233), praised the efforts of the women he fought alongside:

> Thanks mainly to the presence of the girls, I suspect, we were not at all down hearted although recognizing quite well that militarily we were in a hopeless position.

Within days, all other Republican resistance in Dublin had been crushed. Most of those who were not captured fled the city, including IRA Chief of Staff Liam Lynch. Down in Munster, former British garrisons were seized by men whom the Free State Government referred to as "insurgents."

In June, Brighid O'Mullane was down in Sligo on her summer holidays:

> [I] was scarcely a week there when the Four Courts were attacked and the Civil War started. Just as I was thinking what part I could take in it, a Volunteer arrived with a message from the military barracks which had been occupied by the IRA to say there were three officers of Cumann na mBan there who were personal friends of my own. I rushed up immediately to the barracks and found there Sheila Humphreys, Una O'Connor and Peg Cuddihy of my Ranelagh Branch. These had come under orders to take part in the projected invasion of the North which had been agreed upon between Richard Mulcahy and the Republican Army in Dublin had been attacked by the Free State Army, which thus violated the agreement arrived at regarding the attack on the North.[2]

Thus, Brighid joined the Republican forces. Soon, however, with the approach of the victorious Free State troops, orders were received to evacuate the barracks and take to the hills. The women decided to return to Dublin.

Nurse Geraldine O'Donel found herself in the same position. She had been in Hamman's Hotel before its evacuation, but was then sent down to Tipperary with a medical team:

> We went to Clonmel where Seamus Robinson was in Command. It was then all the leaders turned up there, deValera, Childers, Liam Lynch and others. I had my quarters in the Military Barracks where I set up my First Aid Station. All the leaders used to turn up there for meals. I organized Stations in Tipperary town, Rockwell College and Shanbally Castle.... In Clonmel Barracks I would not let our fellows sleep in the beds until I had all the blankets washed. I got in about six women from the town to do this. We had a very big crowd there, a lot had come from Cork. We had a lot of people slightly wounded, torn with barbed wire, etc. Two men were killed and we could do nothing for them.... There was no fighting in Clonmel, but there was outside it.... It was at Shanbally Castle, Clogheen, that the Army broke up into columns and we could be of no further use.[3]

Brighid O'Mullane and her party, with guns hidden away in the trunk of their car, set out to surreptitiously return to Dublin. They were joined along the way by two other Cumann women, Nora Brick and Maggie Doyle. At Carrick-on-Shannon, their car was halted by Free State troops. The women were taken to the barracks, but having charmed the officers, they were eventually cleared to travel on. There could have been a tragedy, though, as Brighid points out:

> The O.C. came out to chat with us as we could not leave the car where our dangerous luggage was. Some of the girls disapproved of our methods and were for shooting the officers with the guns we had, but our arguments got the better of them and they came to see the wisdom of our ruse. We very graciously thanked the officers and parted with them.[4]

Entering Dublin on foot, the party of women walked right into a firefight between Free Staters and Republicans:

> We had got safely as far as South William Street and going down there a burst of firing came up the street towards us, but none of us was hit. We looked down and saw a company of Free State soldiers lined across the street at the other end. We then realized that they were firing at an IRA outpost and that we were directly in the line of fire. I pulled my companions with me into a large doorway to get some kind of cover. To our amazement the door behind us opened and we recognized Mrs. Freeman, the mother of two Cumann na mBan girls of our Ranelagh Branch. She recognized Sheila Humphreys and myself and insisted on us coming into the shelter of her home.

Seeking out Republican headquarters, then temporarily in Suffolk Street, some of the women were sent out again with dispatches. In Brighid's case, this was to the United Services Club in Stephen's Green, ordering them to evacuate the position at once. Later, she and Sheila Humphreys were sent out with papers from Cathal Brugha, which had to be taken to a place of safety:

> We started off from Tara Hall and had only got as far as Lower Gardiner Street, when we were held up by a posse of Free State troops under the command of Paddy Daly. They called on us to halt, but we refused and cycled furiously away. They fired on us, and as we turned a corner, we ran straight into another group of them, who seized us and pulled us off our bicycles. Paddy Daly came up then with his men.[5]

Women searchers were brought up, but O'Mullane and Humphreys put up such a struggle that the searchers gave up. The two women got away on their bicycles with their precious documents undiscovered. As well as transferring documents, O'Mullane also records that she and some of the others also moved a machine gun and a number of rifles between outposts. If caught, they would have been summarily executed, reflecting the tensions of the time. After many adventures, Brighid O'Mullane was eventually arrested in November 1922 and sent to Mountjoy Jail.

Kay Brady, a member of a wealthy Belfast linen manufacturer, and a graduate of University College Dublin, then living in Leeson Street, also acted as a driver, conveying men and arms for the Republican cause. C.S. Andrews recalled one such mission she undertook with him and Ernie O'Malley as her passengers:

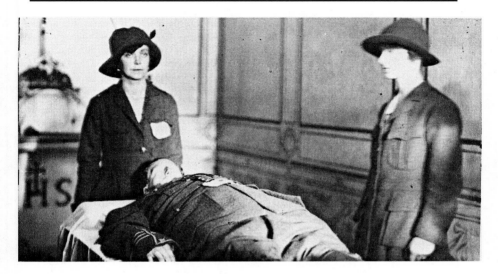

Two women from the anti-treaty Cumann na mBan stand guard over the body of Cathal Brugha.

> I had never known anyone who owned a car except a taxi driver. A car owned and driven by a woman was a complete novelty. Miss Brady and O'Malley indulged in much mutual leg-pulling. I had never seen men and women in that relationship before and was impressed by the fact that her mental agility was much greater than his. My education in the qualities of women had begun and it continued as we drove to Carrickmacross.... In thinking and behavior, she was rather violently feminist—a precursor of women's lib.[6]

Andrews also mentions the admirable part played by Madge Clifford:

> She was personally acquainted with all the members of the Army Council as well as with most of the members of the Provisional Government. Emotionally she was deeply involved in Irish Republicanism; one of the devoted band of women without whose help it would have been impossible to have carried on the Civil War for any length of time.... Watching Madge Clifford in action I realized for the first time that women had a role outside the home.... It never occurred to me that they could operate successfully as administrators or political advisers....[7]

As the struggle was ending in Dublin, Free State forces were pushing into Republican territory in Tipperary and Limerick. On 11th August, General Emmet Dalton and his National troops entered the city of Cork to much rejoicing. On the 20th. more troops under Sean Hales landed at Kinsale, surprising the "Irregulars," who withdrew at once in the face of superior numbers. The Republicans were now fighting a rearguard action. Republican nurse Madge Daly, working at the New Barracks at Limerick, then partly converted into a military hospital, recalled:

When the Republicans evacuated the City, the girls remained in the barracks until the men had got clear, and then returned to their homes, still ready to undertake any duty required of them. Mrs. Hartney, an early and active member, who went to Adare to help the IRA, was shot dead by Free State troops when crossing the yard of the hotel there. Her husband was serving with the Republican forces at the time…. It was the saddest period in our history, the comrades of yesterday fighting and killing one another.[8]

Margaret Duggan, a member of Cumann from Berehaven, County Cork, was also shot dead. She had been caught up in an ambush while in the company of two "Irregulars." In the skirmish, one of the Free State soldiers was wounded. In anger, Captain Hassett of the Free State Army shot her, mortally wounding her, after he saw Margaret talking to a captured IRA man.

The Free State Army, of old IRA Volunteers, was now enlarged by an influx of "Trucilliers"—a derogatory term for men who joined after the war had ended and who now swaggered about the place in their new uniforms. The new pro-treaty force had the decisive advantage of superior armaments, transport, and supplies, provided by the old enemy, Britain. They also had the support of the greater majority of the people, who just wanted an end to it all. As the war progressed, amid reports of atrocities, the Free State forces, by the end of the summer of 1922, held all the main cities and most of the countryside. Then a severe blow was struck against the few surviving Republican guerrillas by the Roman Catholic hierarchy, who excommunicated them. In a country where religion played such a major part in the lives of the people, this was a crushing condemnation. Nonetheless, even when their forces diminished, the Republican guerrillas fought on.

At this point, the Free State Government suffered two major losses. Michael Collins was killed in an ambush at Bealnablath in County Cork, on 22nd August 1922. And previously, President Griffith died of a heart attack on 12th August. Griffith was replaced by William Cosgrave as prime minister (officially titled as president of the executive council). Richard Mulcahy took over as military commander. The Republicans lost Liam Lynch, killed by Free State forces. In mid–October, the Dail passed what was known by the diehard Republicans as the "Murder Bill," which established military courts that had the power to order the execution of combative Republicans. Those caught in arms were shot out of hand, and a policy of ruthless reprisal executions followed. The Republicans fought on, their cause now hopeless. As Madge Daly recorded in her witness statement to the Bureau of Military History:

Soon the jails were filled with Republican prisoners, and conditions in Limerick Jail were deplorable. Our girls did all they could to help the prisoners. In 1922 a number of members of Cumann na mBan were arrested outside Limerick Jail, where they had been waiting for prisoners who were supposed to be allowed to escape…. The conditions under which they were held in custody in Kilmainham and Mountjoy were appalling. I have a number of letters sent out secretly by Nannie Hogan, which describe vividly the brutality to which they were subjected.

Ann (Nannie) Hogan died four weeks after returning home, having been weakened by the hunger strike she had undertaken in jail. Mary McSwiney also followed the suffragette model of the hunger strike. On her twentieth day, she was given the Last Rites. It was only after representation from people in Ireland and abroad that the Free State authorities gave in. She was released after twenty-four days of her hunger strike.

There was unspeakable horror carried out during the civil war—prisoners tortured, or taken out and shot—but the treatment of the women prisoners was beyond experience up to that point. It appears to have been guided by Free State leader W.T. Cosgrave, who declared, "The mainstay of the trouble we have had was the activity of the women." In his view, it was "not possible to consider these women as ordinary females."[9]

The huge numbers of women arrested, some for merely having Republican literature in their homes or for being relatives of IRA men, produced overcrowding in the prisons, in some cases four to a cell. It created enormous pressure on the prison authorities. Tempers became short as the prisoners began to organize and rebel against their imprisonment. Mary McSwiney went on a hunger strike and was released after twenty-one days. With the news that more prisoners were to be brought in, the women barricaded their cell doors with furniture, wedging it so that it was impossible to open the

Maire Comerford (*center*) was released by the Free State Government after a twenty-seven-day hunger strike.

door. Exasperated, the governor of the prison, Paidin O'Keefe, fired his revolver through the spyhole of one cell that contained Brighid O'Mullane, Maire Comerford, and Sighle Humphreys. The bullet lodged in the opposite wall. Tempers cooled when, after several days, reassurance was given by the authorities that no more prisoners would be lodged at Mountjoy. In the spring of 1923, to ease overcrowding, a number of prisoners were transferred to Kilmainham Jail. Here. Brighid O'Mullane was appointed by her fellow prisoners as O.C. of the wing. Right from the start they insisted on their treatment being that accorded to prisoners of war. They objected to their cell doors being locked at night. Getting no response from the prison governor, on one particular night, having received instructions on how to do it themselves, they unscrewed the locks of their cells, all eighty of them, and dropped them through the ventilators onto the outside sill. After a heated discussion between O'Mullaine and the prison governor, Commandant T. O'Neill, it was agreed that the cells would not be locked. There were further protests over their rights as prisoners of war, but they were only resolved after the women went on a hunger strike. With women being taken off to hospital, O'Neill caved in. The women had won. In his favor, O'Mullaine was to write in her witness statement: "In fairness to Commandant O'Neill, I would like to say that his conduct throughout was unimpeachable, and he never broke his word."

There was one particular incident full of poignancy when women from Cumann na Saoirse, former members of Cumann na mBan and former friends of some of the prisoners, were used alongside the wardresses and military police to move some seventy prisoners from Kilmainham to the converted prison at the North Dublin Union. Mary McSwiney was on a hunger strike at the time, and the prisoners refused to go until she was released. The prisoners to be removed had agreed to resist, but not to attack. Dorothy Macardle recounted the distressing incident in *The Kilmainham Tortures,* an undated booklet now in the Kilmainham Gaol collection. She describes the removal as "violent but disorganized." Bridie O'Mullane and Rita Farrelly, the first to be seized, were crushed and bruised "between men dragging them down and men pressing up the stairs." Brighid herself recorded the incident:

> We were dragged from the top landing down the stairway, all of us resisting violently, but eventually having to yield to superior force, and were dragged into a room downstairs to be searched.

Fellow prisoner Una Gordon "clung to the iron bars of the stairs and the men beat her hands with their fists." With her hands free, she was "dragged down the stairs by her hair, her head beaten against the iron bars of the staircase."[10] Other women were struck, as with May Zambra, with an iron bar. Dorothy Macardle recalled her own removal:

... after I had been dragged from the railings, a great hand closed on my face, blinding and stifling me, and thrust me back down to the ground amongst trampling feet.

Amid the brutality and resistance, it took the authorities over five hours to complete their task. Over the coming days, the Republican women prisoners from all around the country were taken to the North Dublin Union, described by inmate Margaret Buckley as "a sort of concentration camp for women." Removals from Mountjoy Jail were equally brutal. Judy Gaughran was flung down the stairs. Maire Comerford had to have three stitches to a head wound; Sighle Humphreys was removed half-conscious; Sorcha Mac-Dermott was knocked to the floor by five female searchers and beaten.

Now without any hope of winning, on 24th May 1923, deValera, former president of Sinn Fein, and Frank Aitken, Liam Lynch's successor as IRA chief of staff, issued the order to the "Soldiers of the Republic, Legion of the Rearguard" to "dump arms." Thus, the civil war was ended, but with neither the surrender of the of the remnants of the IRA nor the recognition of the Free State's legitimacy.

The prisoners were gradually released to return to their homes and families, where they still existed. The number of people who met violent deaths during the civil war, which lasted just under a year, was almost five thousand—far more than during the two and a half years of the war against the British. The civil war became one of those periods about which few people spoke. The memories were there, but no one spoke of it. In 1966, Eoin Neeson's book *The Civil War in Ireland* was published. It was the first history of the civil war. It had taken over forty years before someone had taken the courage to articulate the suffering of that one terrible year.

So, what of Cumann na mBan? Though they had been true to their ideals, they had chosen the wrong side, and in an Irish Free State, following the end of the civil war, suspicion of the movement turned to indifference as their influence waned. Reminiscing in the 1966 edition of the *Capuchin Annual*, Eilis Bean Ui Chonail reflected:

Cumann na mBan is gradually passing into history. Our ranks are, alas! Being depleted. In the city, up and down the country time has been kind in leaving so many old members of Cumann na mBan to pass on their reminiscences.

And thus Cumann na mBan faded, but it did not quite die.

The constitution of the new Irish Free State, drawn up in 1922, guaranteed the rights and equality of women, unlike that of the north, where they would have to wait until 1928. The Free State declared in Article 3 that "every person, without distinction of sex, shall ... enjoy the privileges and be subject to the obligations of such citizenship." In the general election of 1923, five women were elected to the Dail. Perhaps of greater interest in that election was the mandate of the public given to the Free State Government to build upon the Treaty. They gained sixty-three seats; Sinn Fein, led by Eamon deValera, gained forty-six, but because they refused to swear the controversial oath of allegiance to the British monarch, as required in the treaty, they were unable to take their seats in the Dail. Labor gained fourteen seats.

The ruling party now took on a new name, Cumann na nGael, and passed a Public Safety Act giving themselves emergency powers in peacetime to deal with the IRA. In the summer of 1926, deValera formed a new party, Fianna Fail. Constance Markievicz chaired its inaugural meeting in the La Scala Theatre. It was here that deValera declared that he would enter the Dail without taking the oath, on the basis that Cumann na Gael was not the legitimate parliament of the Irish Republic. In the general election of 1927, W.T. Cosgrave's Cumann na nGael was returned to power. Fianna Fail won forty-four seats, plus the support of two independent Republicans. While Cosgrave's party lost its overall majority, winning just forty-seven seats, it was able to count on the support of Labor, Independents, and others. On 23rd June, the elected Fianna Fail deputies sought admission to the Dail chamber but were denied access unless they subscribed full-heartedly to the oath. This they refused to do and were denied access. Legal proceedings were instituted in the High Court to test the validity of the exclusion. Unfortunately, as the case was being adjudicated, Cumann na nGael's justice minister, Kevin O'Higgins, was assassinated. In response, the Cumann na nGael government introduced three new bills. The first gave the government further power to deal with the IRA. The other two were constitutional measures aimed at absentee Fianna Fail deputies. One bill required all candidates in future elections to make a declaration under oath that they would take the Oath of Allegiance and sit in the Dail if elected. The other measure was devised to prevent any attempt by Fianna Fail to press for a referendum on the oath without first taking their seats in the Dail. This was a glorious catch-22 situation, created by the government, but in August a Jesuitical solution was found, which was equally devious. The Fianna Fail deputies would subscribe to the oath with mental reservations. DeValera sold the swearing as an "empty formality." The new deputies entered the Dail on 11th August and pledged to dismantle the constitution of the Irish Free State in order to bring about the cherished Republic. In the Dail. they established alliances with the National League and the Labor Party, eventually forcing a vote of no confidence in the government. Fresh elections were held in the autumn, with Cumann na nGail just hanging on. Cosgrave's government fought another general election in February 1932, on the basis of its past service. Fianna Fail emphasized economic self-sufficiency, the Republican ideal, and the aspiration to reconcile all sections of national opinion. Fianna Fail won seventy-two seats and was returned as the largest party in the Dail. Jennie Wyse Power, suffragette and nationalist, was elected to the senate, retaining her position for nine years. Re-forging its links with the other parties, Fianna Fail formed the new government. DeValera now began breaking links with Britain. He also declared that the state would have a special relationship with the Catholic Church, which was unfortunate to say the least. The Church's attitude toward women, was that their place was in the home, looking after their husbands and children. This undue influence of the Church over the government led to legislation during the 1920s and 1930s that placed restrictions on and chipped away at the rights of citizenship of women.

Caitriona Beaumont has highlighted the subtlety of the change.[11] The 1924 Juries Act allowed women, but not men, to exempt themselves from jury service. The intention was portrayed as being benign in allowing women, busy looking after the home and family, to avoid time-consuming jury service. The Act was in contravention of Article 3 of the Constitution, which placed obligations on both men and women. There was a protest by the Irish Women's Citizen Association, who argued that "women had no right to evade any duties and responsibilities involved in citizenship." The overwhelmingly male-dominated Dail ignored the protest, and the Bill was passed into law. It was the thin end of the wedge. In 1927, a further Act was passed, removing women from the jury lists. Due to widespread protest by women, during the debate in the Dail it was conceded that women could be included on the jury list, if they so applied. This was allowed in the belief that some women, and they were the exception it was suggested, might wish to perform a role in public life.

Other restricting Acts followed. In the Civil Service (Amendment) Act of 1925, women were obliged to resign upon getting married. This, in fact, brought it in line with the British civil service, thus giving the Irish Act its justification. The Conditions of Employment Act, in 1936, was designed to alleviate unemployment in Eire following the Depression. While it had some good points, Article 16 provided ministerial authority to prohibit the employment of women in certain forms of industrial work. It read:

16.—(1) The Minister may in respect of any form of industrial work, after consultation with representatives of employers interested in such form of industrial work and with representatives of workers so interested, by order make regulations either—
  (a) prohibiting the employment of female workers to do such form of industrial work, or
  (b) fixing a proportion which the number of female workers employed by any employer to do such form of industrial work may bear to the number of other workers so employed.

(2) When any regulations made under this section are for the time being in force in respect of any form of industrial work it shall not be lawful for any employer to employ to do such form of industrial work either (as the case may be) any female worker or so many female workers that the number of female workers so employed by such employer bears to the number of other workers so employed a proportion greater than that fixed by such regulations.

(3) If, when any regulations made under this section are for the time being in force, any employer employs a female worker or a number of female workers in contravention of such regulations such employer shall be guilty of an offence under this section.

Helena Molony, still around, was vehement in her protest of the Act, but her bitterness was especially reserved for the Labor leaders who had supported a "capitalist Minister in setting up a barrier against one set of citizens." This was seen by her as the ultimate betrayal by James Connolly's successors. Veteran feminist Hanna Sheehy Skeffington inferred that the Act would throw large numbers out of work and would have scandalous results, forcing women into prostitution. "There was a terrible alternative such unfortunate women might take," she wrote, "and it would be at the door of Mr. Lemass ... if women were driven to take such an alternative."

A new Irish Constitution was drawn up by the deValera government in 1937. Articles 9 and 16 appeared to undermine the position of women in Ireland. They concerned qualification of citizenship and voting rights. Lacking was the phrase—the important phrase—"without distinction of sex." Whether it was deliberate, or merely lazy, in the drawing up of a new constitution, deValera dismissed the phrase as being meaningless. Following widespread protest, the term was inserted in Article 16, and somewhat of a fudge, in Article 45, which related to women in paid work. The pressure brought by educated middle-class women did not perhaps reflect the position of women in Ireland as a whole. The country was enthralled to the Roman Catholic Church. Its teaching emphasized that the domestic role of women was within the family. Social pressure from neighbors forced women to comply. Helena Molony was one who criticized the Church for its stand, and perhaps as a reward for her long-standing socialist commitment, in 1937, she was elected president of the Irish Trade Union Congress. She was only the second woman to hold the office.

In the general election of 1948, Fine Gael, with the assistance of Clann na Poblachta, just about squeezed into government. Leader John Costello, in a bid to look magisterial, took the final step to full independence from Britain by declaring that Ireland was now a republic. In truth, she had been a republic in all but name since 1938. In Costello's coalition government, Dr. Noel Browne of Clann na Poblachta was made minister for health. Browne attempted to introduce free healthcare, following the British model, to expectant and nursing mothers. It became known as the Mother and Child Scheme. The idea was to benefit working-class women in families with limited means. This rather benign piece of legislation brought forth the full fury of the Catholic Church in Ireland, in the shape of John Charles McQuaid, Archbishop of Dublin. He declared the scheme would introduce socialized medicine to Ireland. It would permit the state to meddle in family life. It was not as if the Church was not already doing that in the everyday lives of the citizens with its restrictions and constraints, a series of dos and don'ts. The Church, confusing Christianity with Communism, had its supporters in the Irish Medical Association, who were opposed to the possible introduction of a National Health Service that would interfere in their private practice. The scheme was abandoned, and in protest Browne resigned. The Church continued to dominate in Ireland, and the doctors retained their fees. It was just another betrayal for working-class mothers.

Far away in Rome, Pope John XXIII's Second Vatican Council of 1962–1966 introduced more liberal concepts, based on the realities of the day. The concepts of divorce within the Catholic Church, contraception, and even feminist thought began to be openly discussed.

Fresh hope for the equality of women in Ireland was not to come for another decade, not until Ireland's entry into the European Economic Community (now the European Union) in 1973. Law followed upon law from Brussels. The Anti-Discrimination (Pay) Act of 1974 established the right of women, employed at like work to men, to equal pay. The Employment Equality Act, which came into law in 1977, prohibited discrimination on grounds of sex or marital status in recruitment training, or provision of opportunities for promotion. That same year came the Unfair Dismissals Act, and in 1981 came the Maternity (Protection of Employees) Act, which protected pregnant employees from unfair dismissal.

The Maternity Act was passed in 1981, and it ensured the right of women to return to work following the birth of a child. Other acts, sometimes opposed by elements of the government, were brought into being following pronouncements by the European Court of Justice. Equal rights for women in Ireland have largely been achieved. Coupled to this was the diminishing power of the Roman Catholic Church, brought about by its own hypocrisy and wickedness, exhibited in the exposure of pedophile priests, the Magdalene Laundries, the sale of illegitimate babies to wealthy American Catholic families, and the exposure of the Bishop of Galway, Eamon Casey's long sexual relationship with an American divorcee, that produced a son who was born in 1974.

In 1979, Maire Geoghan-Quinn became the first woman since 1921 to be appointed to a cabinet position within the government. Perhaps the ultimate victory for women, in what many perceived to be still a misogynist Ireland, was the appointment of two women in succession as president: Mary Robinson, serving from 1990 to 1997, and Mary McAleese, from 1997 to 2011. Also in the 1990s, the suffragette struggle was recognized when the Gender Studies building at University College, Dublin, was renamed the Hanna Sheehy Skeffington

Rosie Hackett in old age

Building. It was a pity that her husband, also a feminist, was not also recognized. Hanna was further honored in England when her name and picture, one of fifty-eight British suffragettes, appeared on the plinth of the statue of Millicent Fawcett in Parliament Square, London. It was unveiled in 2018.

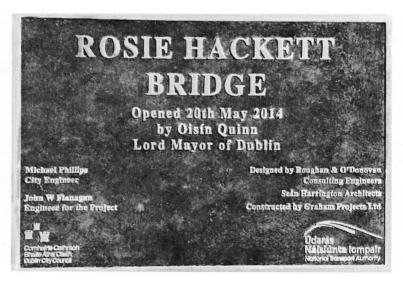

Plate erected on Rosie Hackett Bridge, Dublin

What was perhaps more delightful was that Little Rosie Hackett, working-class Rosie Hackett, was also acknowledged. In May 2014, the latest bridge over the Dublin Liffey was named in her honor. There was an open competition for a name to be given to the bridge. More than 18,000 people took part; there were eighty-five suggestions, whittled down to five—and Rosie Hackett was chosen. Someone once described the bridge as a low, single-span concrete construction, simple and sensitive in design. What I like about it is that benches have been provided for people to quietly sit and contemplate the river and think of the contribution that women have made.

Chapter Notes

Chapter 1

1. Pankhurst, Emmeline, *Suffragette: My Own Story*, 1914. Reprinted by Hesperus Press, London, 2016, p. 21. Manchester-born Lydia Becker was an early leader of the British suffragist movement. She founded the *Women's Suffrage Journal*.

2. Hansard, 1866–67.

3. Unattributed source, Valmcbeath. com/Victorian-era-womens-suffrage, p. 3.

4. The DWSA became the Dublin Women's Suffrage (and Poor Law Guardian) Association, evolving into the Dublin Women's Suffrage & Local Government Association before becoming the Irish Women's Suffrage & Local Government Association.

5. "Report of the Irish Women's Suffrage & Local Government Association," quoted in Quinlan, Carmel, "Onward Hand in Hand," in Ryan, Louise, & Ward, Margaret, *Irish Women & the Vote*, p. 28.

6. Cullen, Mary, "A history of her story," *Irish Times*, 17th Oct. 2012.

7. Quinlan, Carmel, "Onward Hand in Hand," p. 35, in Ryan, Louise, & Ward, Margaret, *Irish Women & the Vote*, p. 35.

8. Cousins, James H., & Margaret E., *We Two Together*, Ganesh & Co., Madras, 1950.

9. Luddy, Maria, "Separate but equal," *Irish Times*, 17th Oct. 2012.

10. Pankhurst, p. 170.

11. "The Tales of the Tullamore Mice," *Irish Citizen*, 26th July 1913. The prison at Tullamore was the favored place for incarcerating suffragettes, though some were imprisoned temporarily in Mountjoy.

12. *Irish Times*, 19th July 1912.

13. **Mary Leigh** was born in Manchester in 1885. She became a member of the WSPU. She was arrested in 1908 for throwing stones at No. 10 Downing Street and sent to Holloway Prison. Once released, she was re-arrested while protesting at the House of Commons and sentenced to three months. In 1909, while on the roof of a building in which Asquith was speaking, she removed some tiles, which she threw down onto the police below. Dragged from the roof, she was given two weeks' imprisonment. Going on a hunger strike, she was forcibly fed through the nose. Barely days out of prison, Mary was re-arrested for throwing stones at David Lloyd George's car. She got two months with hard labor and was force-fed again. In 1911, she was imprisoned for two months for assaulting a policeman, though it was questionable as to who assaulted whom. In July 1912, she traveled to Dublin.

Gladys Evans was born in 1877 into a prosperous middle-class family. Her father was the owner of *Vanity Fair*, a British weekly society magazine. In 1908, Gladys was working for Selfridges, the department store, in London. Later she joined the WSPU and was employed to run their shop. She visited Canada in 1911 to stay with her sister, but she was back in England in 1912. After her release following the incident in Dublin, she emigrated to the United States.

Jennie Baines was born Sarah Jane Hunt in 1866, but she was known as Jennie to her family. She came from a Salvation Army background. She joined the WSPU in 1905 and became a paid organizer in 1908 at £2 a week. Her job was to organize meetings, open new branches of the WSPU, and arrange meetings and rallies. She was noted as a powerful speaker and was well respected as a proponent of action rather than words.

She was arrested and imprisoned for short terms about fifteen times, including six months for unlawful assembly in 1908. After the Dublin experience, she went on to bomb train carriages parked in a siding. Arrested, she was found guilty and sent to Holloway Prison. She was force-fed, but becoming ill, was released. She emigrated to Australia.

Mabel Capper was born at Chorlton on Medlock, near Manchester, in 1888. She was born into a suffragette family. Her father was secretary of the Manchester branch of the Men's League for Women's Suffrage. Her mother was an active member of the Women's Social and Political Union. Mabel joined the WSPU in 1907 and moved down to London the following year. In October of that year, she was arrested, along with the younger Pankhursts and others, following the attempt to invade the House of Commons. She spent one month in prison. In July 1909, she was arrested for disrupting a meeting in Edinburgh, addressed by Lloyd George. After a six-day hunger strike, she was released. In August, she was again arrested, along with Mary Leigh, on a charge of disorderly conduct, assaulting the police and breaking windows while in Birmingham. In Winson Green Prison, she was forcibly fed. Further arrests followed over the next two years. In July, she traveled with others to Dublin. Following the declaration of war in 1914, Mabel Capper joined the Volunteer Aid Detachment. She later became a pacifist.

14. Lytton, "Prison and Prisoners," 1914, quoted in Jenkins, Lyndsey, *Lady Constance Lytton…*, London, 2015, pp. 142–3.

15. Ryan, Louise, *Winning the Vote for Women*, p. 25.

16. National Archive Ireland, GPB/SFRG/1/5 Barbara Hoskins, 7th Feb. 1913. Quoted in Sarah-Beth Watkins, *Ireland's Suffragettes*, p. 45.

17. Francis Sheehy Skeffington, a known pacifist, was proceeding home after trying to prevent further looting in the city. He was being followed by a group of people. As he approached Portobello Bridge, he was stopped by a picket of the Royal Irish Rifles, who had orders to prevent crowds from gathering. Sheehy Skeffington was arrested as a possible ringleader and taken to Portobello barracks. Here he was interviewed by Captain J.C. Bowen-Colthurst. Later that evening, Bowen-Colthurst was ordered to occupy the premises of businessman James Kelly. He took Sheehy Skeffington with him as a form of hostage. As the soldiers proceeded along the road, they came upon two lads, Laurence Byrne and James Coade. Without provocation or explanation, Bowen-Colthurst shot and mortally wounded Coade. The patrol then moved on to Kelly's. Here, two occupants, Patrick McIntyre and Thomas Dickson, were taken into custody. Returning to the barracks, and without any form of trial, Bowen-Colthurst ordered their execution by firing squad. Later, Major Sir Francis Vane, in overall charge of the barracks, returned and discovered what had happened. He immediately informed the authorities in Dublin Castle of what he considered to be murder. After some prevarication, Bowen-Colthurst was court-martialed, but found guilty but insane. He was sent to Broadmoor Mental Hospital, but he was released less than two years later. He was quietly resettled in Canada, where he died in 1965.See: McKenna, Joseph, *Voices from the Easter Rising*, pp. 281–4.

18. Kelly, Vivien, "Irish Suffragettes at the time of the Home Rule crisis," *History Ireland,* Issue 1 (Spring 1996) vol. 4.

Chapter 2

1. Mary E. Daly, "Working-class housing in Scottish and Irish cities on the eve of World War I," in Connolly, Houston, & Morris, *Conflict, Identity and Economic Development*, p. 218.

2. 1911 Census, Belfast and Dublin.

3. John P. Swift, "The Last Years," [Ed.] Nevin, Donal, *Lion of the Fold*, 1998, p. 92.

4. Clarkson, J. Dunsmore, *Labour and Nationalism in Ireland*, New York, 1925, p. 225.

5. McGarry, Feargal, "Helena Maloney: a revolutionary life," *History Ireland*, Vol. 21, No. 4, 2013.

6. *Irish Citizen*, Jan. 1918.

7. McGarry.

8. McAuliffe, Mary [Ed.], "Rosie," in Devine, Francis, *Working in a Rose Garden…* pp. 41–2.

9. Jane Shanahan Military Service Pension. File REF10154, Military Archives.

10. O'Brien, Nora Connolly, *Portrait of a Rebel Father* (1975 ed.), pp. 156–7.

11. Moriarty, Theresa, "Larkin and the

Women's Movement," in Nevin, Donal [Ed.], James Larkin, *Lion of the Fold*, p. 98.

12. O'Faolain, Sean, *Constance Markievicz*, Cresset Women's Voices, Century Hutchinson, London, 1934 (reprint 1987) p. 117.

13. For more detail on Jacobs and its female strikers, see McAuliffe, Mary [ed.], "Rosie," and Yeates, Padraig, *Lockout.*

14. Helena Molony, Bureau of Military History, Witness Statement 391. Professor Fergus A. D'Arcy also makes reference to the personality clash in his paper, "Larkin and the Dublin Lock-Out," in Levin, Donal, James Larkin, *Lion of the Fold*, p. 45.

15. White, Jack, *Misfit, An Autobiography*, p. 261.

16. Women who joined the Irish Citizen Army:

Barrett, Mrs.	Joyce, Mrs.
(Connolly)	Lynn, Kathleen
O'Reilly, Molly	Carney, Winifred
Ryan, Margaret	ffrench-Mullen,
Cavanagh, Maeve	Madeleine
Brady, Bridge	Kelly, Annie
Norgrove, Mrs.	Molony, Helena
Walsh, Martha	Grennan, Julia
Hackett, Rosie	Gifford, Nellie
Davis, Bridget	Kempson, Lily
Shanahan, Jinny	Norgrove, Emily
Caffrey, Chris	O'Farrell, Elizabeth
Hyland, Mary	Gough, Bridget
Lynch, Bessie	Seery, Kathleen
Perolz, Maria	Connolly, Nora
Devereux, Mary	Connolly, Ina

Source: R.M.Fox & Ann Matthews & etc.

17. O'Brien, Nora Connolly, p. 154.

18. It has been alleged that Markievicz paid for all the food out of her own pocket, selling her jewelry and taking out loans. She was also connected with running an Inghinidhe na h'Eireann soup kitchen to feed poor schoolchildren.

19. Sean O'Casey, later to become a playwright, was originally born John Cassidy. Though a Protestant, he became a fervent nationalist and was a member of the Gaelic League. As a working man, O'Casey was an early member of the Irish Transport and General Workers' Union, founded by James Larkin. O'Casey was the first to write a history of the ICA, which was published in 1919.

20. O'Cathasaigh, P.O., *The Story of the Irish Citizen Army*, p. 52.

21. White, Misfit, p. 304.

22. O'Cathasaigh, p. 34.

Chapter 3

1. Ward, Margaret, *Unmanageable Revolutionaries*, London, 1983, p. 14.

2. Hearne, Dana [Ed.] Anna Parnell, *Tale of a great sham,* Dublin, p. 90.

3. Helena Molony Witness Statement BMH 391.

4. For details on this case, see: McKenna, Joseph, *The Irish-American Dynamite Campaign*, pp. 72–88 and 148–155.

5. Ibid., pp. 28–60.

6. Mrs. Sidney Czira, Witness Statement BMH 909. While in America, Sidney Gifford was briefly married to a Hungarian émigré, Arpad Czira. Sidney returned to Ireland with her son Finian in 1921, thereafter referring to herself as Mrs. Sidney Czira.

7. Maeve McGarry, Witness Statement BMH 826.

8. Czira.

9. Mrs. Richard Mulcahy Witness Statement BMH 399. Minnie Ryan, a former fiancée of Sean MacDiarmada, married General Richard Mulcahy, IRA, in 1920.

10. The separation of women and men was more traditional than misogynist. The churches, both Catholic and Protestant, had a tradition of segregation of the sexes, and this overlapped into public life.

11. Cal McCarthy, *Cumann na mBan and the Irish Revolution*, pp. 12–13, puts forward the case that the formation of C.mBan was not as spontaneous as has been supposed. Thomas MacDonagh, feminist and senior IRB man, had put forward the concept of establishing a female paramilitary force. In this, he was supported by Tom Clarke. Bulmer Hobson, IRB man and cofounder of the Fianna Eirean, informed Molly Reynolds of the intention to do so. At the time, Hobson was sharing an office at 12 D'Olier Street, Dublin, with her father.

12. *Capuchin Annual* 1966, Eilis ni Chorra, *A Rebel Remembers*, pp. 292–3.

13. Nora Connolly O'Brien Witness Statement BMH 286.

14. Molly Reynolds, Cumann na mBan, Witness Statement BMH 195.

15. Margaret Kennedy Witness Statement BMH 185. Na Fianna Eireann (Soldiers of Ireland) was founded in 1909 by Bulmer Hobson and Constance Markievicz. It was

a nationalist boy scout movement. The boys were steeped in Irish culture. See: McKenna, *Voices from the Rising*, pp. 22–27.

16. Captain Seamus Pounch, Fianna Eireann Witness Statement BMH 267.

17. Eileen Walsh, Cumann na mBan, Witness Statement BMH 480.

18. Eily O'Hanrahan O'Reilly Witness Statement BMH 270.

19. Nan Nolan, Witness Statement BMH 1441.

20. *Capuchin Annual* 1966, Sean T. O'Ceallaigh, Arthur Griffith, p.140.

Chapter 4

1. Elis Ni Riain, Witness Statement 568.

2. Bridget Diskin, Witness Statement 484.

3. Bessie Cahill, Witness Statement 1,143.

4. Coogan, T.P., 1916: *The Easter Rising*, p. 94.

5. Seamus Kavanagh, Witness Statement 208.

6. Nancy Power Wyse, Witness Statement 541.

7. Helena Molony, Witness Statement 391.

8. Nora Connolly O'Brien, James Connolly, *Portrait of a Rebel Father*, pp. 298–9.

9. R.M. Fox, in his *History of the ICA*, lists twenty-seven women. Ann Matthews, in her Irish Citizen Army, lists twenty-eight. The extra woman would appear to be Maria Perolz, who acted as a courier between the garrisons and beyond.

10. Ruaidhri Henderson, Witness Statement 1686.

11. Annie Norgrove, Hanratty Papers, Kilmainham Gaol Museum.

12. Molony Witness Statement 391.

13. "A Nurse in Dublin Castle: a first hand account by a VAD Nurse," *Blackwood's Magazine*, Dec. 1916.

14. Fox, *History of the Irish Citizen Army*. P144.

15. James Coughlan, Witness Statement 304.

16. Annie O'Brien Cumann na mBan, Witness Statement 805.

17. Robert Holland, F. Company, 4th Battalion, Witness Statement 280. The Miss "Cumiskey" mentioned by Holland may perhaps be a trick of memory. After all, he was recalling events some twenty years

prior. There is no mention of her in McAuliffe & Gillis's edited book, *Richmond Barracks: 1916*, nor in Cal McCarthy's *Cumann na mBan & the Irish Revolution*.

18. Aine O'Rahilly, Witness Statement 333.

19. Catherine Rooney (nee Byrne), Cumann na mBan, Witness Statement 648.

20. Diary of Geraldine Fitzgerald, National Archives, Kew, London, War Office Papers 35/207.

21. Aoife deBurca, Witness Statement 359.

22. Catherine Byrne, Witness Statement 648.

23. Frank Robbins, ICA, Witness Statement 585.

24. Margaret Skinnider, *Doing My Bit for Ireland*, New York: Century, 1917.

25. Ibid.

26. Nora O'Daly, "The Women of Easter Week," *An tOglac*, 1926.

27. Rosie Hackett, Witness Statement 546.

28. Aine Ryan, Cumann na mBan, Witness Statement 887.

29. *Easter Week Diary of Miss Lily Stokes*, Nonplus, Dublin, 1916.

30. Captain Aine Heron, Cumann na mBan, Witness Statement 296.

31. Ui Chonail, Eilis Bean, "A Cumann na mBan recalls Easter Week," *Capuchin Annual* 1966.

32. Aoife deBurca, Witness Statement 359.

33. William Daly, E. Company, 2nd Battalion, Witness Statement 291.

34. Ibid.

35. Lily Stokes, *Easter Diary*.

36. Skinnider, *Doing My Bit for Ireland*.

37. Molly Reynolds, Witness Statement 195.

38. Aoife de Burca, Nurse, Cumann na mBan, Witness Statement 359.

39. Ibid.

40. Seamus Daly, F. Company, 2nd Battalion, Witness Statement 360.

41. Caufield, Max, *The Easter Rebellion*, p. 319.

42. Catherine Rooney, nee Byrne, Cumann na mBan, Witness Statement 648.

43. Aine Ryan, Cumann na mBan, Witness Statement 887.

44. "The Surrender: An Account of Miss Elizabeth O'Farrell, who bore Pearse's message to General Lowe," in *Dublin 1916*, edited

by Roger McHugh (London: Arlington Books, 1976).

45. *"A Nurse in Dublin Castle."*

46. Eileen Costello, Gaelic League, Witness Statement 1184.

47. "The Surrender."

48. Sean Kennedy, C. Company, 1st Battalion, Witness Statement 842.

49. Rose McNamara, Cumann na mBan, Witness Statement 482.

50. *The Anglo-Celt,* 6th May 1916, p. 1, and Witness Statement 805.

51. Rosie Hackett, Witness Statement 546.

52. "The Mexican"—Eamon de Valera (1882–1975). Born George de Valeros in New York, on 14th October 1882. His father was Jaun Vivion de Valera, a Spanish-born artist from the Basque Country in Spain. His mother was Catherine Coll from Bruree, County Limerick. Lack of evidence of a marriage certificate would suggest that he was illegitimate, at a time when these things mattered. George was taken to Ireland upon the death of his father and brought up by his grandmother. By 1901, he was known as Edward deValera. With the rise of Gaelic nationalism, he changed his first name to Eamon.

53. Ui Chonail, Eilis Bean, p. 276.

54. Mary Colum, from *Life and Dreams,* 1928, reproduced in Roger McHugh, *Dublin, 1916.*

55. Lynch, Patricia, *Workers' Dreadnought,* May 1916, reproduced in Roger McHugh, *Dublin 1916,* p. 317.

56. Emily Norgrove memoir, Hanratty Papers, Kilmainham Gaol Museum. See also Ann Matthews, *The Irish Citizen Army,* p. 144.

57. Brian Barton, *The Secret Court Martial Records of the Easter Rising,* p. 100. See also Leon O'Broin, *W.E. Wylie and the Irish Revolution, 1916–1921,* p. 27. There is no reference in the trial to this outburst.

Chapter 5

1. Conlon, Lil, *Cumann na mBan & the Women of Ireland,* pp. 33–4.

2. Ibid., p. 35.

3. Coogan, Tim Pat, Michael Collins, p. 61.

4. Seumus Daly, Volunteer, 2nd Battalion and IRB man, Witness Statement 360.

5. Skinnider, Margaret, *Doing My Bit for Ireland,* Century, New York, 1917, p. 25.

6. Sean O'Duffy, A. Company, 1st Battalion, Witness Statement 313.

7. Seamus Daly, F. Company, 2nd Battalion, Witness Statement 360.

8. Related incidents are taken from Lil Conlan, pp. 68–72.

9. Mrs. Linda McWhinney (nee Kearns), Witness Statement 404.

10. To confuse the British should they discover the leak, Collins gave Lily Mernin the code-name of "Little Gentleman," sometimes abbreviated to "Lt. G." This abbreviation, "Lt. G.," confused Richard Bennett, author of *The Black & Tans,* pp. 102–104, who believed "Lt. G." to be one "Lieutenant G.," a British officer.

11. Keohane, Leo, *Captain Jack White,* p. 184. Jack White, as he was generally known, was born James Robert White, the son of Field Marshal Sir George White V.C. That he had influence within the British Establishment is confirmed in that he was often a dinner guest of King Edward VII and a friend of H.G. Wells, G.B. Shaw, Arthur Conan Doyle, and corresponded with Tolstoy.

12. Eilis Bean Ui Chonaill (nee Na Riain), Cumann na mBan, Witness Statement 568.

13. Ni Chorra, Eilis, "A Rebel Remembers," *The Capuchin Annual* 1966, p. 297.

14. *Lord Riddell, War Diary, 1914–1918,* Ivor Nicholson & Watson, London, p. 130.

15. *Nationality.* See also: Cal McCarthy, *Cumann na mBan,* pp. 99–100.

16. Some Sinn Fein members had successfully been elected to more than one seat. Eoin MacNeill had been elected both in Derry City and the National University of Ireland. Eamon deValera had been elected to East Clare and West Mayo, and Liam Mellows was elected to East Galway and North Meath.

17. See: Maire Comerford, *The First Dail,* 1969, note 1, p. 12.

18. Alice M. Cashell, Republican judge, Witness Statement 366.

19. *Irish Times,* 15th July 1920.

20. Margaret Sweeney, Cumann na mBan, Witness Statement 1267.

21. Helena Molony, ICA, Witness Statement 391.

22. Brighid O'Mullane, Cumann na mBan, Witness Statement 450.

23. Bessie Cahill (nee Harrington), Cumann na mBan, Witness Statement 1143.

Chapter 6

1. Kathleen Boland, Cumann na mBan, Witness Statement 586.

2. Dr. Alice Barry, Witness Statement 723.

3. Catherine Rooney nee Byrne, Cumann na mBan, Witness Statement 648.

4. Mary Flannery Woods, Witness Statement 624.

5. Mary Rigney, Sinn Fein, Witness Statement 752.

6. Mary Flannery Woods.

7. Margaret "Peg" Broderick-Nicholson, Cumann na mBan, Witness Statement 1682. Perhaps surprisingly, in what appeared to be a strong Republican family, Peg's brother was an officer in the British Army. Of him she relates: "...the job I most hated was enticing British soldiers down the docks in order to have them relieved of their arms by the Volunteers, one of whom, an officer, happened to be my brother."

8. Margaret Sweeney, Cumann na mBan, Witness Statement 1267.

9. Mrs. K. O'Callaghan, Witness Statement 688.

10. See: the handwritten note of Michael J. Feeley RIC., Witness Statement 68, and Adrian Hoar, *In Green & Red: the Lives of Frank Ryan*, p. 168. Nathan, the son of a Jew, was brought up as a Christian, only asserting his Jewish heritage midway during World War I. He claimed to be the only Jewish officer to serve in the Brigade of Guards during the war. This, however, was untrue. His commission as an officer was in the less-glamorous Cycling Section of the Royal Warwickshire Regiment. After the demobilization from the Auxiliaries, Nathan had a number of "dead-end jobs," before reasserting himself as a soldier, to fight with some distinction in the International Brigade in Spain. Fellow Brigadista Kit Conway, a former IRA man and leading figure in the Irish section within the British Battalion, recognized him and refused to serve under him: "Comrades, we are Being blackguarded. They've put the Black and Tans to command us," he announced. As a consequence, the Irish contingent transferred to the American Battalion. Nathan was mortally wounded by a bomb at the battle around Guadarrama. He died on 15th July 1937.

11. Loyalist wives and the wives of British officers also suffered. Perhaps the most brutal was the shooting of Captain Kennlyside on Bloody Sunday, when the Squad and others eliminated a large section of British Intelligence in Dublin. As Squad member Mick O'Hanlon prepared to shoot him, Kennlyside's wife threw herself in front of her husband, trying to prevent his killing. Mick Flanagan, the leader of the group, pushed her to one side and shot the British agent in her presence. At 119 Morehampton Road, Donnybrook, members of the Squad raided that house in order to assassinate another British agent, Donald Lewis McClean. McClean's wife was present at the time, and he begged his intended killers not to shoot him in his wife's presence. Showing some humanity, they agreed, and he was taken upstairs, where he was shot and killed.

12. Margaret Sweeney, Cumann na mBan, Witness Statement 1267.

13. Linda Kearns, "In Times of Peril," *Belfast Magazine*, No. 16, March 1995.

14. Mrs. Margaret "Peg" O'Callaghan, Witness Statement 747.

15. Miss Annie Barrett, telephone operator, Witness Statement 1133.

16. Mrs. Margaret "Peg" O'Callaghan. On 19th December 1919, the Squad (an assassination division of the IRA) assisted by some Volunteers from Tipperary, including Dan Breen, ambushed a convoy of cars at Phoenix Park in which General Sir John French was traveling. They targeted the wrong car, and so Lord French escaped. In the attack, Volunteer Martin Savage was shot dead, and Breen was badly wounded.

17. Annie Ryan, Cumann na mBan, Witness Statement 887.

18. Eilis Bean Ui Chonaill nee Ryan, Cumann na mBan, Witness Statement 568. That a parlor maid was required for a named castle official is of some significance. Andy Cope, the assistant undersecretary, had been sent by Prime Minister Lloyd George to gauge the temperature among the Sinn Fein leadership in the runup to the truce. Miss McDonagh, it would seem, was used as a conduit between Michael Collins and Andy Cope. British Intelligence in Ireland, in the shape of Captain R. D. Jeune, became aware that something was afoot, when the house of Republican John O'Connor was raided, and a letter on Dublin Castle paper was discovered. It read: "Dear Mr. O'Connor, I am having the papers you require sent to you. Yours sincerely, A.W. Cope."

19. "Periscope, The Last Days of Dublin Castle," *Blackwood's* magazine, August 1922.

20. Lily Mernin worked for Irish Intelligence under the alias of "Little Gentleman," sometimes abbreviated to "Lt. G." Undetected, but strongly suspected, she was dismissed from the British Service in February 1922, and was awarded two years' pension at the lowest rank. She then took up a position with the Irish Army, based at Clancy Barracks. Lily never married, but she traveled to London in June 1922, to secretly give birth to a son, widely believed to have been fathered by her cousin Piaras Beaslai. Lily retired in February 1952. She died five years later, on 18th February 1957, and was buried with full military honors.

21. Lily Mernin, shorthand typist, Dublin Castle, Witness Statement 441.

Chapter 7

1. Madge Daly, Witness Statement 855.

2. Brighid O'Mullane, Witness Statement 485. In an attempt to defuse the situation, Michael Collins had proposed to Liam Lynch, then commandant of the breakaway IRA, that the Free Staters and the Republicans should come together in a covert operation to invade the north. The Free State Army had obtained arms officially from the British. These would have had traceable numbers stamped into them. So, an arrangement was made whereby the Free State Army would swap their arms for untraceable Republican arms. Thus, if any were captured, there would be no comeback against the Free State government. These arrangements had been put in place during the truce.

3. Geraldine O'Donel, nurse with the Republicans during the civil war, Witness Statement 861.

4. Brighid O'Mullane, Cumann na mBan, Witness Statement 485.

5. Paddy Daly was in charge of the Squad, an IRA assassination team. He was involved in an ambush against Lord French during the War of Independence. During the Civil War, Daly led troops in the Free State's successful campaign against Republican positions in Kerry and Tralee. He was particularly noted for his cruelty toward prisoners. Daly was later appointed a major-general in the Free State Army.

6. Andrews, C. S., *Dublin Made Me*, p. 257.

7. Ibid., pp. 262–3.

8. Madge Daly, Witness Statement 855.

9. Sinead McCoole, *No Ordinary Women*, p. 98.

10. Ibid., pp. 122–3.

11. "After the Vote: Women, citizenship and the campaign for gender equality in the Irish Free State (1922–1943)," in Ryan & Ward, *Irish Women and the Vote*.

Bibliography

Primary Sources

Bureau of Military History, Witness Statements.
Oireachtas Members Database.

Books

Andrews, C.S., *Dublin Made Me*, Lilliput Press, Dublin, 2001.
Bennett, Richard, *The Black and Tans*, Spellmount Ltd., Chalford, 2007.
Bentham, Jeremy, *Plan of Parliamentary Reform*, R. Hunter, London, 1817.
Boylan, Henry [ed.], *A Dictionary of Irish Biography*, Gill & MacMillan, Dublin, 1998.
Breen, Dan, *My Fight for Irish Freedom*, Anvil Books, 1964.
Caufield, Max, *The Easter Rebellion*, Four Square Books, London, 1965.
Childers, Erskine, *Military Rule in Ireland*, Talbot Press, Dublin, 1920.
Coffey, Thomas M., *Agony at Easter*, Penguin Books, London, 1969.
Comerford, Maire, *The First Dail*, Joe Clarke, Dublin, 1969.
Conlon, Lil, *Cumann na mBan and the Women of Ireland*, Kilkenny People, Kilkenny, 1969.
Connolly, James, *Labour in Irish History*, New Books, Dublin, 1967.
_____, *Labour, Nationality & Religion*, New Books, Dublin, 1969.
_____, *Socialism & Nationalism*, Three Candles, Dublin, 1948.
Coogan, Tim Pat, *Michael Collins*, Hutchinson, London, 1990.
_____, *1916: The Mornings After*, Head of Zeus, London, 2015.
Dalton, Charles, *With the Dublin Brigade*, Mercier Press, Dublin, 2014.
Dwyer, T. Ryle, *The Squad*, Mercier Press, Cork, 2005.
Fifty Years of Liberty Hall, Sign of the Three Candles, Dublin, 1959 [No author given].
Fox, R. M., *The History of the Irish Citizen Army*, James Duffy & Co., Dublin, 1943.
_____, *Rebel Irishwomen*, Progress House, Dublin, 1935.
Foy, Michael T., *Michael Collins's Intelligence War*, Sutton Publishing, Thrupp, 2006.
Gleeson, James, *Bloody Sunday*, Lyons Press, Guilford, Connecticut, 2004.
Hart, Peter [ed.], *Irish Narratives*, Cork University Press, 2002.
Hopkinson, Michael, *The Irish War of Independence*, Gill & McMillan, Dublin, 2004.
Keohane, Leo, *Captain Jack White*, Merrion Press, Sallins, 2014.
Larkin, Emmet, *James Larkin*, New English Library, London, 1968.
MacAonghusa, Proinsias, and O'Reagain, Liam, *The Best of Connolly*, Mercier, Cork, 1967.
MacLochlainn, Piaras F., *Last Words*, Government of Ireland, 2006.
Matthews, Ann, *The Irish Citizen Army*, Mercier Press, Cork, 2014.
_____, *Renegades: Irish Republican Women 1900-1922*, Mercier Press, Dublin 2010.
McAuliffe, Mary, & Gillis, Liz, *Richmond Barracks, 1916*, Dublin City Council, 2016.

_____, Mary [ed.], *Rosie*, Arlen House, Dublin, 2015.

McCarthy, Cal, *Cumann na mBan and the Irish Revolution*, Collins Press, Cork, 2014.

McCoole, Sinead, *No Ordinary Women*, O'Brien Press, Dublin, 2008.

McHugh, Roger [ed.], *Dublin 1916*, Arlington, Dublin, 1966.

McKenna, Joseph, *Guerrilla Warfare in the Irish War of Independence*, McFarland & Co., 2011.

_____, *Voices from the Easter Rising*, McFarland & Co., Jefferson, 2017.

McMahon, Paul, *British Spies & Irish Rebels*, Boydell Press, Woodbridge, 2008.

Neligan, David, *The Spy in the Castle*, Prendeville Publishing Ltd., London, 1999.

Nevin, Donal [ed.], *James Larkin, Lion of the Fold*, Gill & McMillan, Dublin, 1998.

1916 Rebellion Handbook, Mourne River Press, 1998.

O'Brien, Nora Connolly, *Portrait of a Rebel Father*, Four Masters, Dublin, 1975.

O'Cathasaigh, P.O., *The Story of the Irish Citizen Army*, Maunsel & Co., Dublin [Undated].

O'Conchubhair, Brian [ed.], *Dublin's Fighting Story*, Mercier Press, Cork, 2009.

O'Faolain, Sean, *Constance Markievicz*, Century Hutchinson, London, 1987.

O'Farrell, Mick, *The 1916 Diaries*, Mercier, Cork, 2014.

O'Malley, Ernie, *On Another Man's Wound*, Anvil Books, Dublin, 1979.

Ryan, Annie, *Comrades*, Liberties Press, Dublin, 2007.

Ryan, Louise, *Winning the Vote for Women*, Four Courts Press, Dublin, 2018.

Ryan, Louise, and Ward, Margaret, *Irish Women and the Vote*, Irish Academic Press, Newbridge, 2018.

Ryan, Meda, *The Day Michael Collins Was Shot*, Poolbeg Press, 1989.

_____. *Michael Collins and the Women Who Spied for Ireland*, Mercier Press, Dublin, 2006.

_____. *Tom Barry*, Mercier Press, Cork, 2005.

Sheehan, William, *Fighting for Dublin*, Collins Press, Cork, 2007.

Skinnider, Margaret, *Doing My Bit for Ireland*, General Books, Memphis, 2012.

Townsend, Charles, *Easter 1916*, Penguin Books, 2006.

Walsh, Maurice, *Bitter Freedom*, Faber & Faber, 2015.

Watkins, Sarah-Beth, *Ireland's Suffragettes*, History Press Ireland, Dublin, 2014.

Yeates, Padraig, *A City in Turmoil*, Gill & McMillan, Dublin, 2015.

Periodicals and Newspapers

An tOglac, 1926

Belfast magazine, No. 16

Blackwood's magazine, Dec. 1916

Capuchin Annual, 1936, 1966

Feminist Review, 1982

Irish Citizen

Irish Independent

Irish Times

Kerryman, 1968–9

Times (London)

Index

223